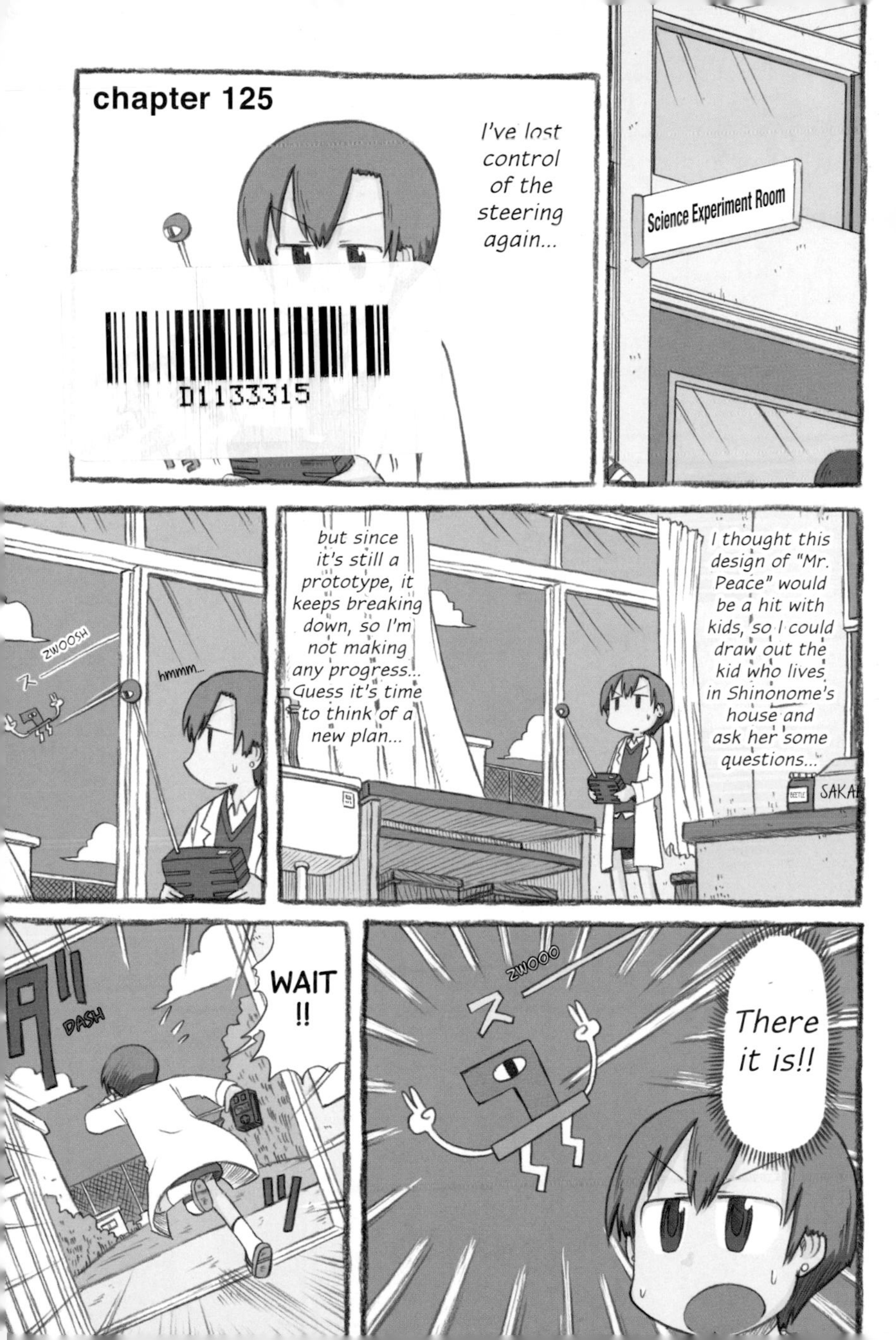
Science Experiment Room
chapter 125
I've lost control of the steering again...
I thought this design of "Mr. Peace" would be a hit with kids, so I could draw out the kid who lives in Shinonome's house and ask her some questions...
but since it's still a prototype, it keeps breaking down, so I'm not making any progress... Guess it's time to think of a new plan...
BEETLE
SAKA
ZWOOSH
hmmm...
ZWOOO
There it is!!
WAIT !!
DASH

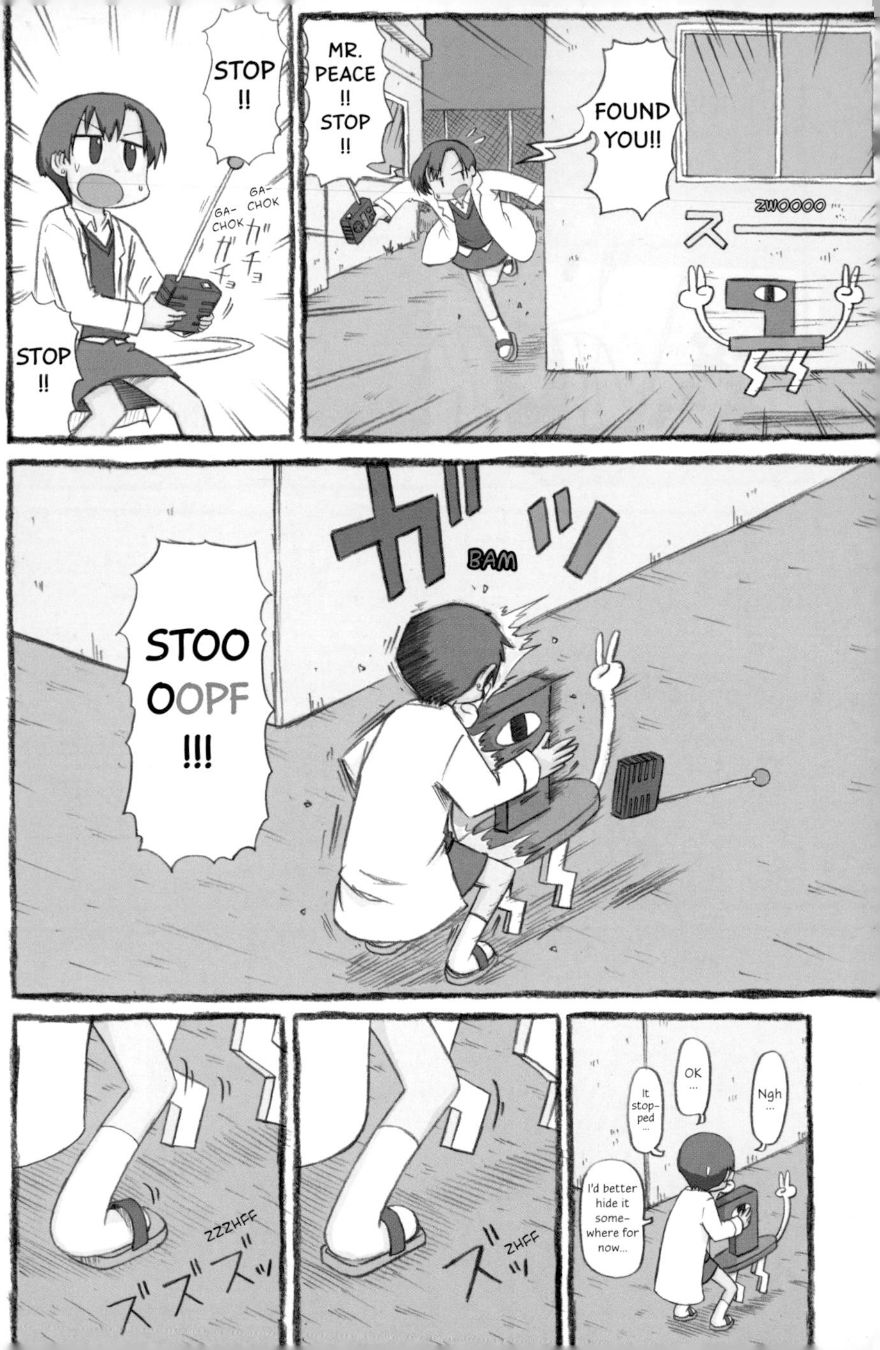
FOUND YOU!!
スー
ZWOOOO
MR. PEACE!! STOP!!
STOP!!
ガチョガチョ
GA-CHOK GA-CHOK
STOP!!
ガッ
BAM
STOOOOPF!!!
Ngh...
OK...
It stop-ped...
I'd better hide it some-where for now...
ズッ
ZHFF
ズズズッ
ZZZHFF

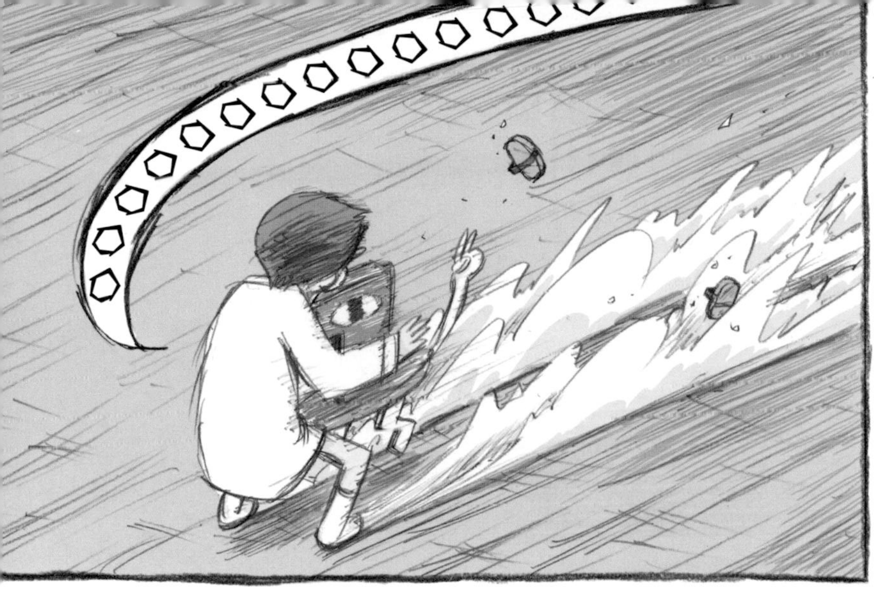

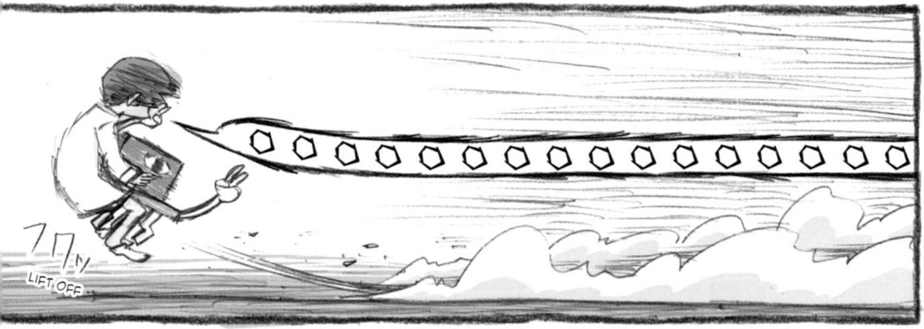
フワッ
LIFT OFF

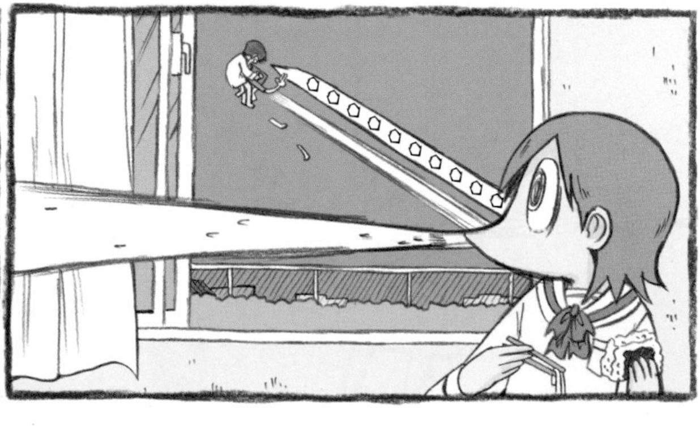

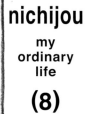

nichijou

my ordinary life

(8)

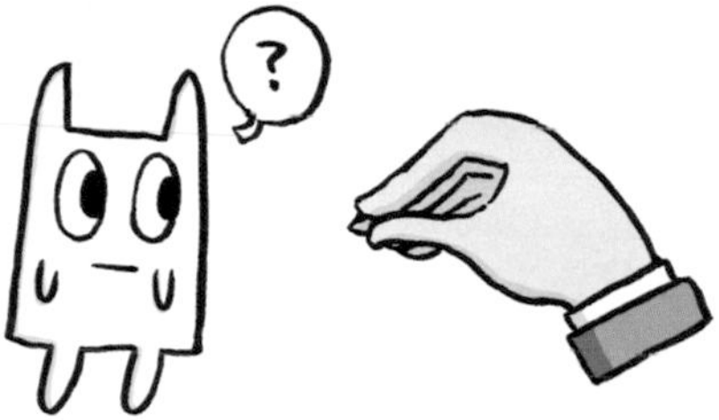

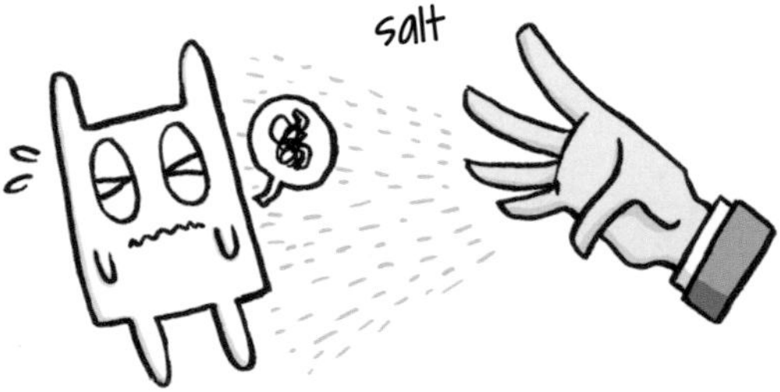
salt

chapter 126

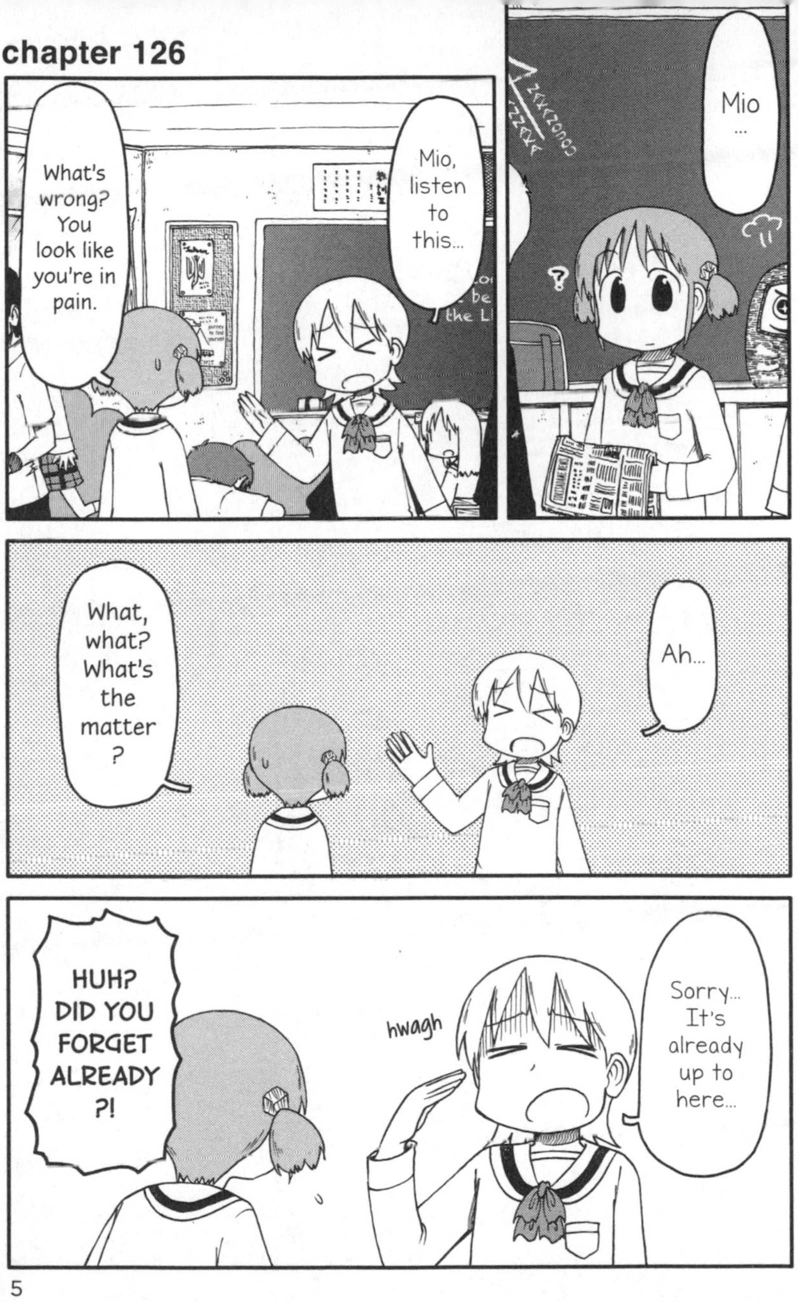

Mio...
Mio, listen to this...
What's wrong? You look like you're in pain.
Ah...
What, what? What's the matter?
Sorry... It's already up to here...
hwagh
HUH? DID YOU FORGET ALREADY?!

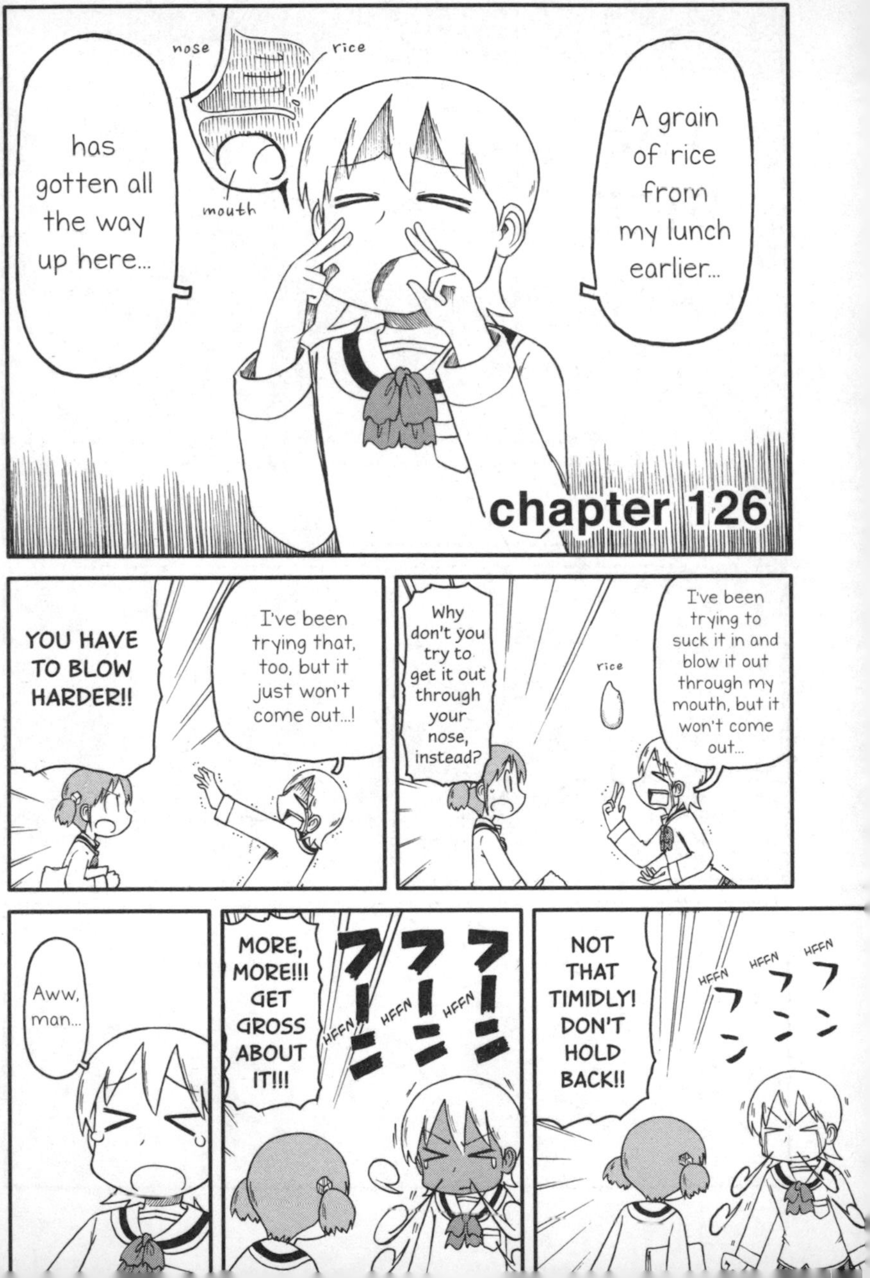
A grain of rice from my lunch earlier...
nose
rice
mouth
has gotten all the way up here...
chapter 126
I've been trying to suck it in and blow it out through my mouth, but it won't come out...
rice
Why don't you try to get it out through your nose, instead?
I've been trying that, too, but it just won't come out...!
YOU HAVE TO BLOW HARDER!!
NOT THAT TIMIDLY! DON'T HOLD BACK!!
HFFN
HFFN
HFFN
HFFN
HFFN
HFFN
MORE, MORE!!! GET GROSS ABOUT IT!!!
Aww, man...

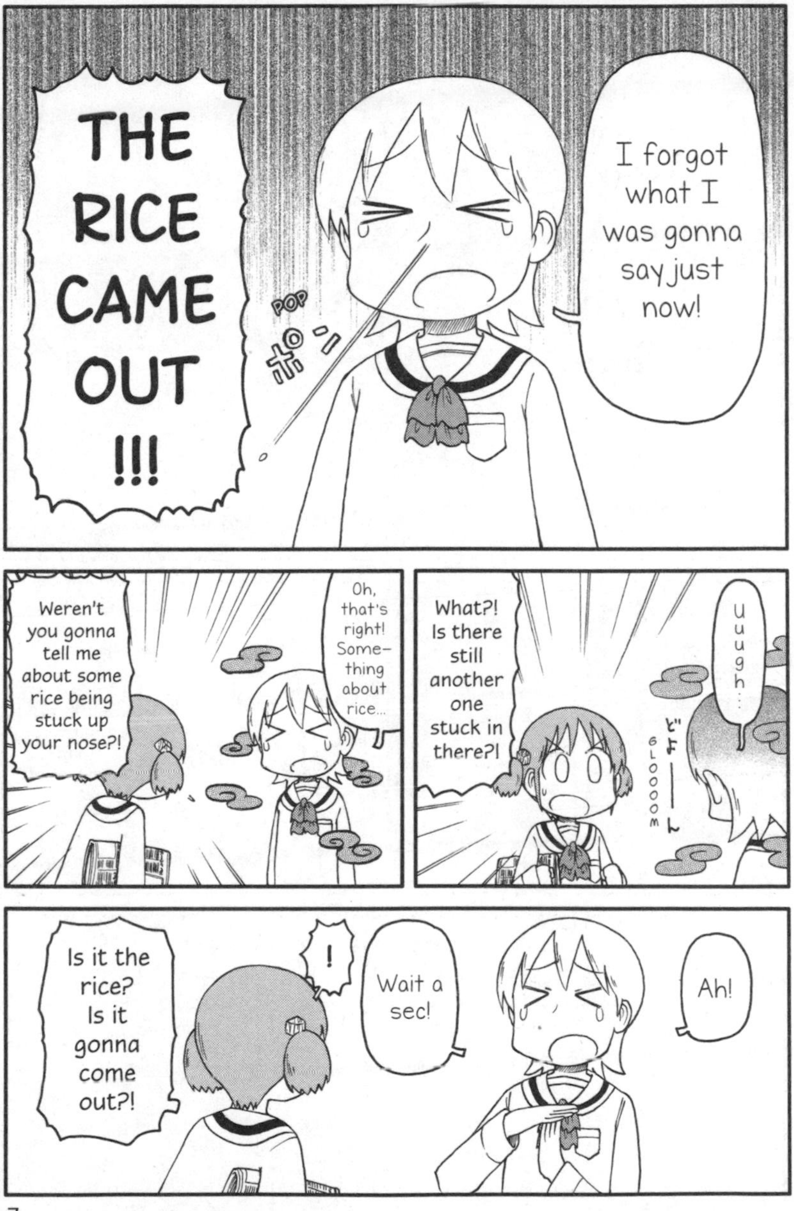
I forgot what I was gonna say just now!
POP
ポン
THE RICE CAME OUT !!!
Uuugh...
GLOOOOM
どよーん
What?! Is there still another one stuck in there?!
Oh, that's right! Something about rice...
Weren't you gonna tell me about some rice being stuck up your nose?!
Ah!
Wait a sec!
!
Is it the rice? Is it gonna come out?!

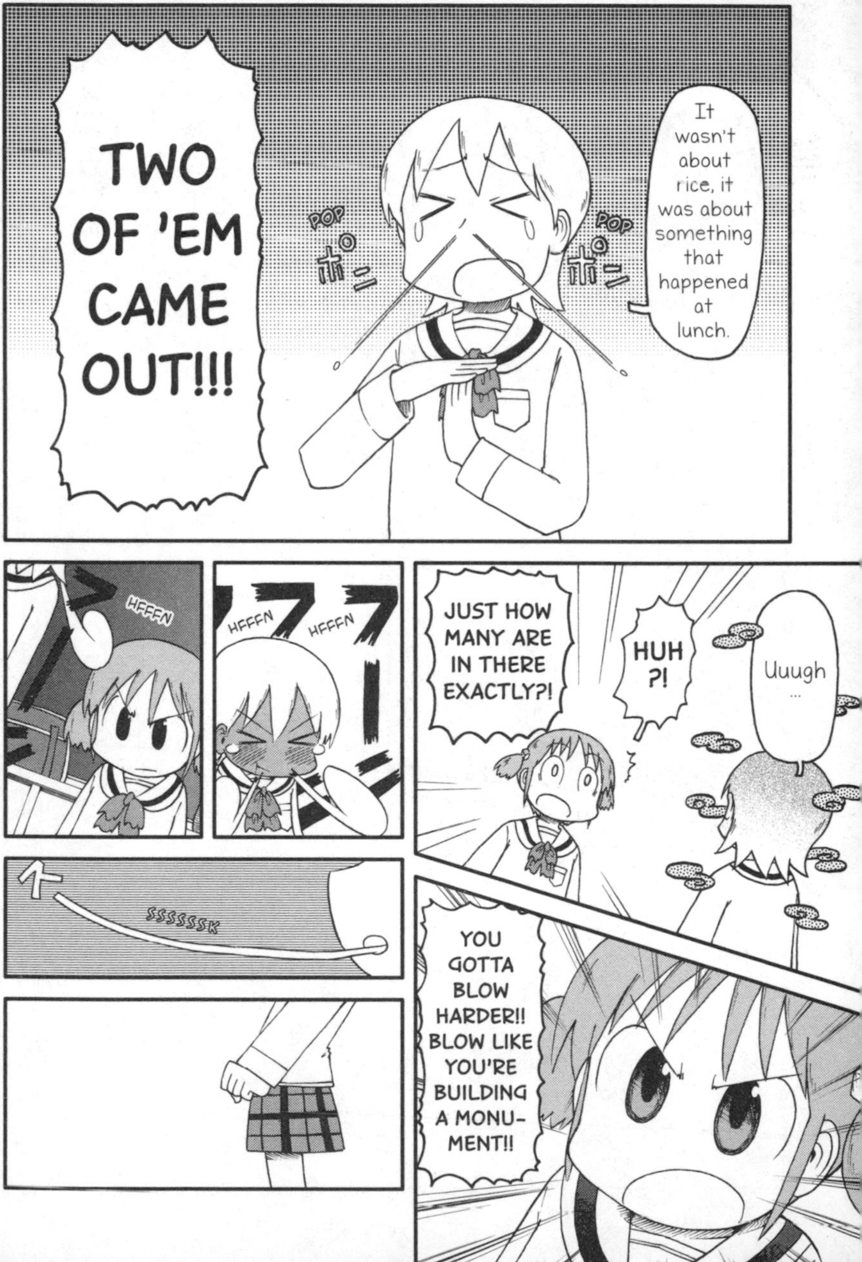
It wasn't about rice, it was about something that happened at lunch.
POP
POP
TWO OF 'EM CAME OUT!!!
Uuugh ...
HUH ?!
JUST HOW MANY ARE IN THERE EXACTLY?!
YOU GOTTA BLOW HARDER!! BLOW LIKE YOU'RE BUILDING A MONUMENT!!
HFFFN
HFFFN
HFFFN
SSSSSSK

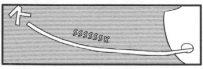

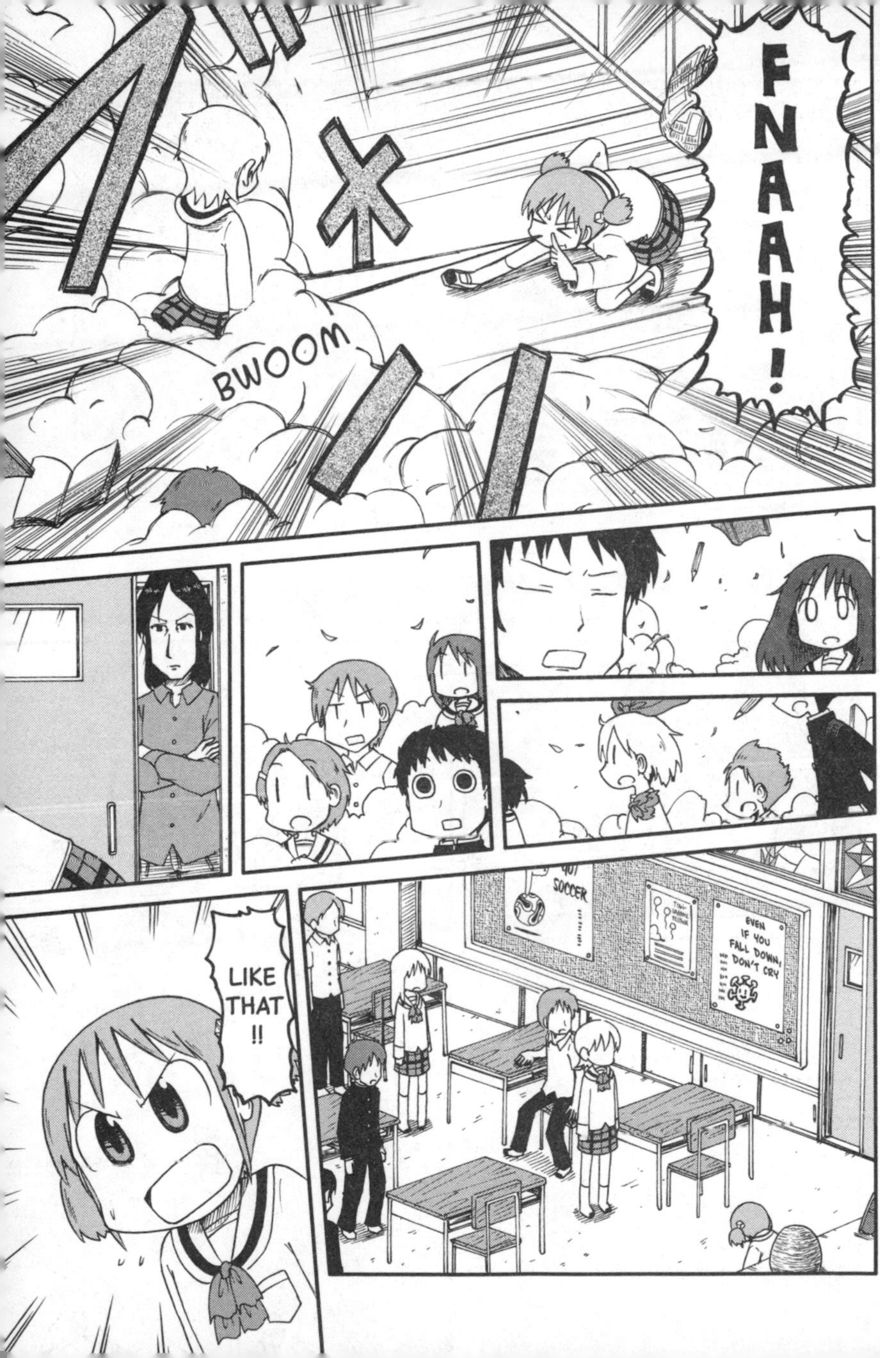
FNAH!
BWOOM
SOCCER
EVEN IF YOU FALL DOWN, DON'T CRY
LIKE THAT !!

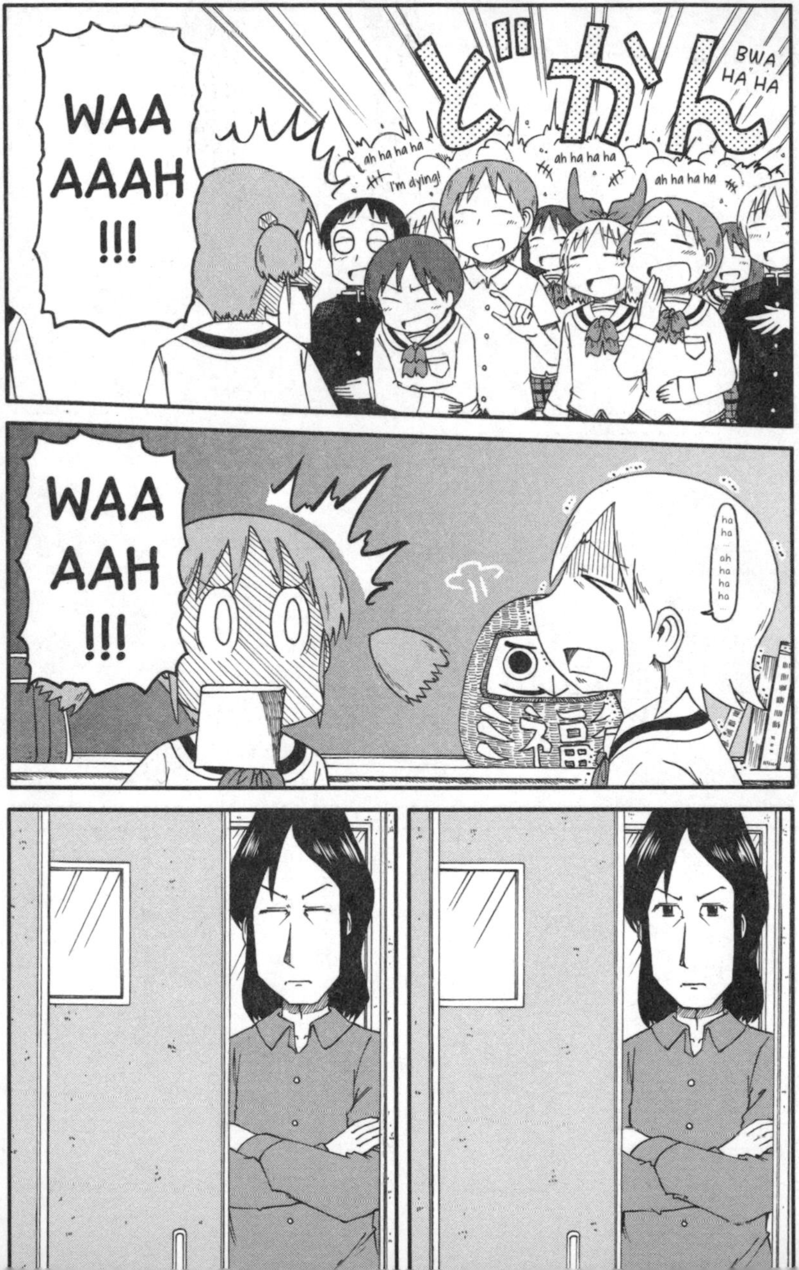
BWA HA HA
どかん
ah ha ha ha ha
ah ha ha ha
ah ha ha ha
I'm dying!
WAA AAAH !!!
ha ha ... ah ha ha ha ha ...
WAA AAH !!!

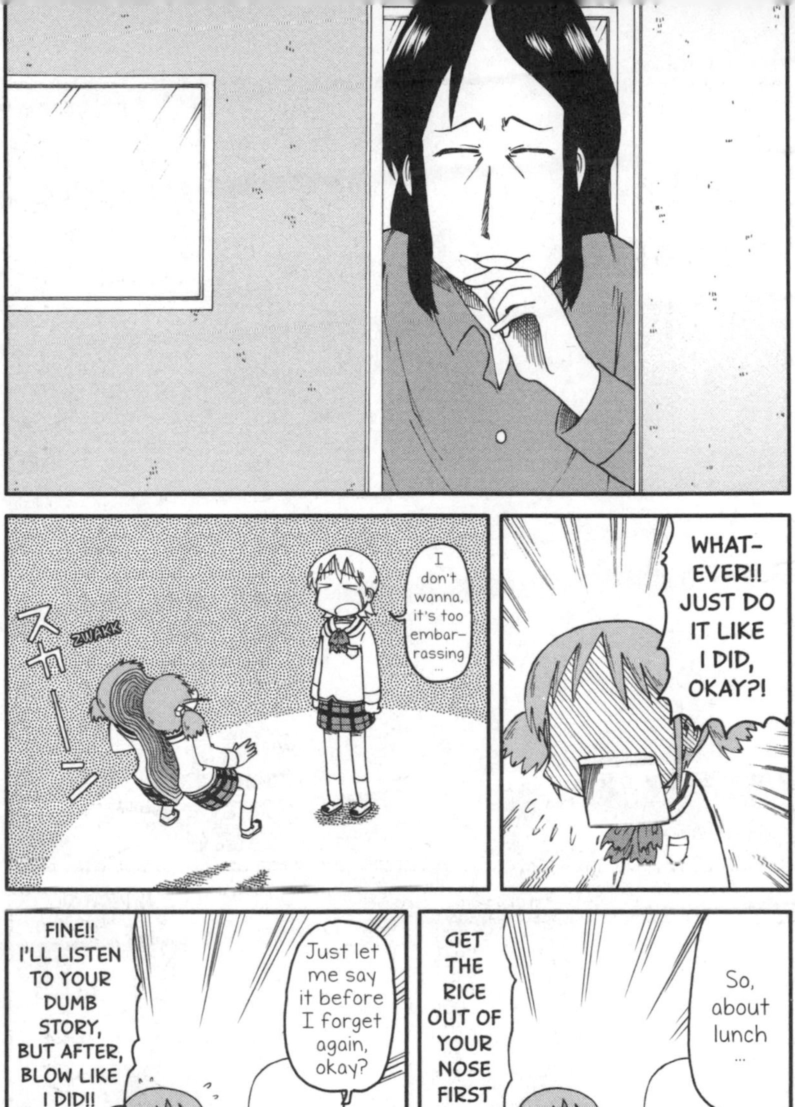
WHAT-EVER!! JUST DO IT LIKE I DID, OKAY?!
I don't wanna, it's too embarrassing ...
ZWAKK
So, about lunch ...
GET THE RICE OUT OF YOUR NOSE FIRST !!
Just let me say it before I forget again, okay?
FINE!! I'LL LISTEN TO YOUR DUMB STORY, BUT AFTER, BLOW LIKE I DID!!

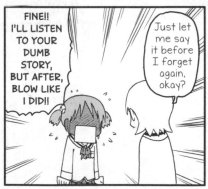

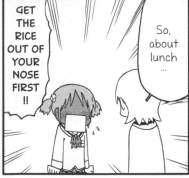

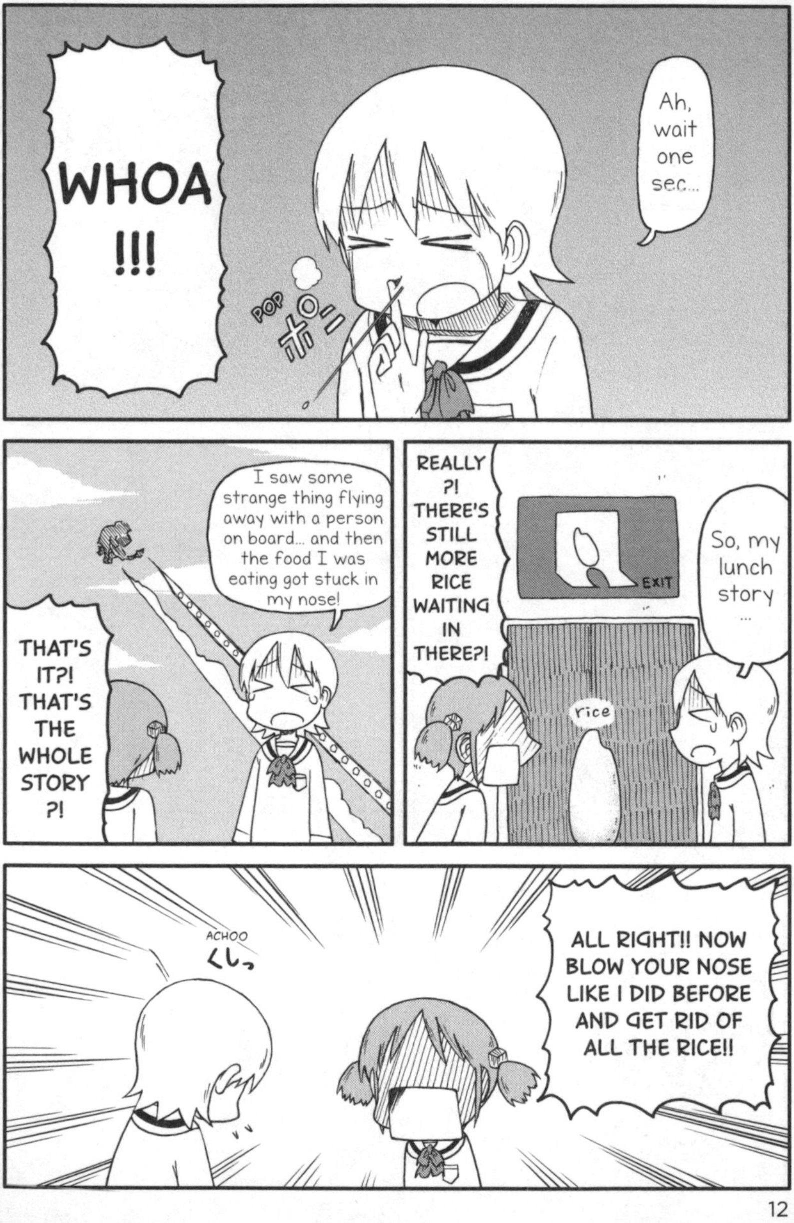
Ah, wait one sec...
POP ポンッ
WHOA !!!
So, my lunch story ...
EXIT
REALLY ?! THERE'S STILL MORE RICE WAITING IN THERE?!
rice
I saw some strange thing flying away with a person on board... and then the food I was eating got stuck in my nose!
THAT'S IT?! THAT'S THE WHOLE STORY ?!
ALL RIGHT!! NOW BLOW YOUR NOSE LIKE I DID BEFORE AND GET RID OF ALL THE RICE!!
ACHOO くしっ

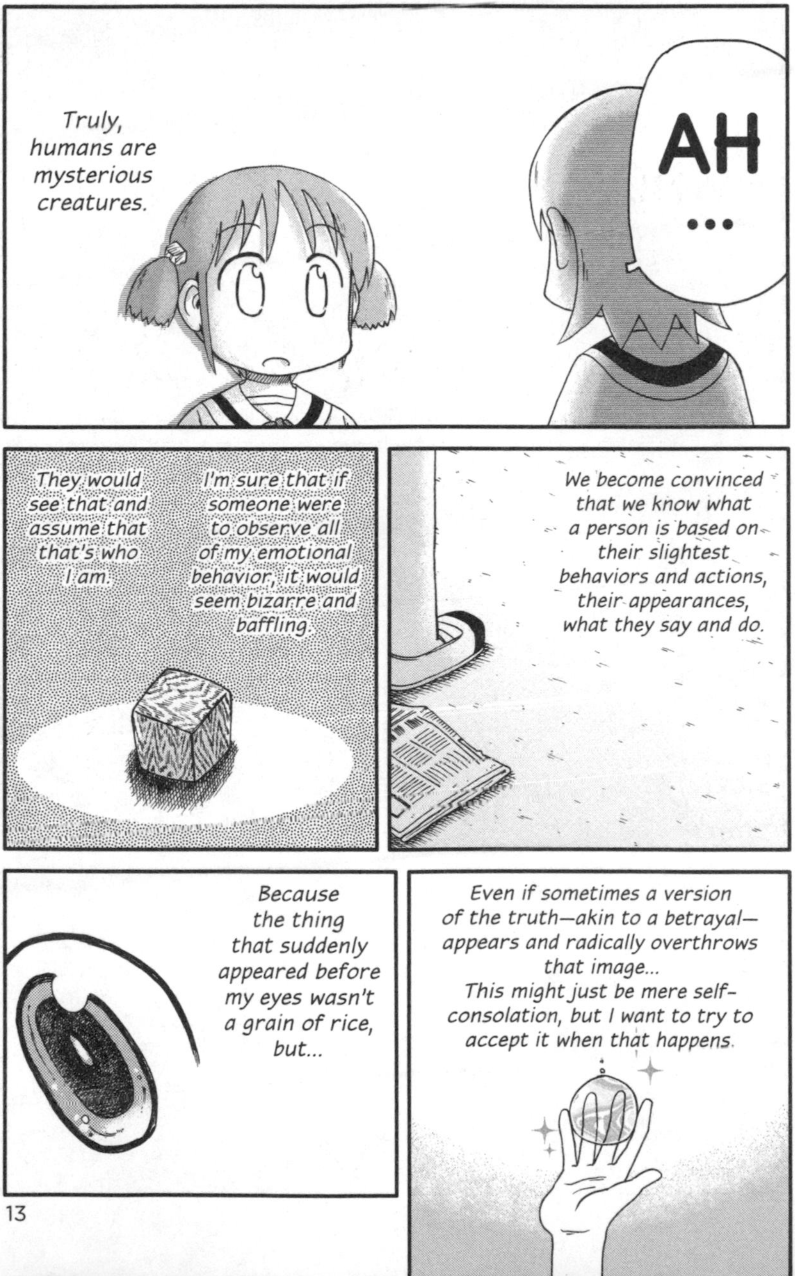
AH
...
Truly, humans are mysterious creatures.
We become convinced that we know what a person is based on their slightest behaviors and actions, their appearances, what they say and do.
I'm sure that if someone were to observe all of my emotional behavior, it would seem bizarre and baffling.
They would see that and assume that that's who I am.
Even if sometimes a version of the truth—akin to a betrayal—appears and radically overthrows that image...
This might just be mere self-consolation, but I want to try to accept it when that happens.
Because the thing that suddenly appeared before my eyes wasn't a grain of rice, but...

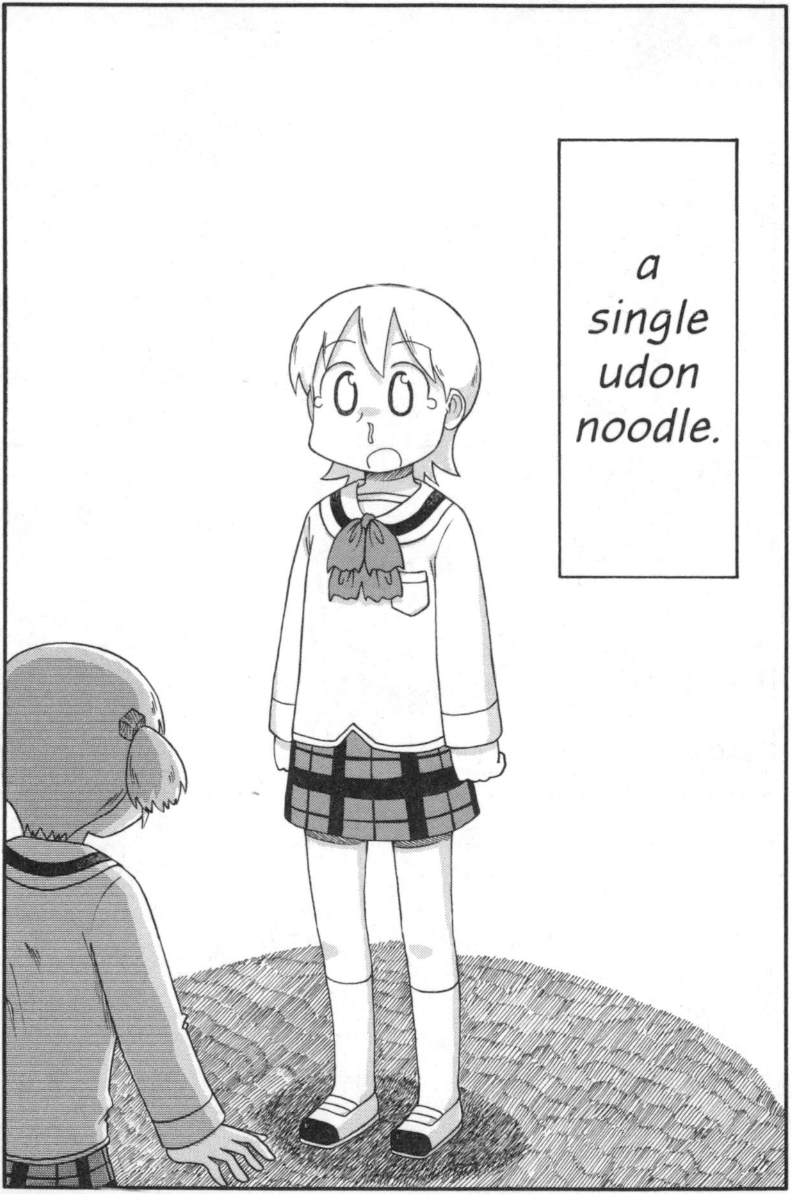
a single udon noodle.

chapter 126: end

chapter 127

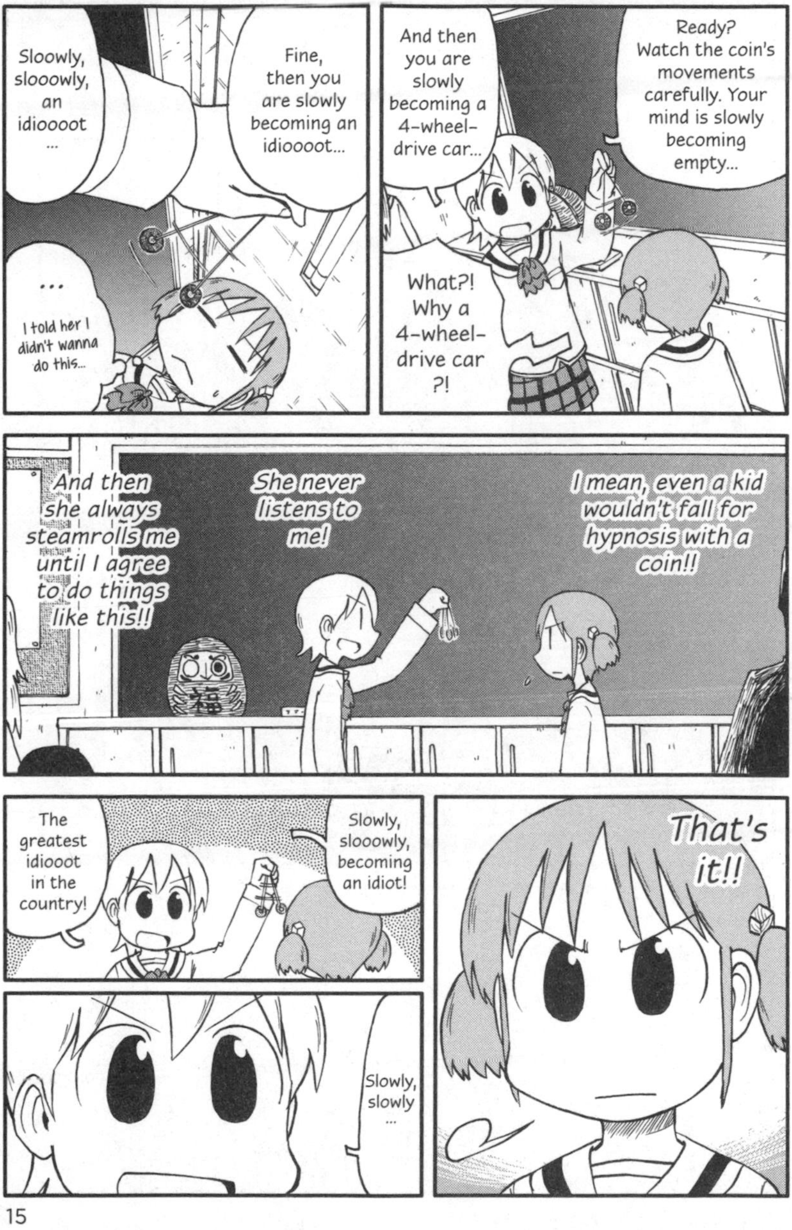

Ready? Watch the coin's movements carefully. Your mind is slowly becoming empty...
And then you are slowly becoming a 4-wheel-drive car...
What?! Why a 4-wheel-drive car ?!
Fine, then you are slowly becoming an idioooot...
Sloowly, slooowly, an idioooot ...
...
I told her I didn't wanna do this...
I mean, even a kid wouldn't fall for hypnosis with a coin!!
She never listens to me!
And then she always steamrolls me until I agree to do things like this!!
That's it!!
Slowly, slooowly, becoming an idiot!
The greatest idiooot in the country!
Slowly, slowly ...

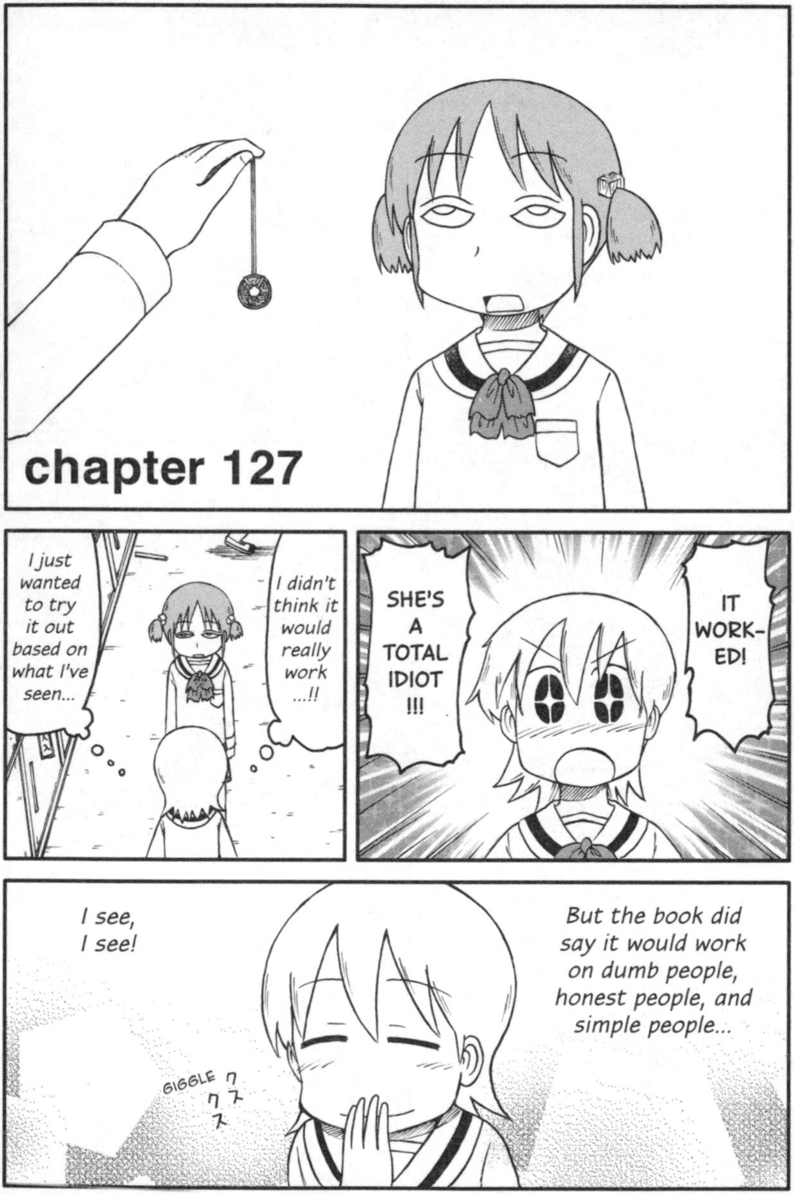
chapter 127
IT WORKED!
SHE'S A TOTAL IDIOT!!!
I didn't think it would really work ...!!
I just wanted to try it out based on what I've seen...
But the book did say it would work on dumb people, honest people, and simple people...
I see, I see!
GIGGLE クスクス

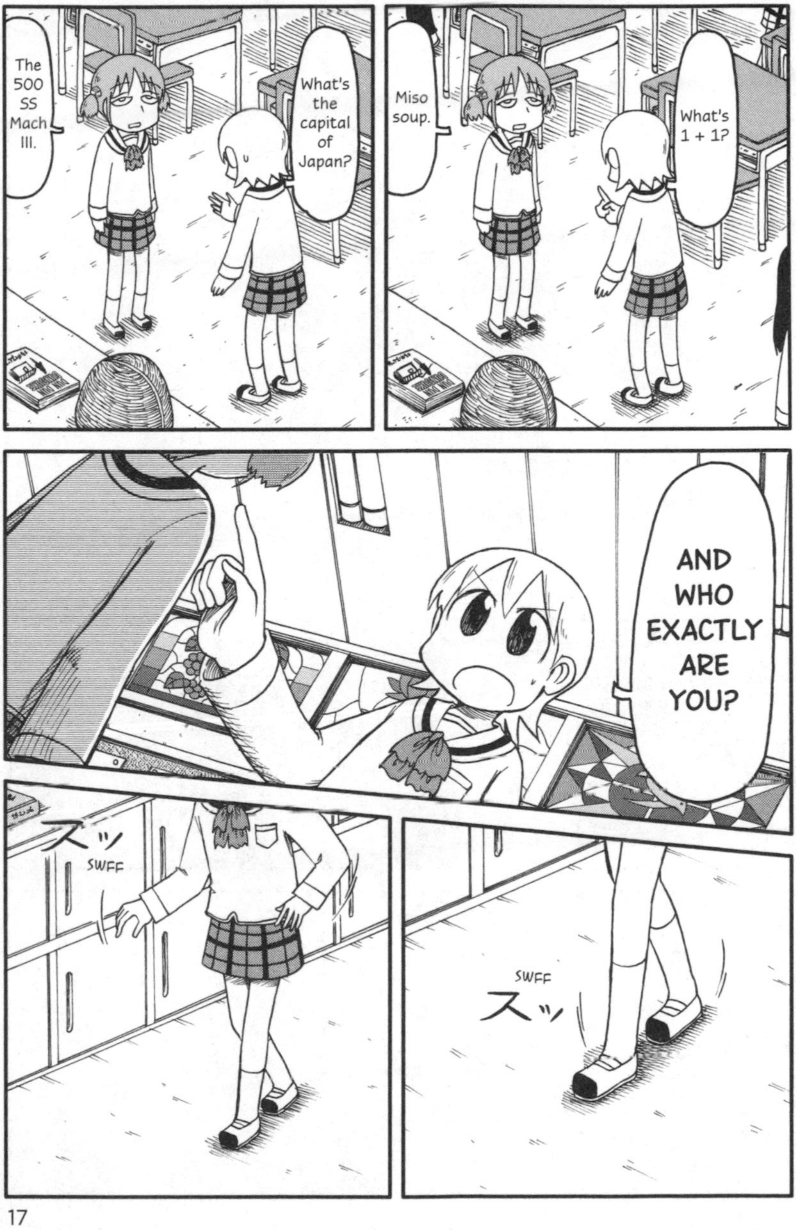
What's 1 + 1?
Miso soup.
What's the capital of Japan?
The 500 SS Mach III.
AND WHO EXACTLY ARE YOU?
スッ
SWFF
スッ
SWFF

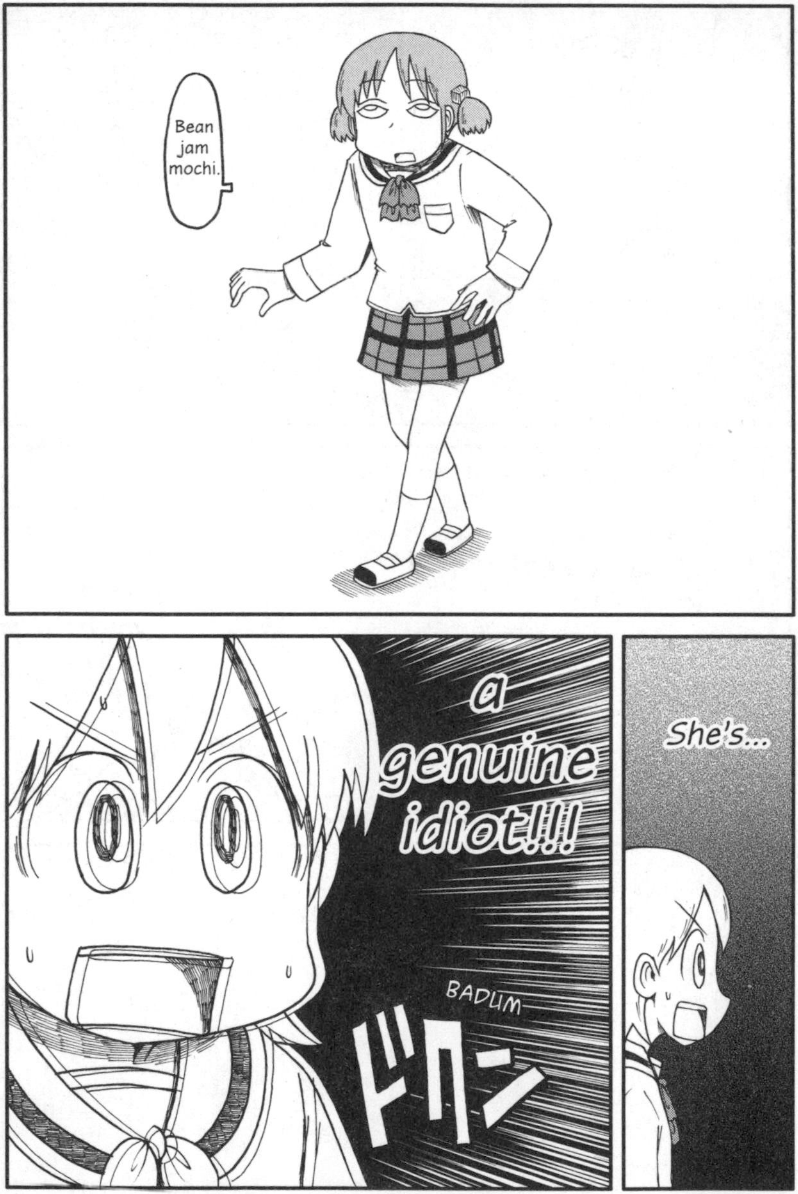
Bean jam mochi.
She's...
a genuine idiot!!!
BADUM
ドクン

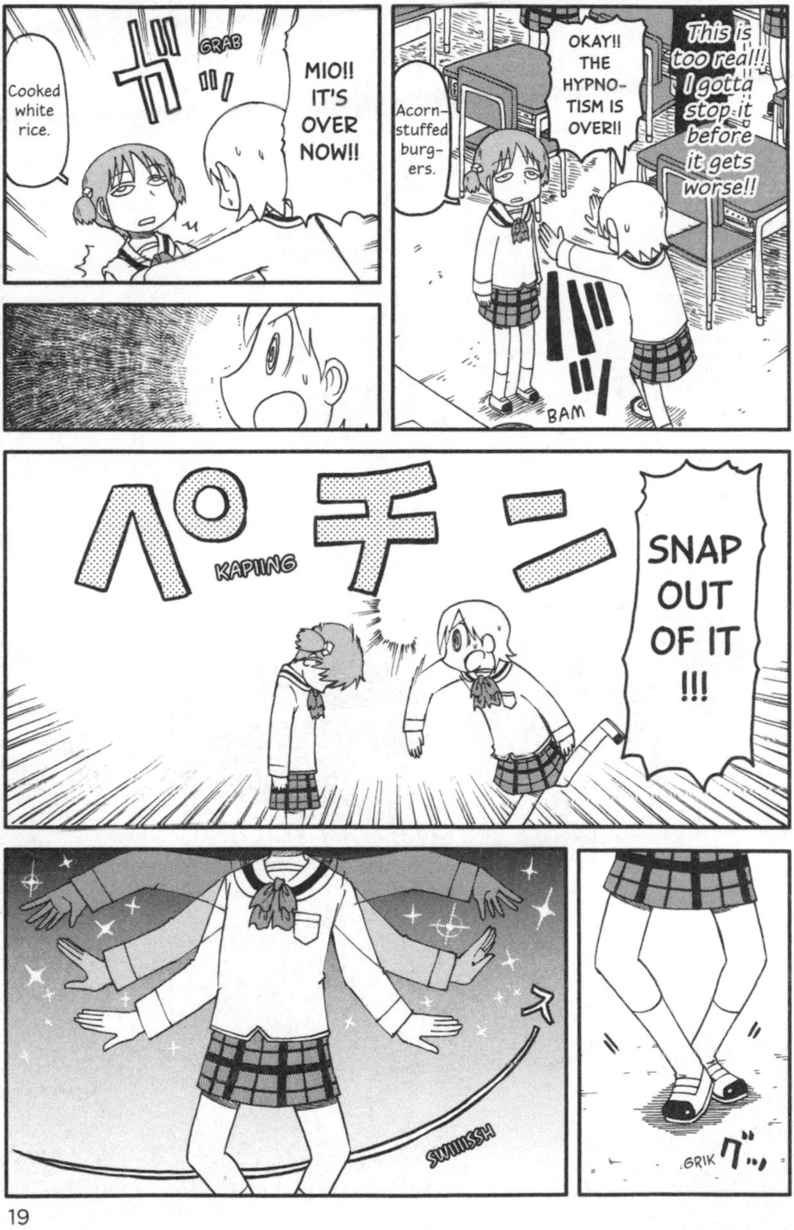
This is too real!! I gotta stop it before it gets worse!!
OKAY!! THE HYPNOTISM IS OVER!!
Acorn-stuffed burgers.
BAM
MIO!! IT'S OVER NOW!!
GRAB
Cooked white rice.
SNAP OUT OF IT !!!
ペチン
KAPIING
GRIK
SWIIIISSH

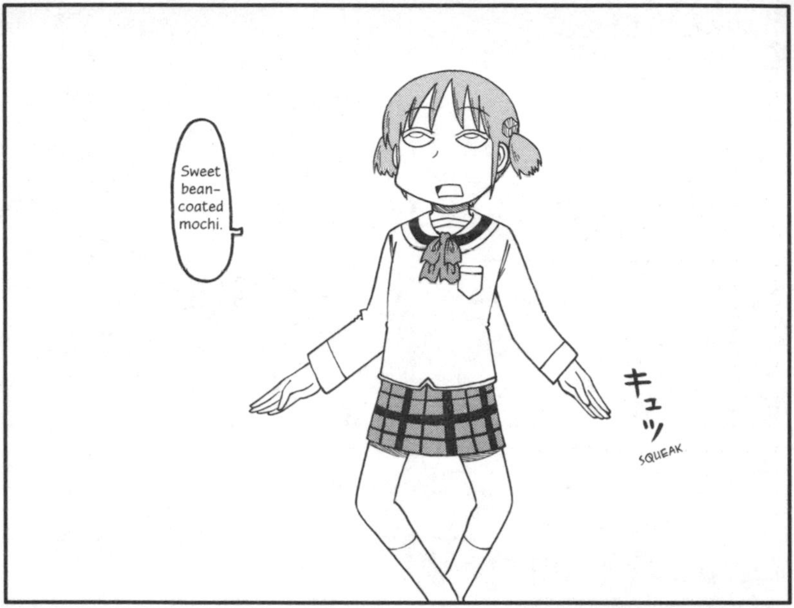
Sweet bean-coated mochi.
キュッ
SQUEAK
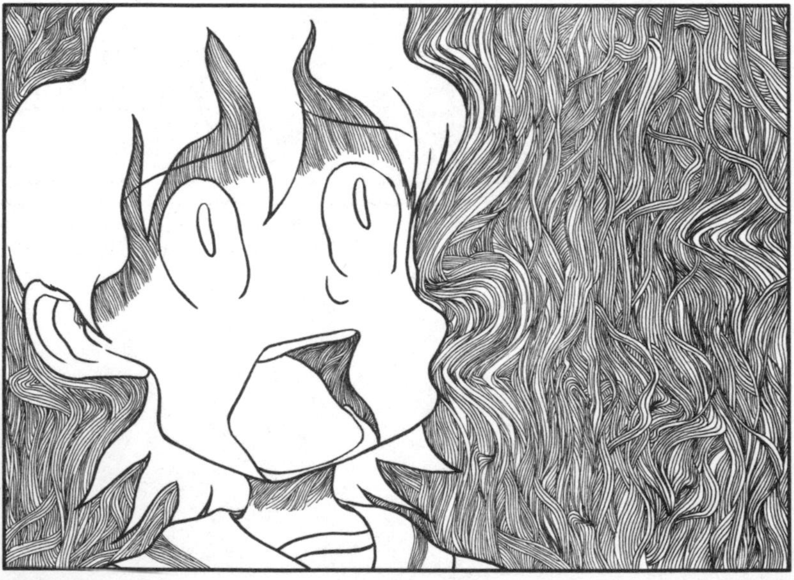

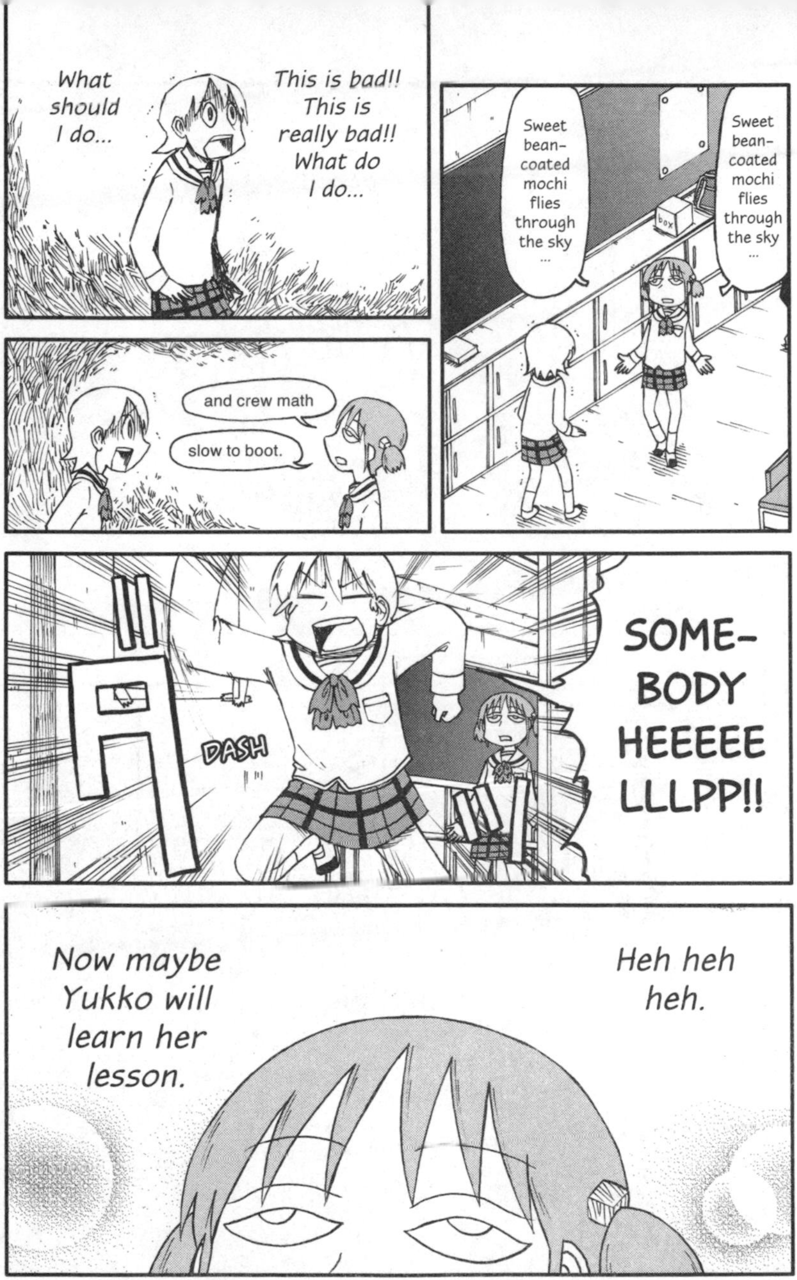

Sweet bean-coated mochi flies through the sky ...
Sweet bean-coated mochi flies through the sky ...
This is bad!! This is really bad!! What do I do...
What should I do...
and crew math
slow to boot.
SOME-BODY HEEEEE LLLPP!!
DASH
Heh heh heh.
Now maybe Yukko will learn her lesson.

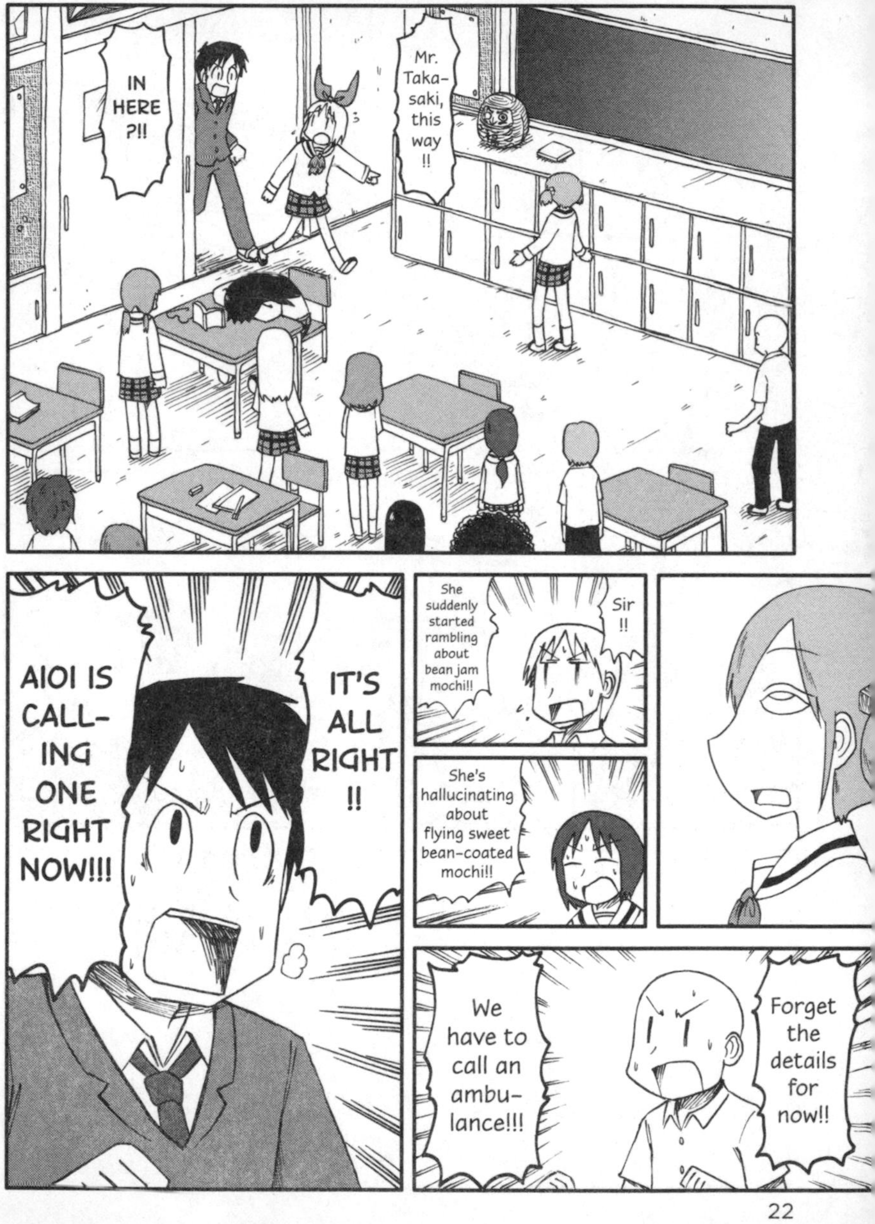

Mr. Takasaki, this way!!
IN HERE?!!
Sir!!
She suddenly started rambling about bean jam mochi!!
She's hallucinating about flying sweet bean-coated mochi!!
Forget the details for now!!
We have to call an ambulance!!!
IT'S ALL RIGHT!!
AIOI IS CALLING ONE RIGHT NOW!!!

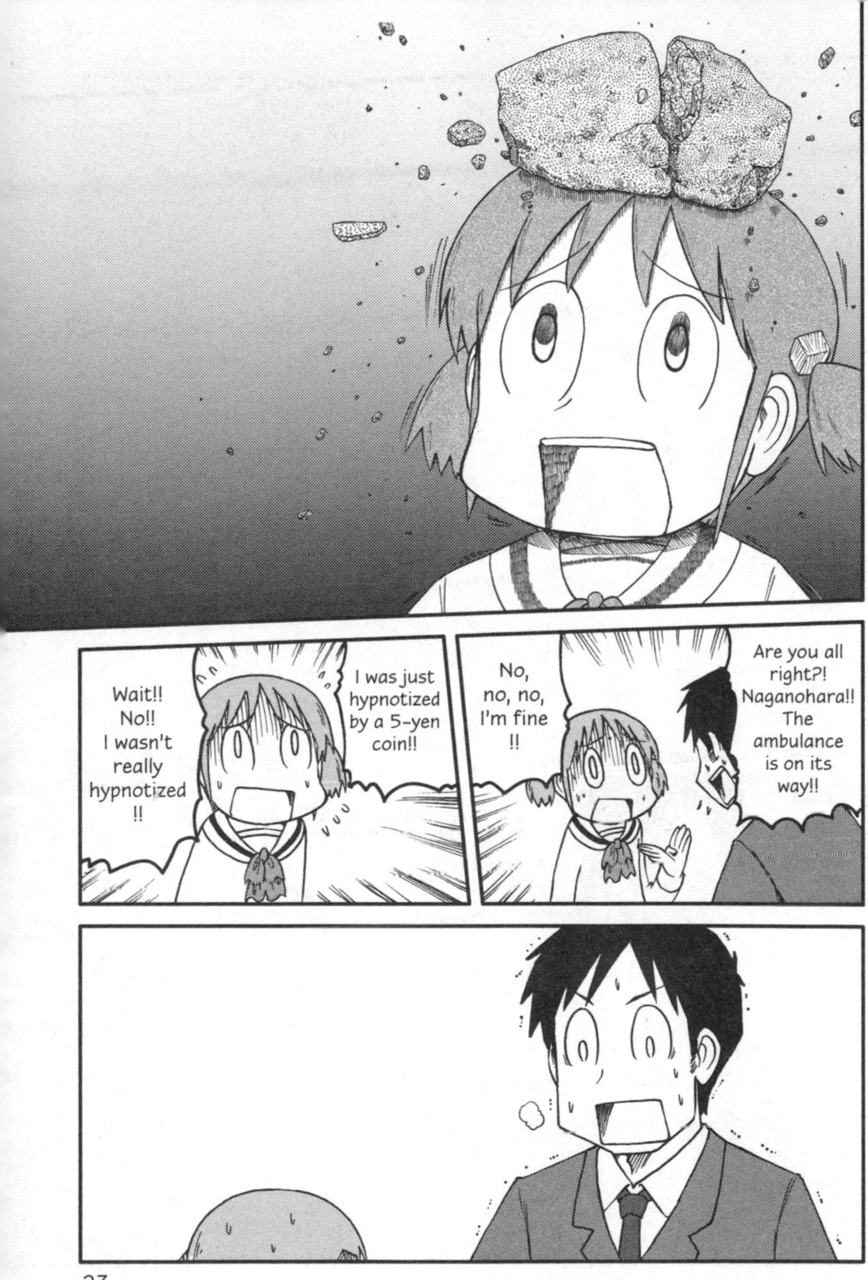
Are you all right?! Naganohara!! The ambulance is on its way!!
No, no, no, I'm fine !!
I was just hypnotized by a 5-yen coin!!
Wait!! No!! I wasn't really hypnotized !!

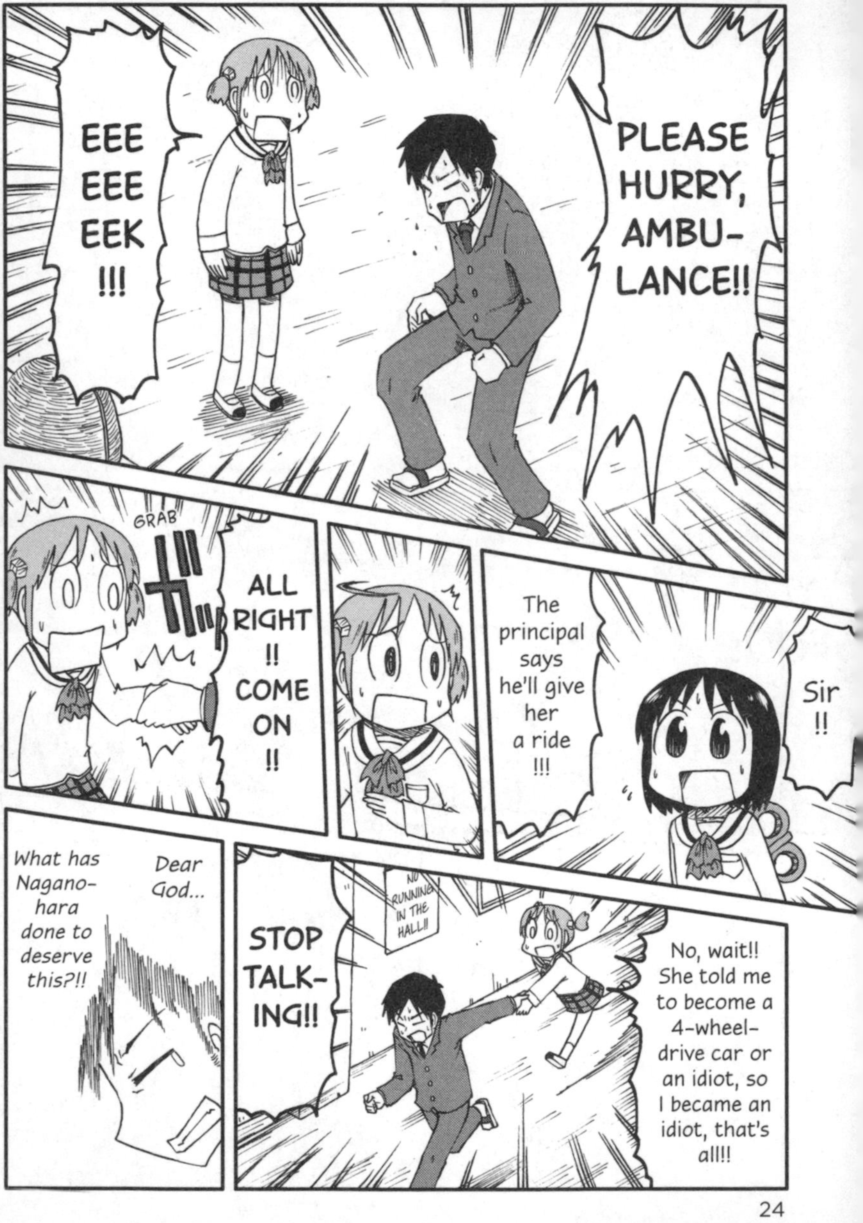
PLEASE HURRY, AMBU-LANCE!!
EEE EEE EEK !!!
Sir !!
The principal says he'll give her a ride !!!
ALL RIGHT !! COME ON !!
GRAB
No, wait!! She told me to become a 4-wheel-drive car or an idiot, so I became an idiot, that's all!!
NO RUNNING IN THE HALL!!
STOP TALK-ING!!
Dear God...
What has Nagano-hara done to deserve this?!!

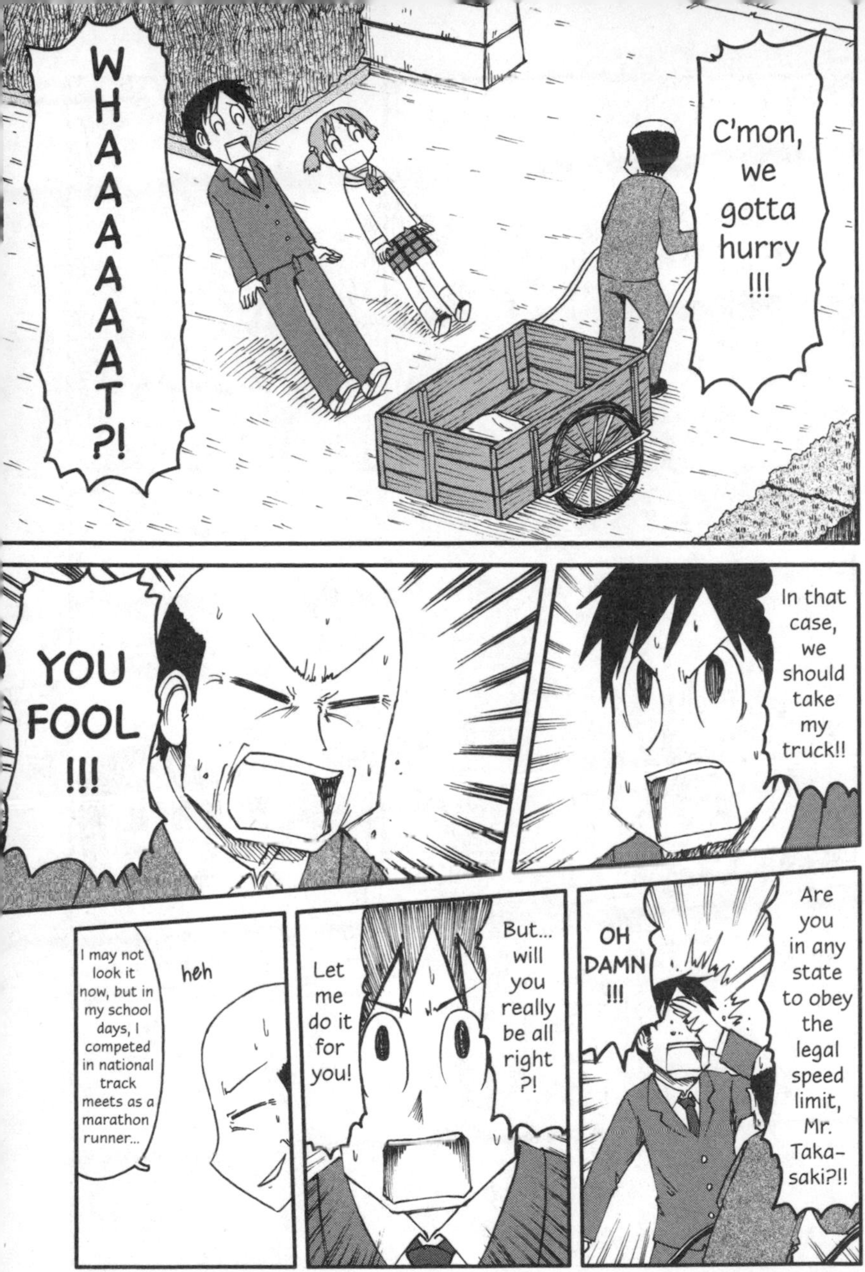
C'mon, we gotta hurry!!!
WHAAAAAAAT?!
In that case, we should take my truck!!
YOU FOOL!!!
Are you in any state to obey the legal speed limit, Mr. Takasaki?!!
OH DAMN!!!
But... will you really be all right?!
Let me do it for you!
heh
I may not look it now, but in my school days, I competed in national track meets as a marathon runner...

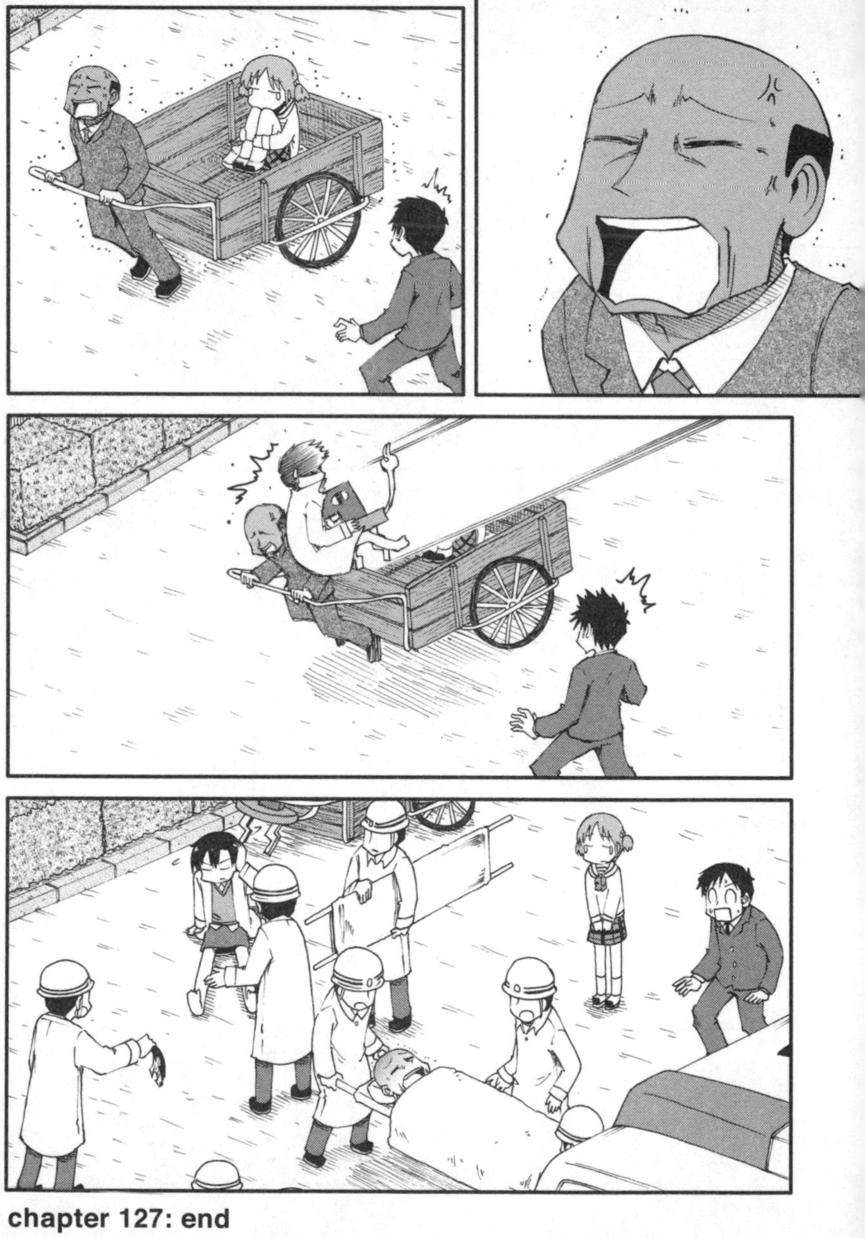

chapter 127: end

chapter 128

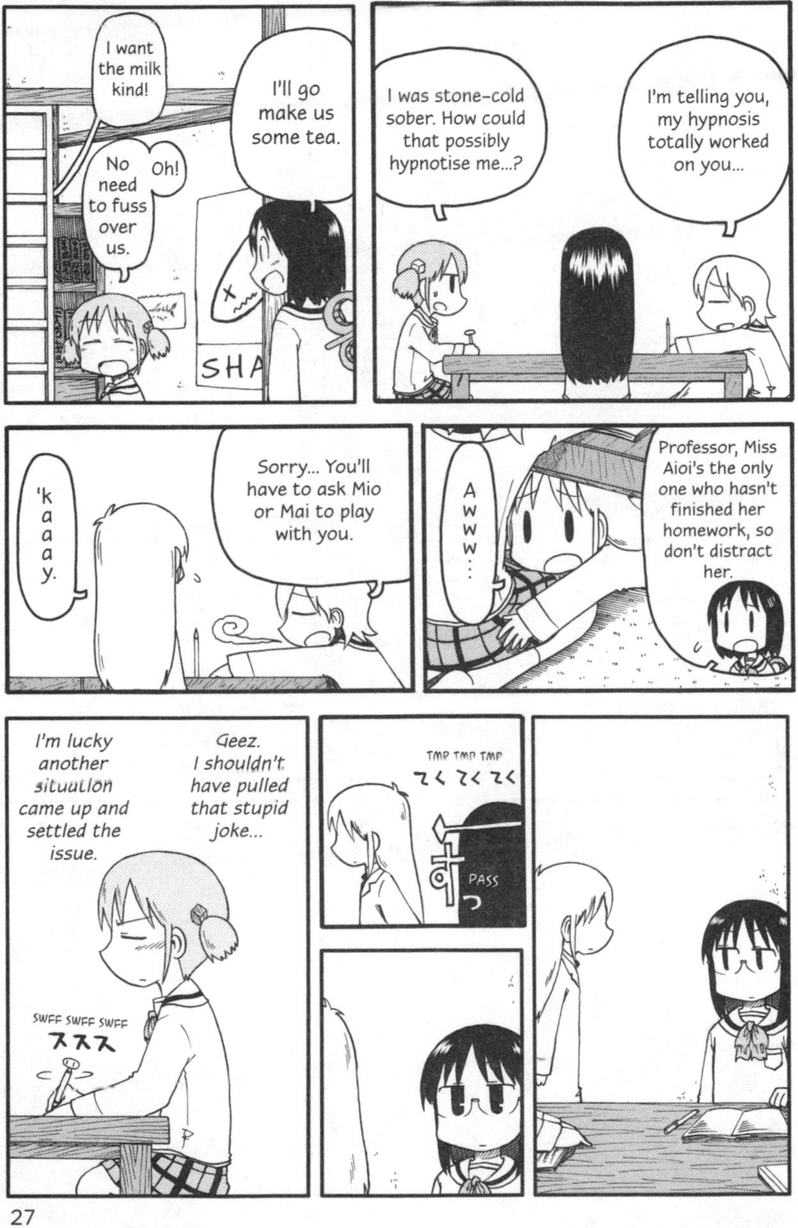

I'm telling you, my hypnosis totally worked on you...
I was stone-cold sober. How could that possibly hypnotise me...?
I'll go make us some tea.
I want the milk kind!
Oh!
No need to fuss over us.
SHA
Professor, Miss Aioi's the only one who hasn't finished her homework, so don't distract her.
Awww...
Sorry... You'll have to ask Mio or Mai to play with you.
'kaaay.
TMP TMP TMP
てくてくてく
PASS
すっ
Geez. I shouldn't have pulled that stupid joke...
I'm lucky another situation came up and settled the issue.
SWFF SWFF SWFF
ススス

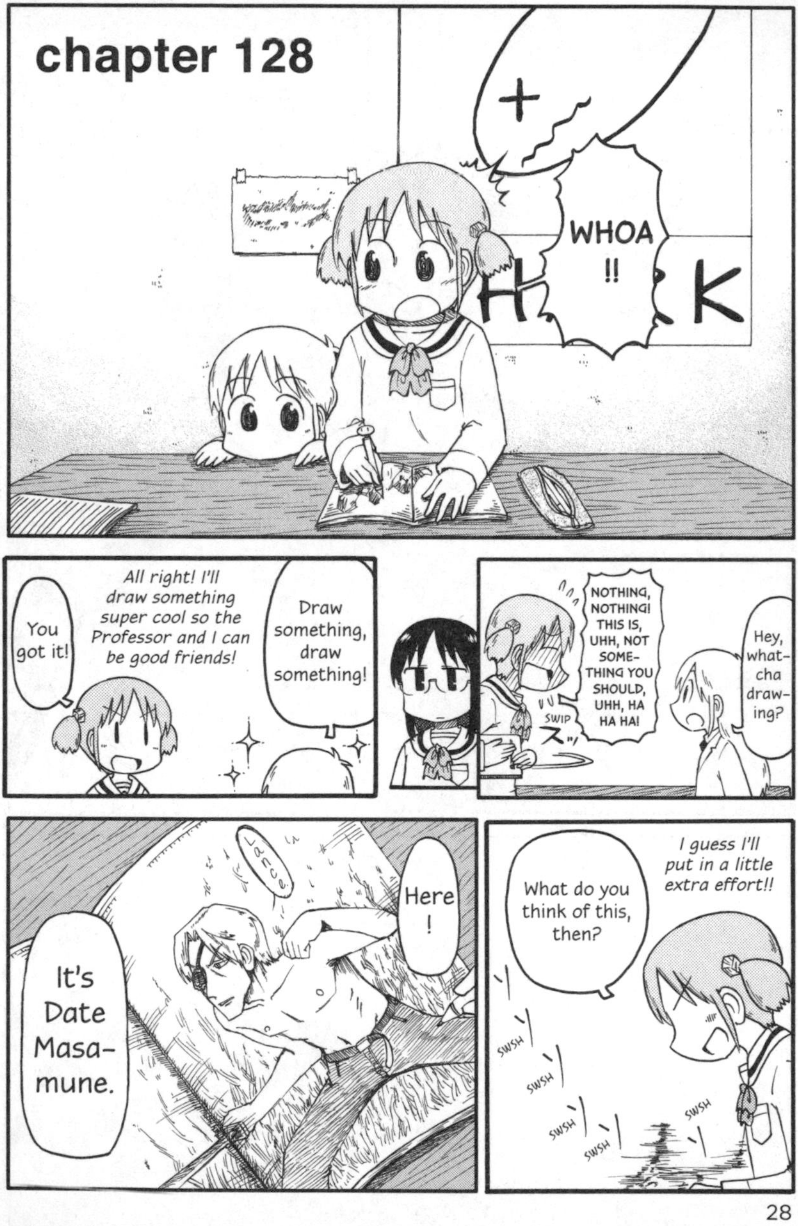
chapter 128
WHOA !!
H K
Hey, whatcha drawing?
NOTHING, NOTHING! THIS IS, UHH, NOT SOMETHING YOU SHOULD, UHH, HA HA HA!
SWIP
Draw something, draw something!
All right! I'll draw something super cool so the Professor and I can be good friends!
You got it!
I guess I'll put in a little extra effort!!
What do you think of this, then?
SWSH
SWSH
SWSH
SWSH
SWSH
Here!
Lance
It's Date Masamune.

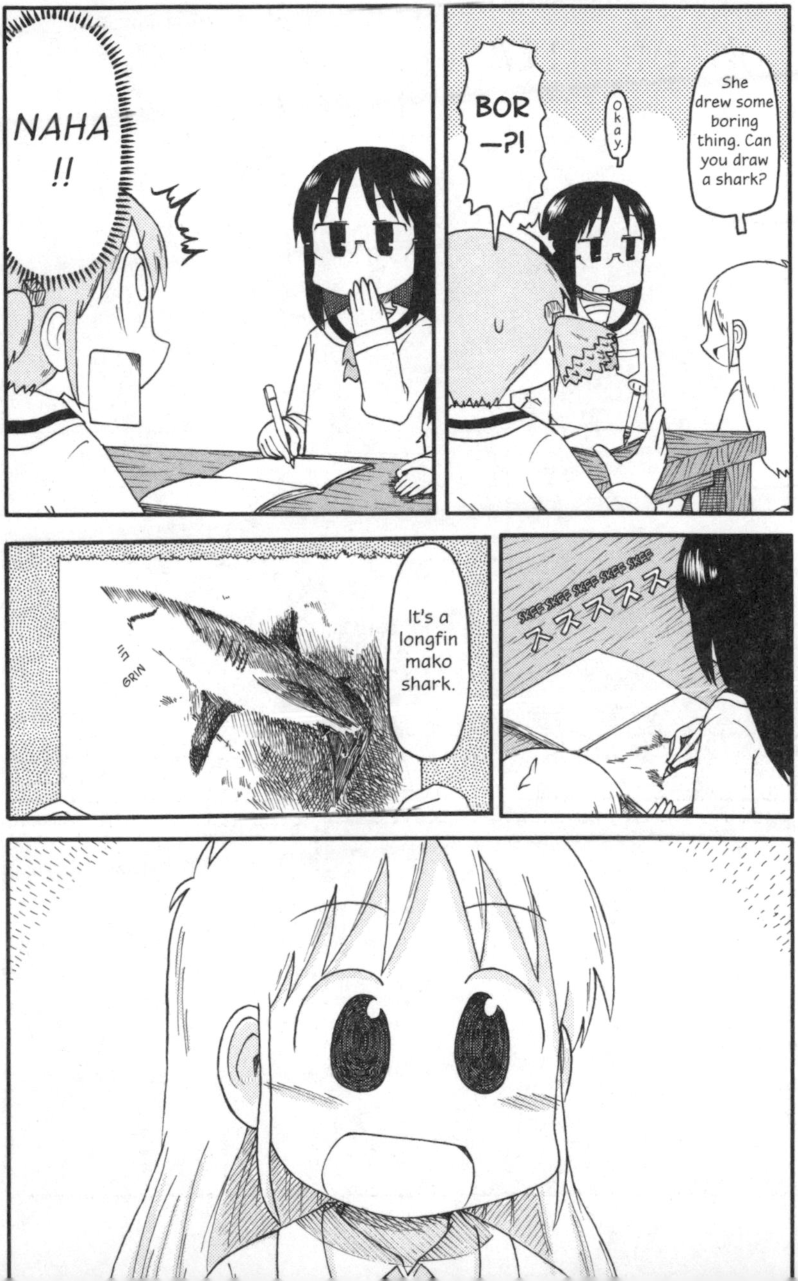
She drew some boring thing. Can you draw a shark?
Okay.
BOR—?!
NAHA!!
SKFF SKFF SKFF SKFF SKFF
ススススス
It's a longfin mako shark.
GRIN

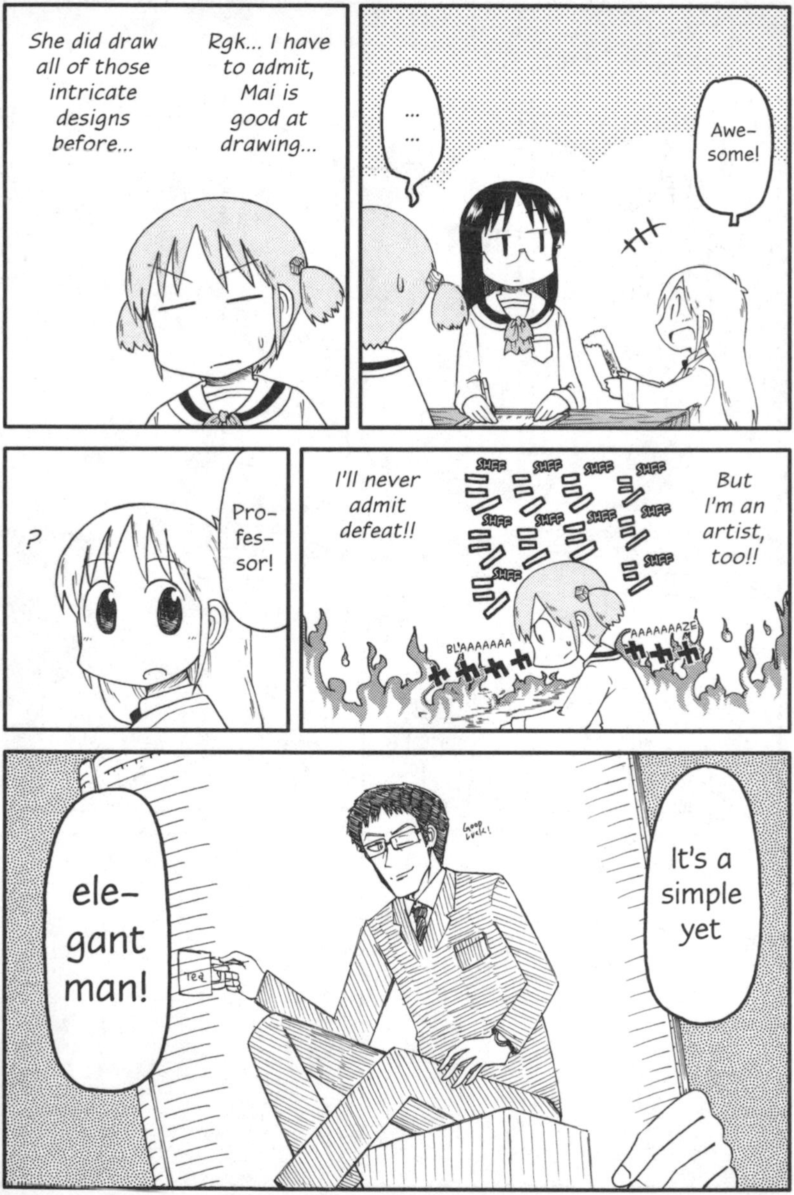
Awe-some!
…
…
Rgk... I have to admit, Mai is good at drawing...
She did draw all of those intricate designs before...
But I'm an artist, too!!
SHFF
I'll never admit defeat!!
BLAAAAAAA
AAAAAAAZE
Pro-fes-sor!
?
It's a simple yet
Good Luck!
ele-gant man!
Tea

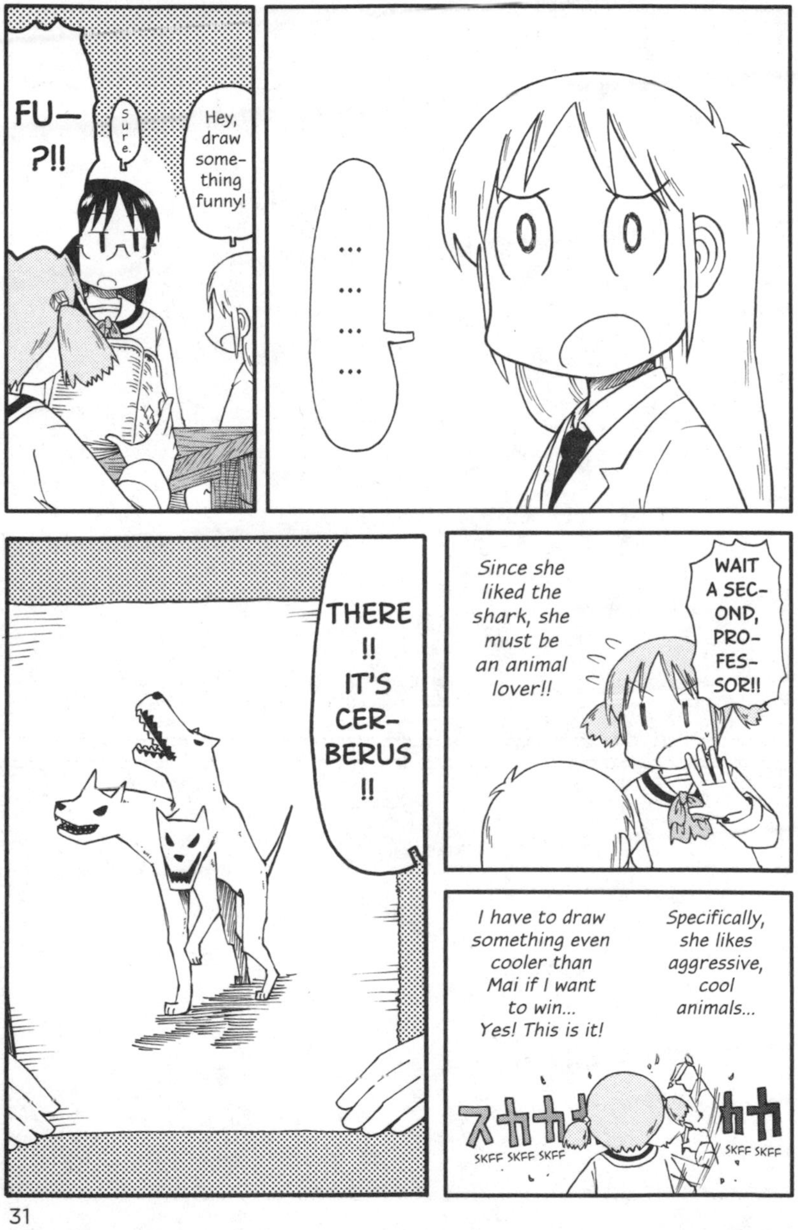
……
……
Hey, draw something funny!
Sure.
FU—?!!
WAIT A SECOND, PROFESSOR!!
Since she liked the shark, she must be an animal lover!!
Specifically, she likes aggressive, cool animals...
I have to draw something even cooler than Mai if I want to win... Yes! This is it!
カカ
SKFF SKFF
スカカ
SKFF SKFF SKFF
THERE!! IT'S CERBERUS!!

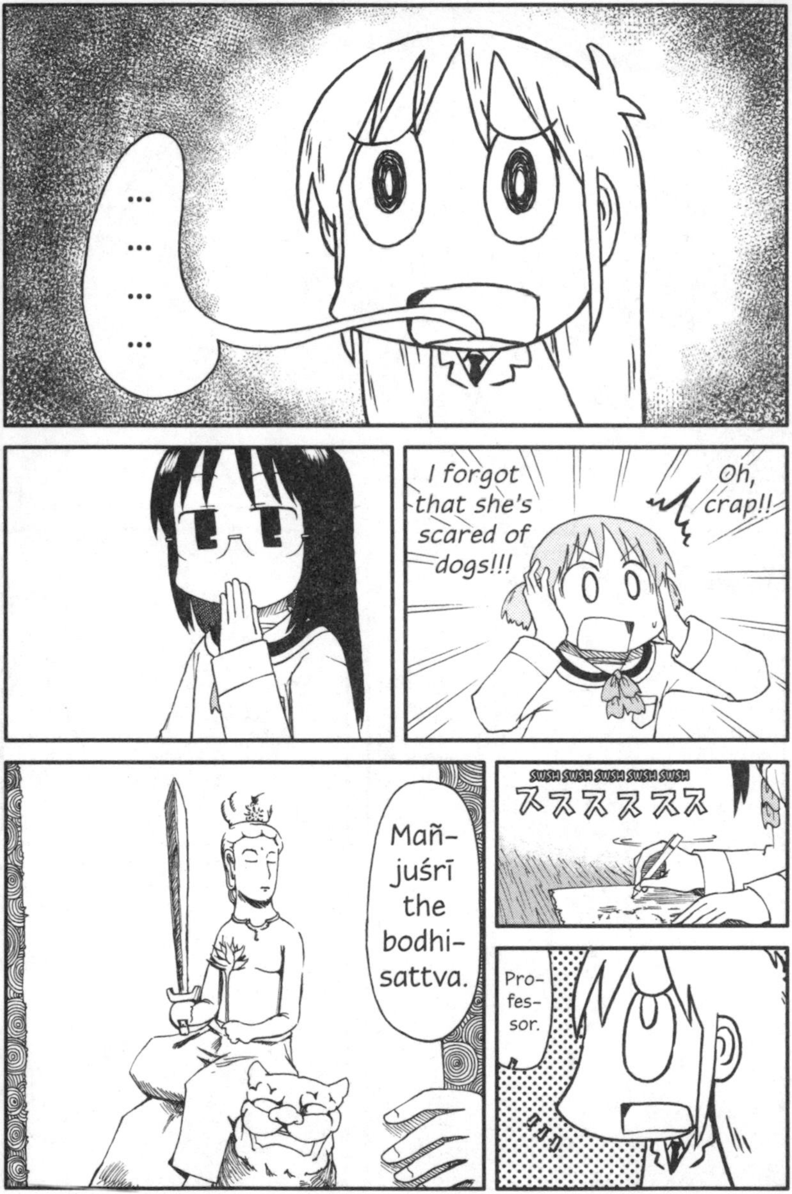
… … … …
Oh, crap!!
I forgot that she's scared of dogs!!!
SWSH SWSH SWSH SWSH SWSH
スススススス
Pro-fes-sor.
Mañ-juśrī the bodhi-sattva.

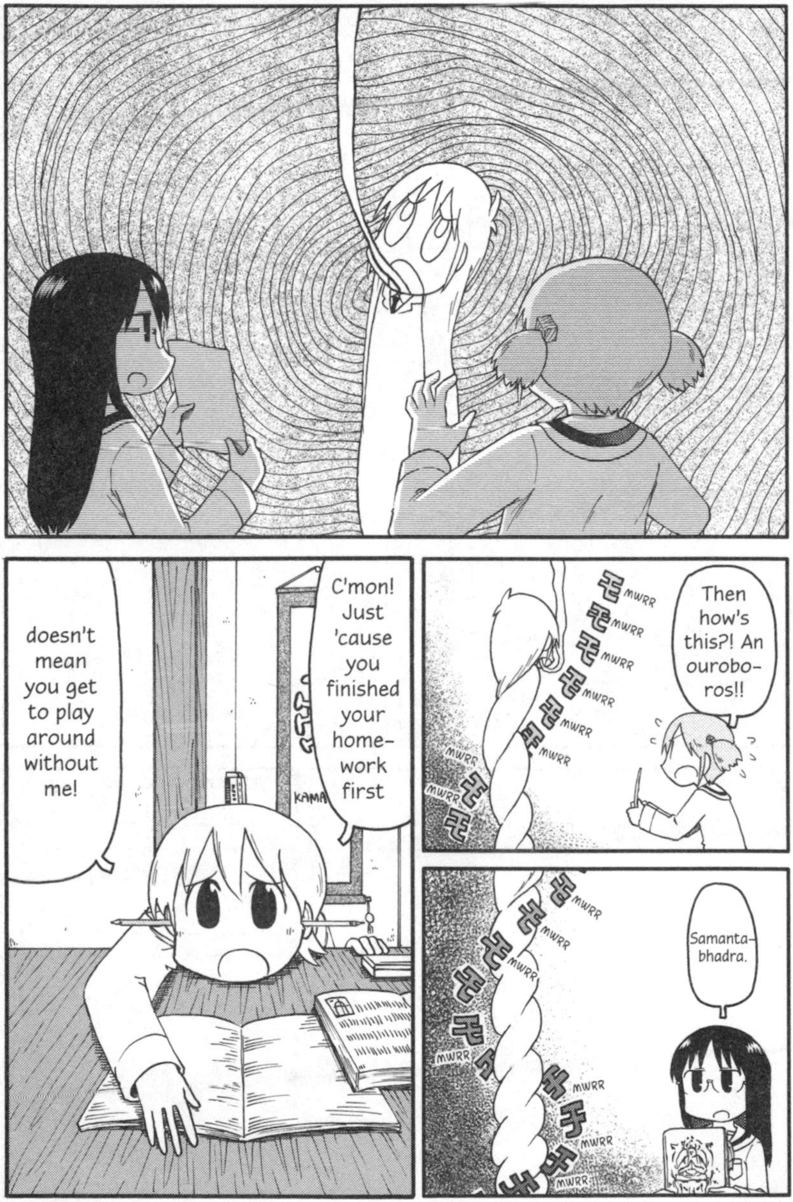
MWRR MWRR MWRR MWRR MWRR MWRR MWRR MWRR
Then how's this?! An ourobo-ros!!
MWRR MWRR MWRR MWRR MWRR MWRR
Samanta-bhadra.
C'mon! Just 'cause you finished your home-work first
KAMA
doesn't mean you get to play around without me!

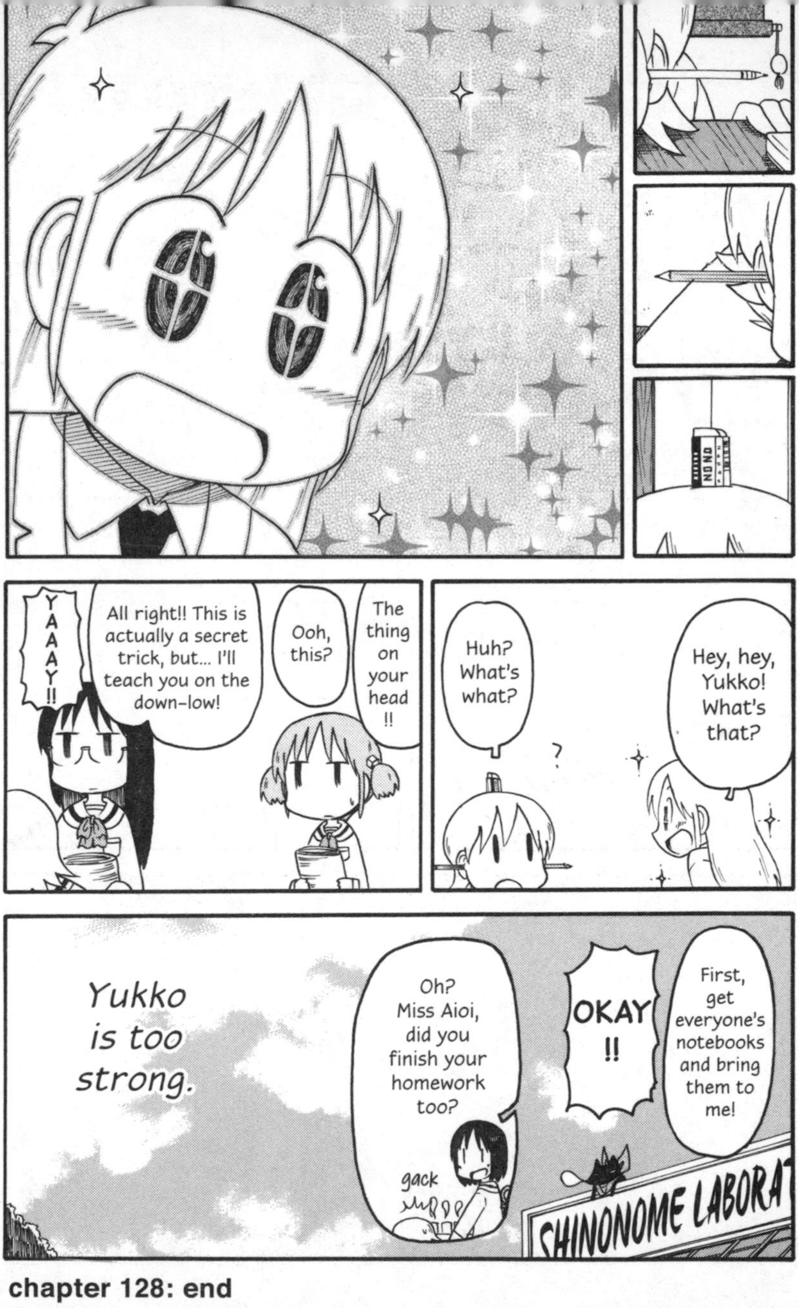
Hey, hey, Yukko! What's that?
Huh? What's what?
?
The thing on your head!!
Ooh, this?
All right!! This is actually a secret trick, but... I'll teach you on the down-low!
YAAAAY!!
First, get everyone's notebooks and bring them to me!
OKAY!!
Oh? Miss Aioi, did you finish your homework too?
gack
SHINONOME LABORAT
Yukko is too strong.

chapter 128: end

pter 129

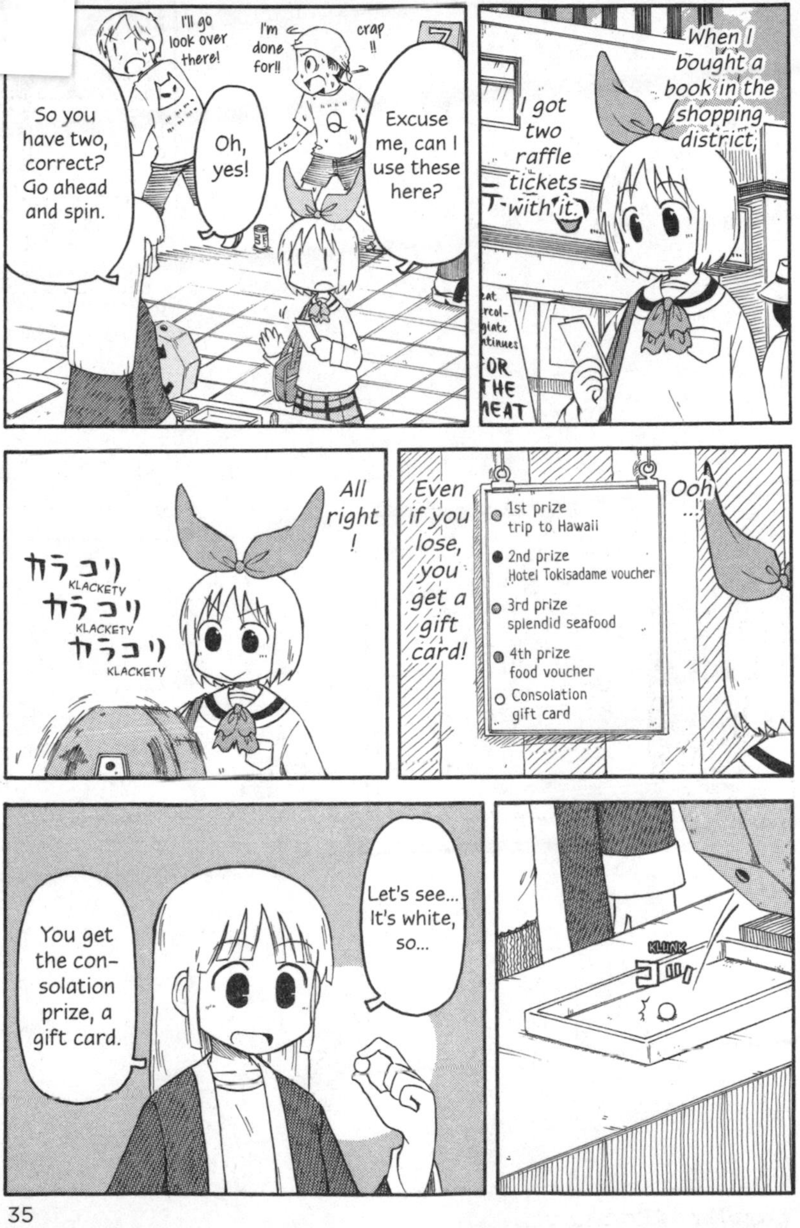

When I bought a book in the shopping district,
I got two raffle tickets with it.
FOR THE MEAT
Excuse me, can I use these here?
crap!!
I'm done for!!
I'll go look over there!
Oh, yes!
So you have two, correct? Go ahead and spin.
Ooh...
Even if you lose, you get a gift card!
1st prize trip to Hawaii
2nd prize Hotel Tokisadame voucher
3rd prize splendid seafood
4th prize food voucher
Consolation gift card
All right!
カラコリ KLACKETY
カラコリ KLACKETY
カラコリ KLACKETY
KLUNK
Let's see... It's white, so...
You get the consolation prize, a gift card.

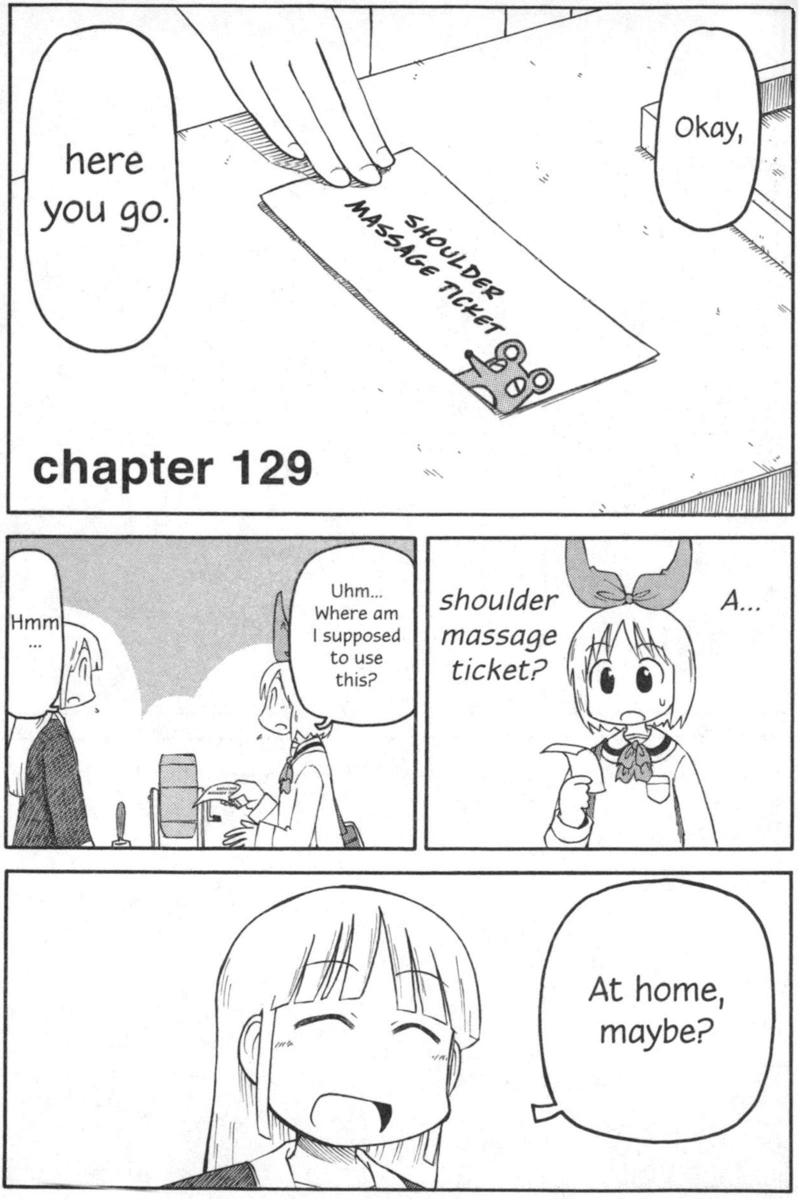
Okay,
here you go.
SHOULDER MASSAGE TICKET
chapter 129
A...
shoulder massage ticket?
Uhm... Where am I supposed to use this?
Hmm...
At home, maybe?

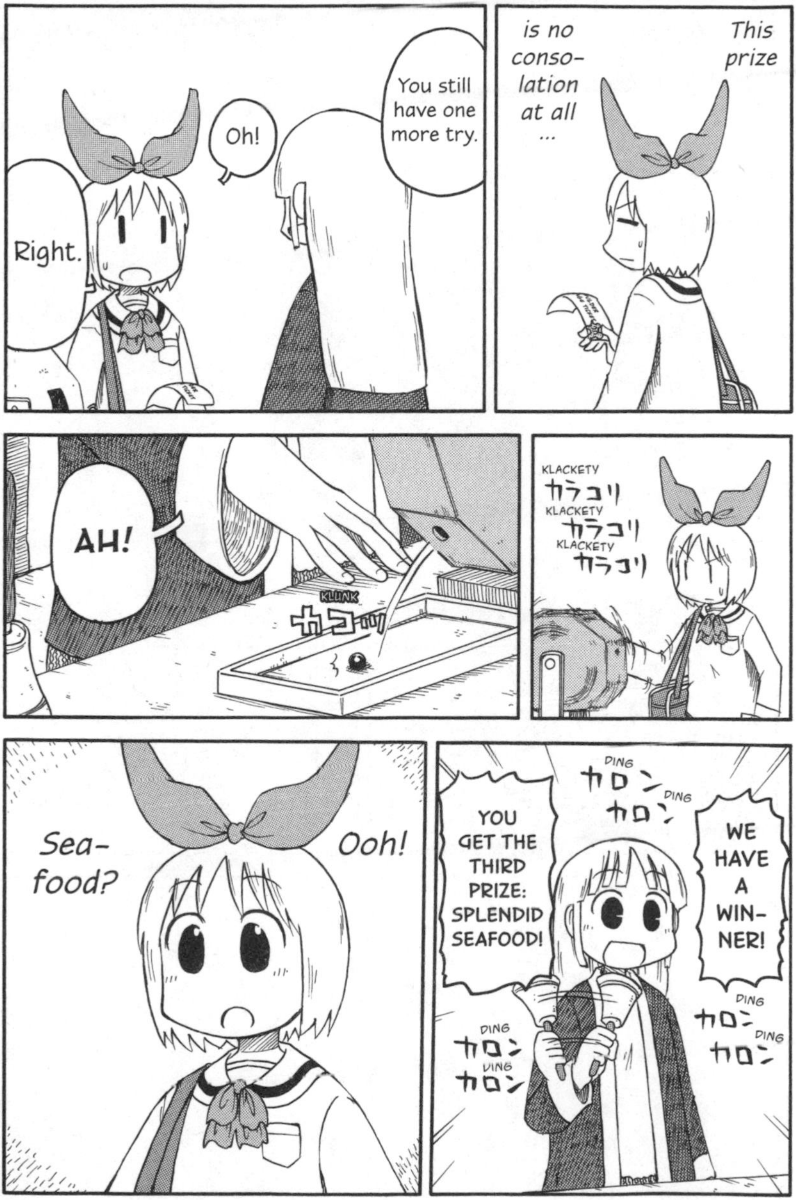
This prize is no consolation at all ...
You still have one more try.
Oh!
Right.
KLACKETY
カラコリ
KLACKETY
カラコリ
KLACKETY
カラコリ
KLUNK
カコッ
AH!
DING
カロン
DING
カロン
WE HAVE A WINNER!
YOU GET THE THIRD PRIZE: SPLENDID SEAFOOD!
DING
カロン
DING
カロン
DING
カロン
DING
カロン
Ooh!
Sea-food?

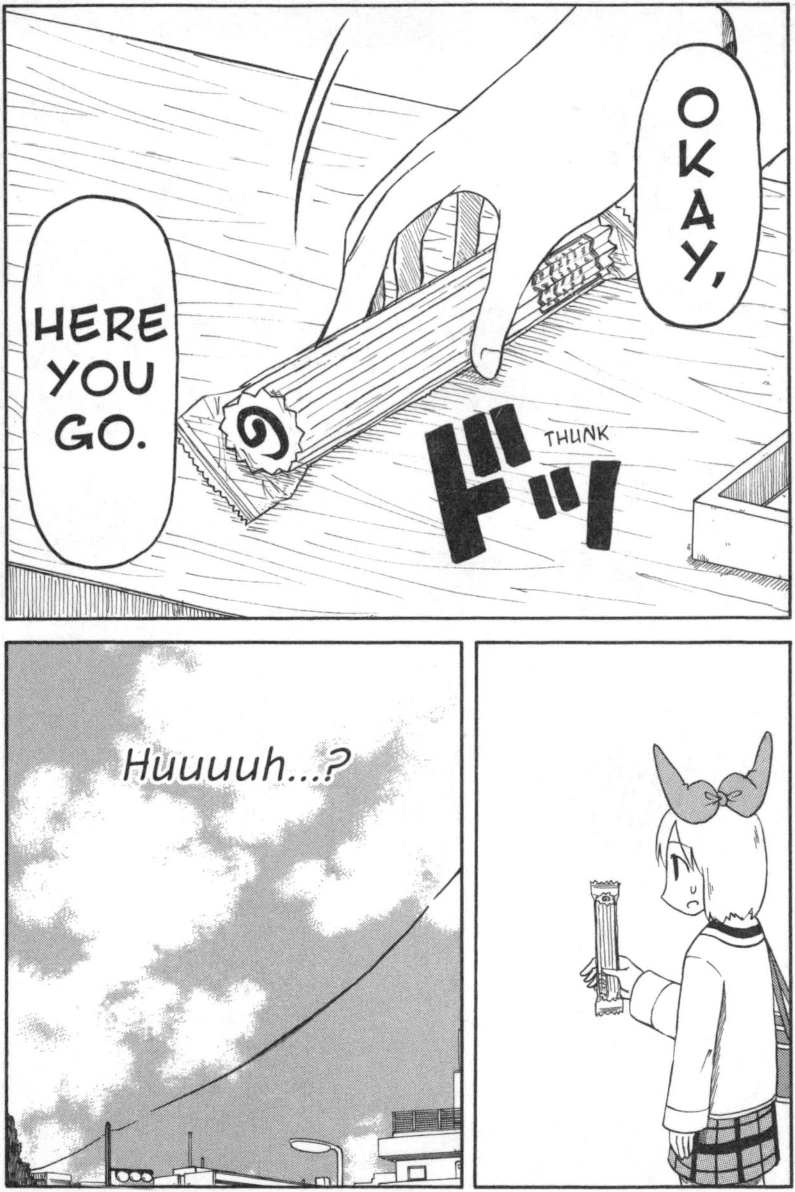
OKAY,
HERE YOU GO.
ドッ
THUNK
Huuuuh...?

chapter 129: end

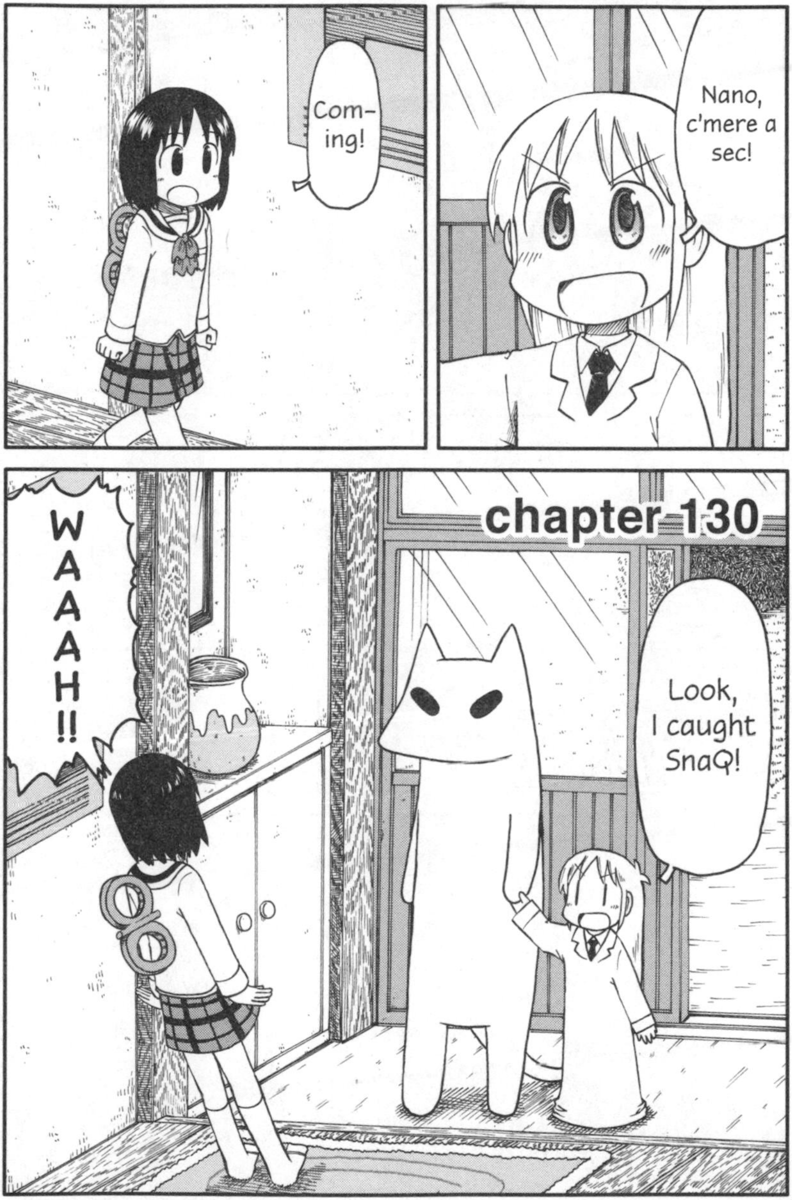
Nano, c'mere a sec!
Com-ing!
chapter 130
Look, I caught SnaQ!
WAAAAH!!

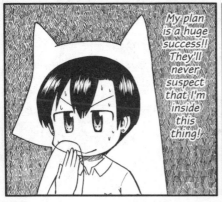

Heh heh heh heh heh ...
My plan is a huge success!! They'll never suspect that I'm inside this thing!
Dressing up as the mascot of this kid's favorite snack was a stroke of genius.
I don't need Mr. Peace anymore, wherever he flew off to.
On top of being woven with Kevlar and aramid fibers, this suit is even protected with a trauma plate.
Now if I get attacked by the daruma, the homunculus, or the sentry robot, I'll be able to stay safe!
Even if I blunder into an adhesion trap like last time,
I can just take off the suit and escape! Heh heh heh... It's flawless!
もが FLAIL
もが FLAIL
もが FLAIL
もが FLAIL
I'm sure the kid will behave if I give her some snacks.
Then I'll use Nano Shinonome's naïveté to my advantage and finally steal the blueprints, wherever they are!!
ピカ
GLINT

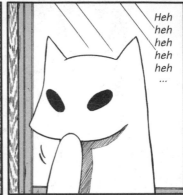

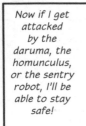

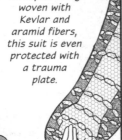

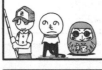

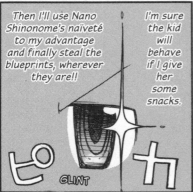

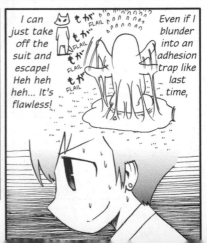

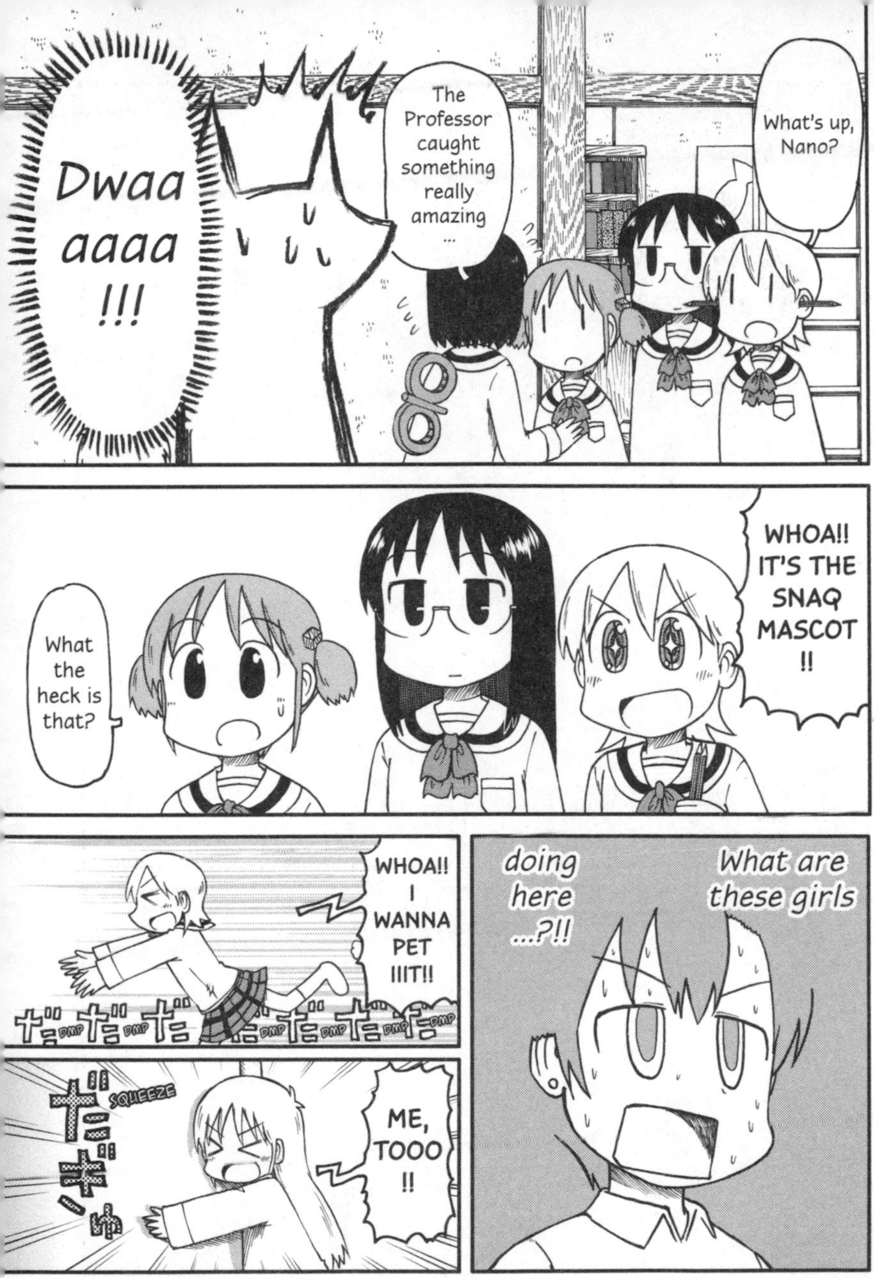
What's up, Nano?
The Professor caught something really amazing ...
Dwaaaaaa!!!
WHOA!! IT'S THE SNAQ MASCOT!!
What the heck is that?
What are these girls doing here ...?!!
WHOA!! I WANNA PET IIIT!!
DMP DMP DMP DMP DMP DMP
ME, TOOO!!
SQUEEZE

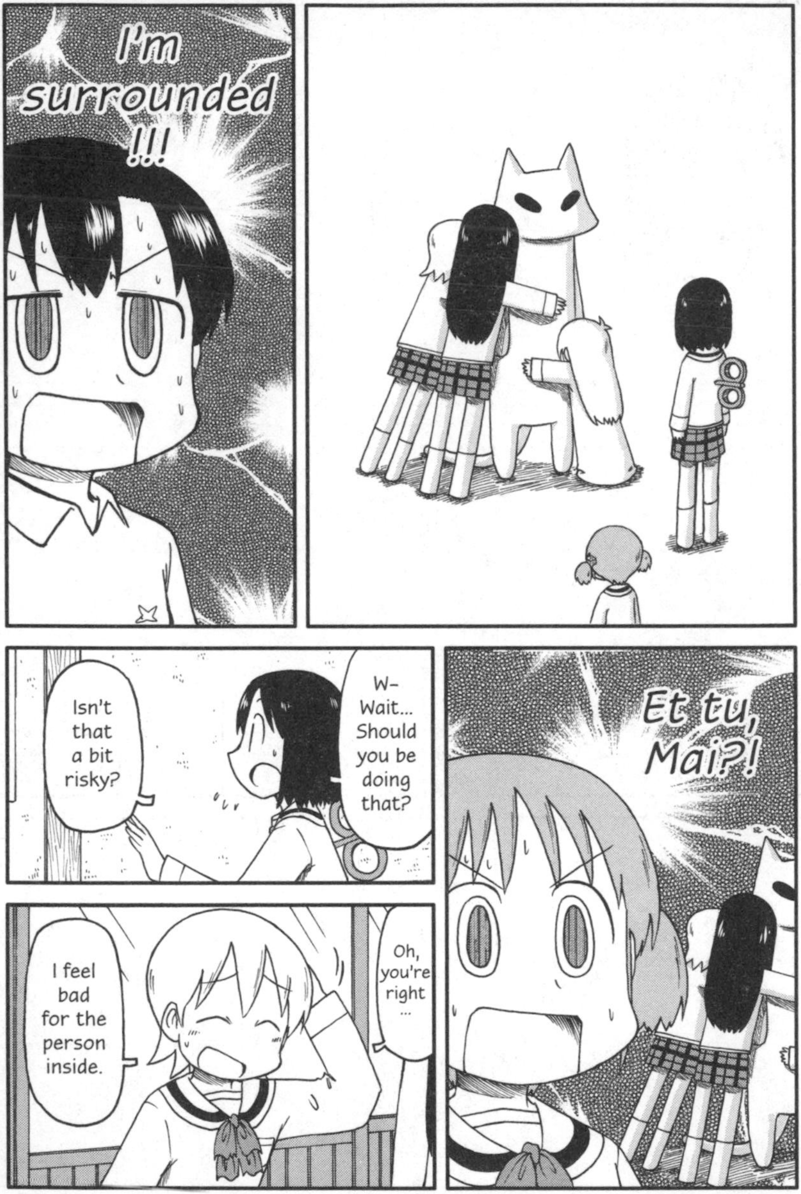
I'm surrounded!!!
Et tu, Mai?!
W- Wait... Should you be doing that?
Isn't that a bit risky?
Oh, you're right ...
I feel bad for the person inside.

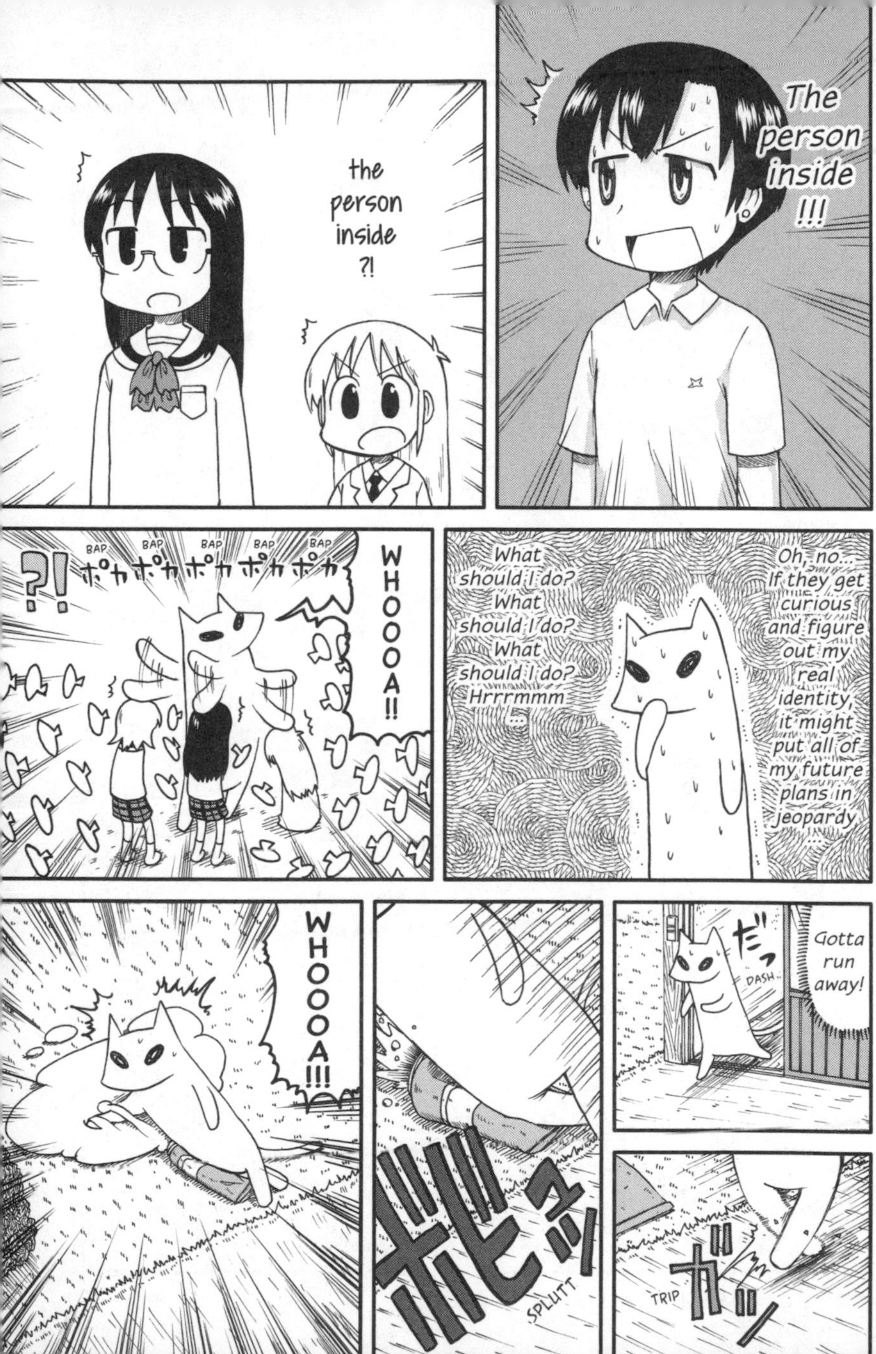
The person inside !!!
the person inside ?!
Oh, no... If they get curious and figure out my real identity, it might put all of my future plans in jeopardy...
What should I do? What should I do? What should I do? Hrrrmmm...
WHOOOOA!!
ポカポカポカポカポカ
BAP BAP BAP BAP BAP
?!
Gotta run away!
ダッ
DASH
ガッ
TRIP
ボヒュッ
SPLUTT
WHOOOOA!!!

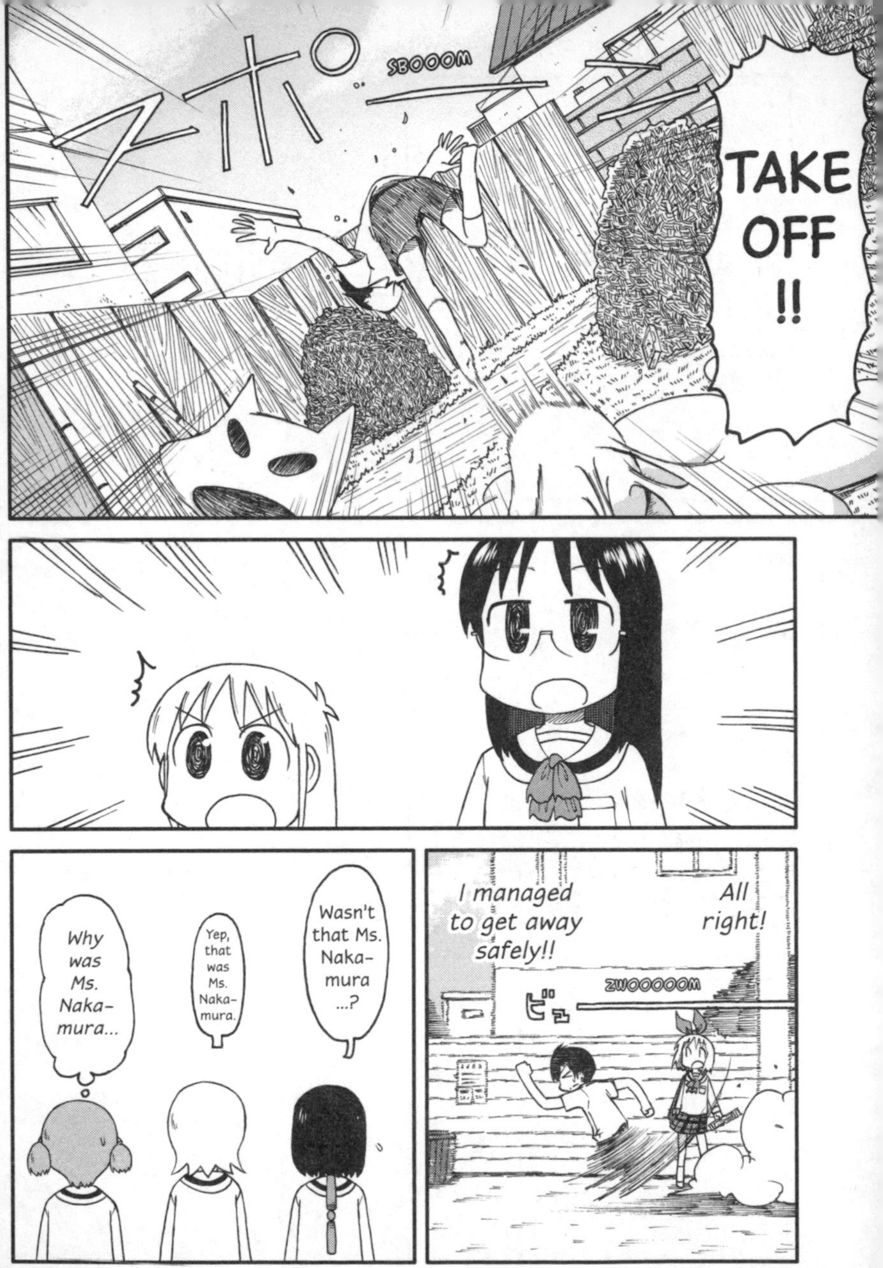

スポー
SBOOOM
TAKE OFF !!
All right!
I managed to get away safely!!
ビュ
ZWOOOOOM
Wasn't that Ms. Naka-mura ...?
Yep, that was Ms. Naka-mura.
Why was Ms. Naka-mura...

chapter 130: end

nichijou

keiichi arawi

ordinary shorts 15

two people, one coat

All right, time to eat!
LIFT
ひょい
Yep, yep, just gonna grab these chopsticks like so...
Then I'm gonna peel off the fish's skin, like so...
PEEL
... Then I'll just... separate the meat...
スススススス
SFF SFF SFF SFF SFF SFF
from the bones... so it's... easy to eat...
COME ON!! MAI!!
SFF SFF
ススス
スススス
ススススス
SFF SFF SFF
STOP BEING SO PERFECT WITH THIS!!

coincidental finale

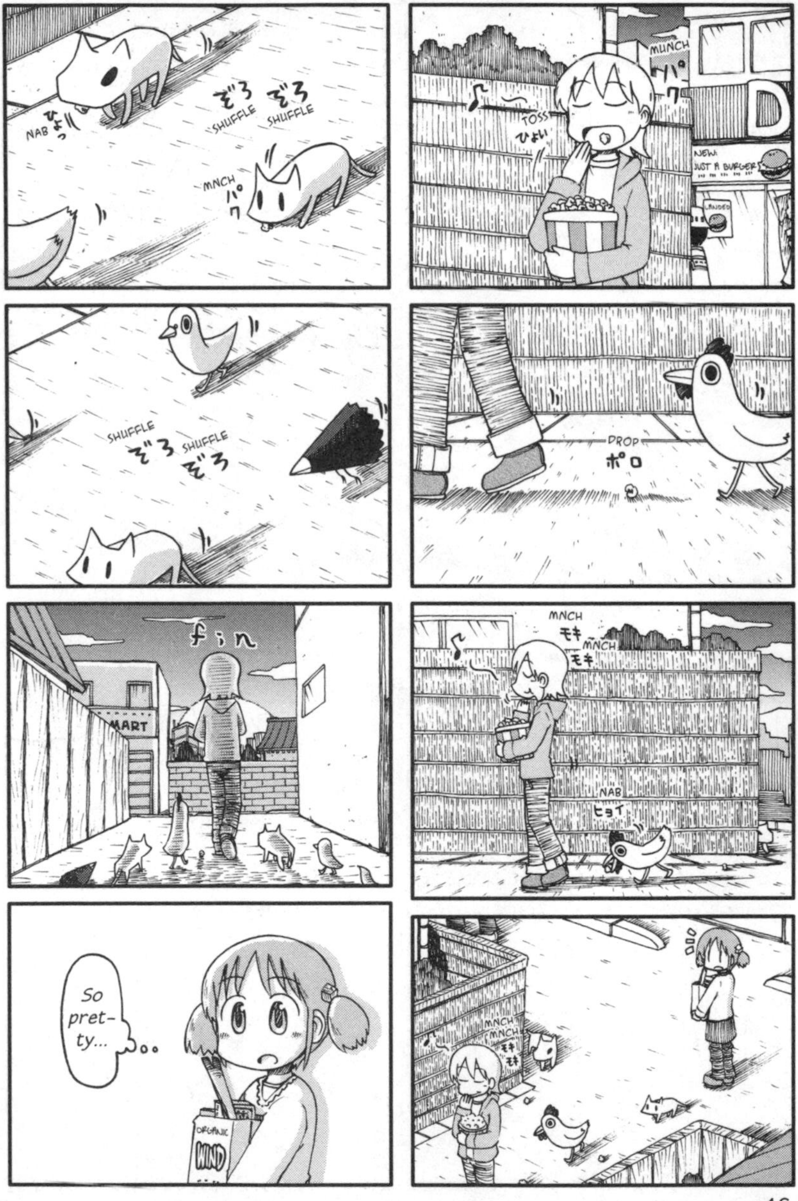

MUNCH
パク
TOSS
ひょい
D
NEW! JUST A BURGER
LANDED
NAB
ひょっ
ぞろ ぞろ
SHUFFLE SHUFFLE
MNCH
パク
DROP
ポロ
SHUFFLE
ぞろ
SHUFFLE
ぞろ
MNCH
モキ
MNCH
モキ
NAB
ヒョイ
fin
MART
MNCH
MNCH
モキ
モキ
So pret-ty...
ORGANIC
WIND

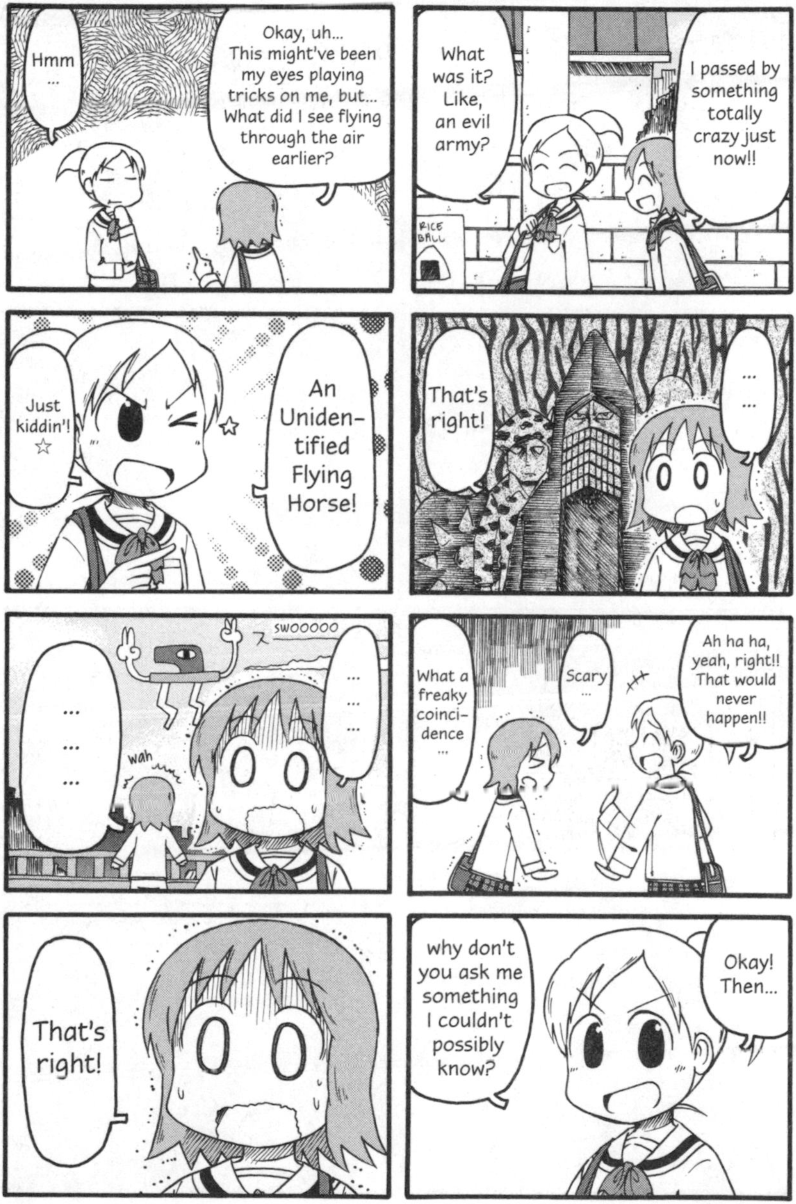
I passed by something totally crazy just now!!
What was it? Like, an evil army?
... ...
That's right!
Ah ha ha, yeah, right!! That would never happen!!
Scary ...
What a freaky coinci-dence ...
Okay! Then...
why don't you ask me something I couldn't possibly know?
Okay, uh... This might've been my eyes playing tricks on me, but... What did I see flying through the air earlier?
Hmm ...
An Uniden-tified Flying Horse!
Just kiddin'! ☆
... ...
SWOOOOO
wah
... ...
That's right!

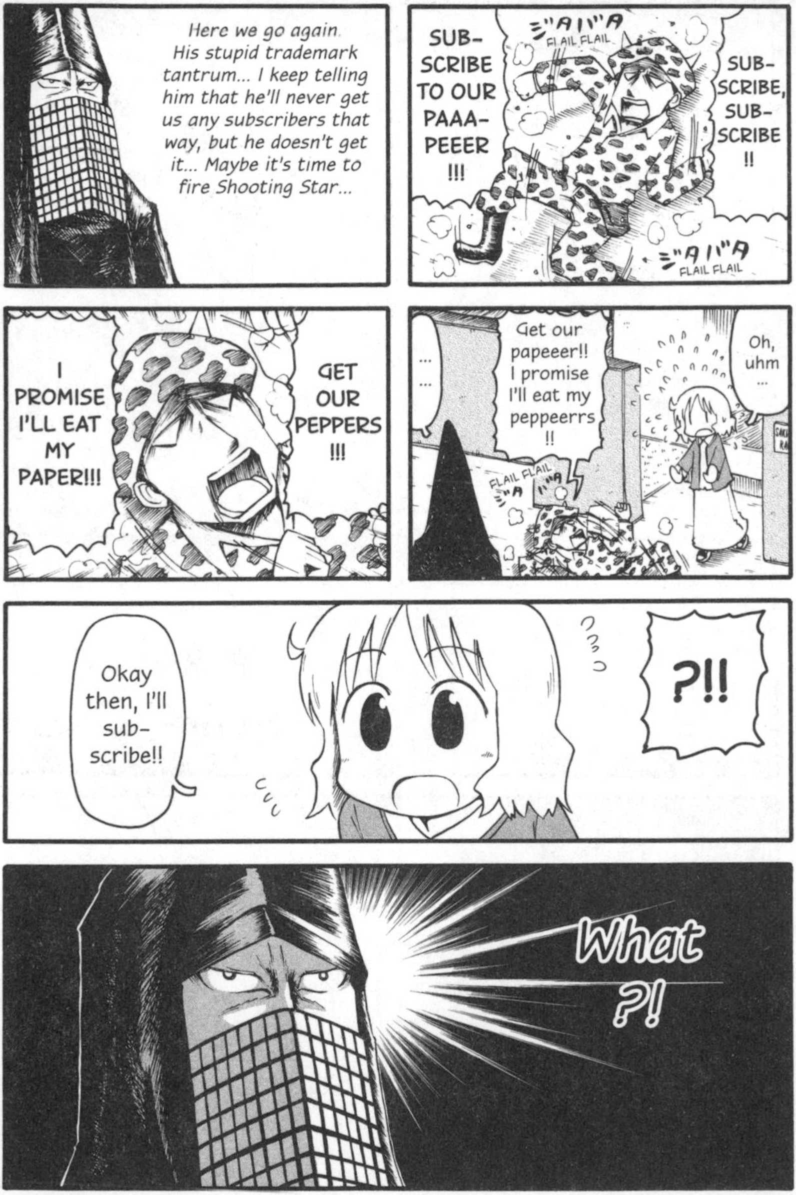
SUB-SCRIBE, SUB-SCRIBE !!
ジタバタ FLAIL FLAIL
SUB-SCRIBE TO OUR PAAA-PEEER !!!
ジタバタ FLAIL FLAIL
Here we go again. His stupid trademark tantrum... I keep telling him that he'll never get us any subscribers that way, but he doesn't get it... Maybe it's time to fire Shooting Star...
Oh, uhm ...
Get our papeeer!! I promise I'll eat my peppeerrs !!
... ...
FLAIL FLAIL
GET OUR PEPPERS !!!
I PROMISE I'LL EAT MY PAPER!!!
?!!
Okay then, I'll sub-scribe!!
What ?!

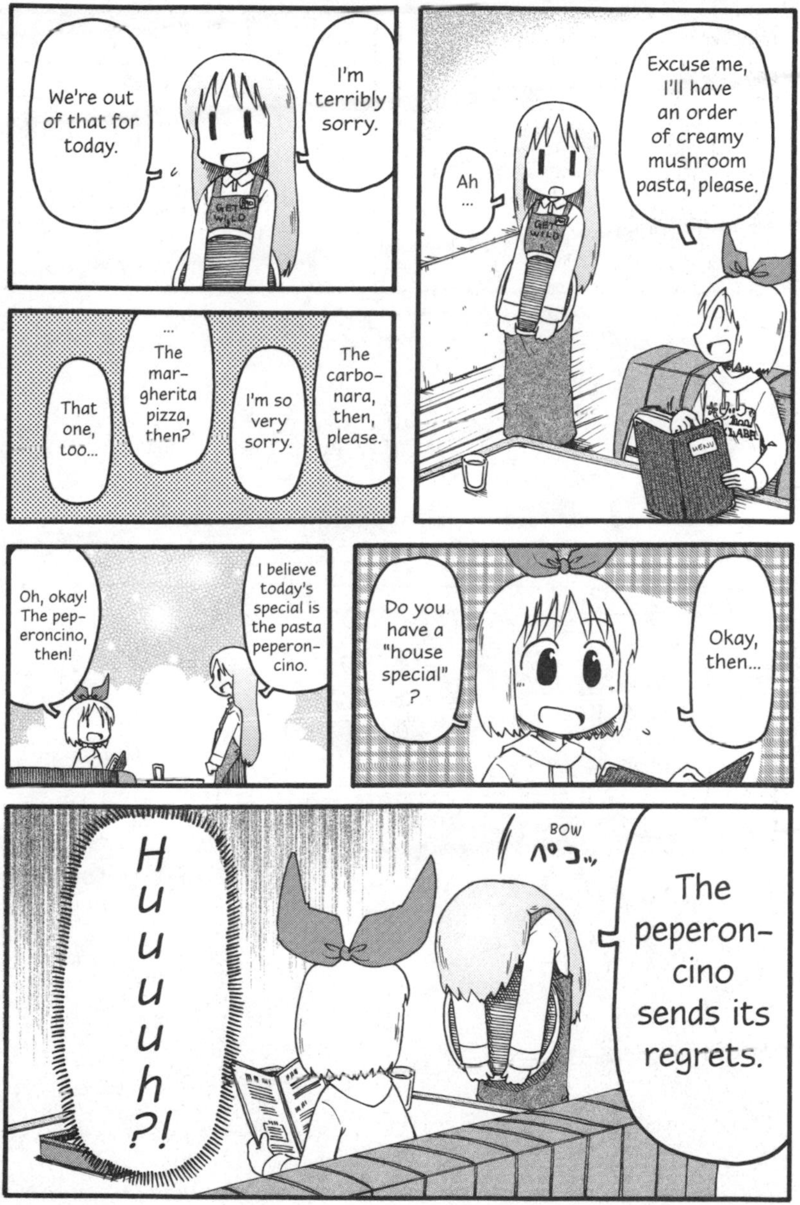
Excuse me, I'll have an order of creamy mushroom pasta, please.
Ah ...
MENU
I'm terribly sorry.
We're out of that for today.
The carbonara, then, please.
I'm so very sorry.
... The margherita pizza, then?
That one, too...
Okay, then...
Do you have a "house special"?
I believe today's special is the pasta peperoncino.
Oh, okay! The peperoncino, then!
The peperoncino sends its regrets.
BOW
ペコッ
Huuuuh?!

get wild cafe

CINNAMO...	
HOT COCOA	¥500
MILKSHAKE	¥400
WEINER COFFEE	¥400
LEMON SQUASH	¥400

the tragedy of shooting star

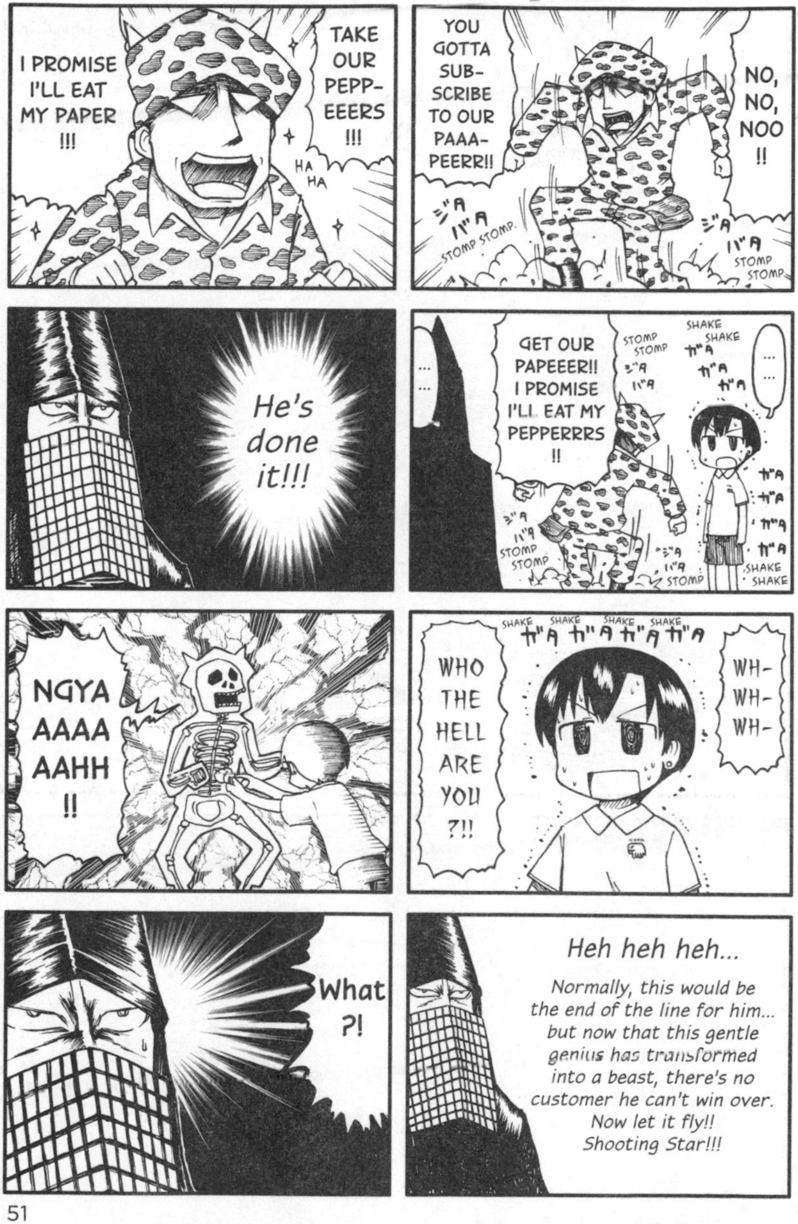
NO, NO, NOO !!
YOU GOTTA SUB-SCRIBE TO OUR PAAA-PEERR!!
ジタ バタ STOMP STOMP
ジタ バタ STOMP STOMP
......
SHAKE SHAKE ガタ ガタ ガタ
STOMP STOMP ジタ バタ
GET OUR PAPEEER!! I PROMISE I'LL EAT MY PEPPERRRS !!
......
ガタ ガタ ガタ ガタ SHAKE SHAKE
ジタ バタ STOMP STOMP
ジタ バタ STOMP
WH- WH- WH-
SHAKE SHAKE SHAKE SHAKE ガタ ガタ ガタ ガタ
WHO THE HELL ARE YOU ?!!
Heh heh heh...
Normally, this would be the end of the line for him... but now that this gentle genius has transformed into a beast, there's no customer he can't win over. Now let it fly!! Shooting Star!!!
TAKE OUR PEPP-EEERS !!!
I PROMISE I'LL EAT MY PAPER !!!
HA HA
He's done it!!!
NGYA AAAA AAHH !!
What ?!

the baby black mamba from that one time randomly came back from its journey!!

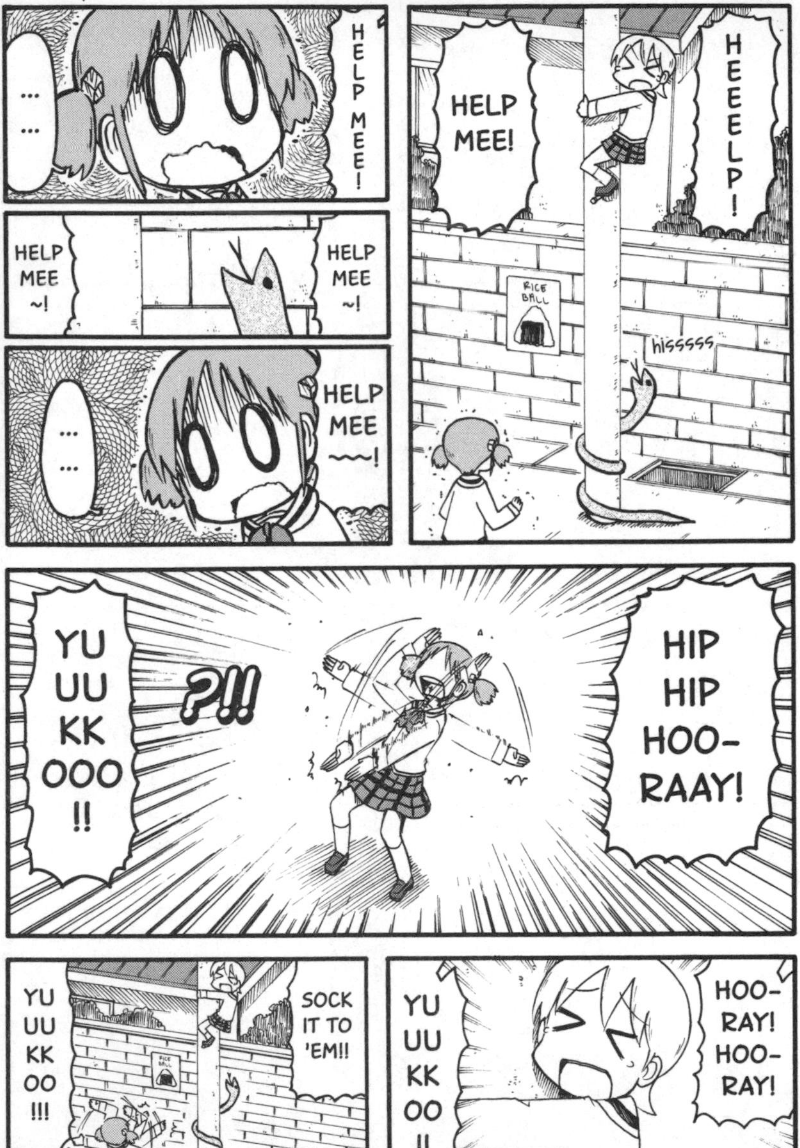
HEEEELP!
HELP MEE!
RICE BALL
hissssss
HELP MEE!
...
...
HELP MEE ~!
HELP MEE ~!
HELP MEE ~~~!
...
...
HIP HIP HOO-RAAY!
?!!
YUUUKKOOO!!
HOO-RAY! HOO-RAY!
YUUUKKOO!!
SOCK IT TO 'EM!!
RICE BALL
YUUUKKOO!!!

ordinary shorts 15: end

chapter 131

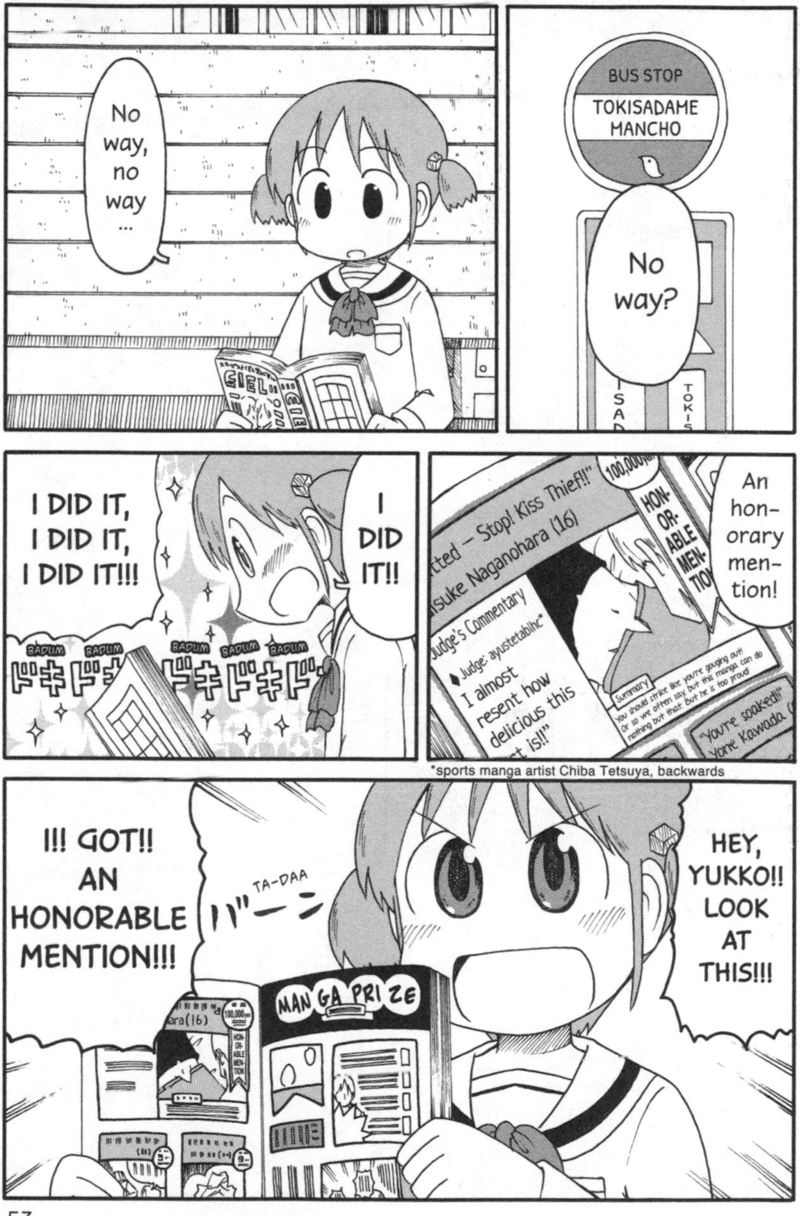
BUS STOP
TOKISADAME MANCHO
No way?
No way, no way ...
An honorary mention!
100,000yen
Judge's Commentary
Judge: ayustetabihc*
I almost resent how delicious this
Summary
You should strike like you're gouging out! Or so we often say, but this manga can do nothing but that. But he is too proud!
I DID IT!!
I DID IT, I DID IT, I DID IT!!!
BADUM
BADUM
BADUM
BADUM
BADUM
HEY, YUKKO!! LOOK AT THIS!!!
TA-DAA
!!! GOT!! AN HONORABLE MENTION!!!
MANGA PRIZE

*sports manga artist Chiba Tetsuya, backwards

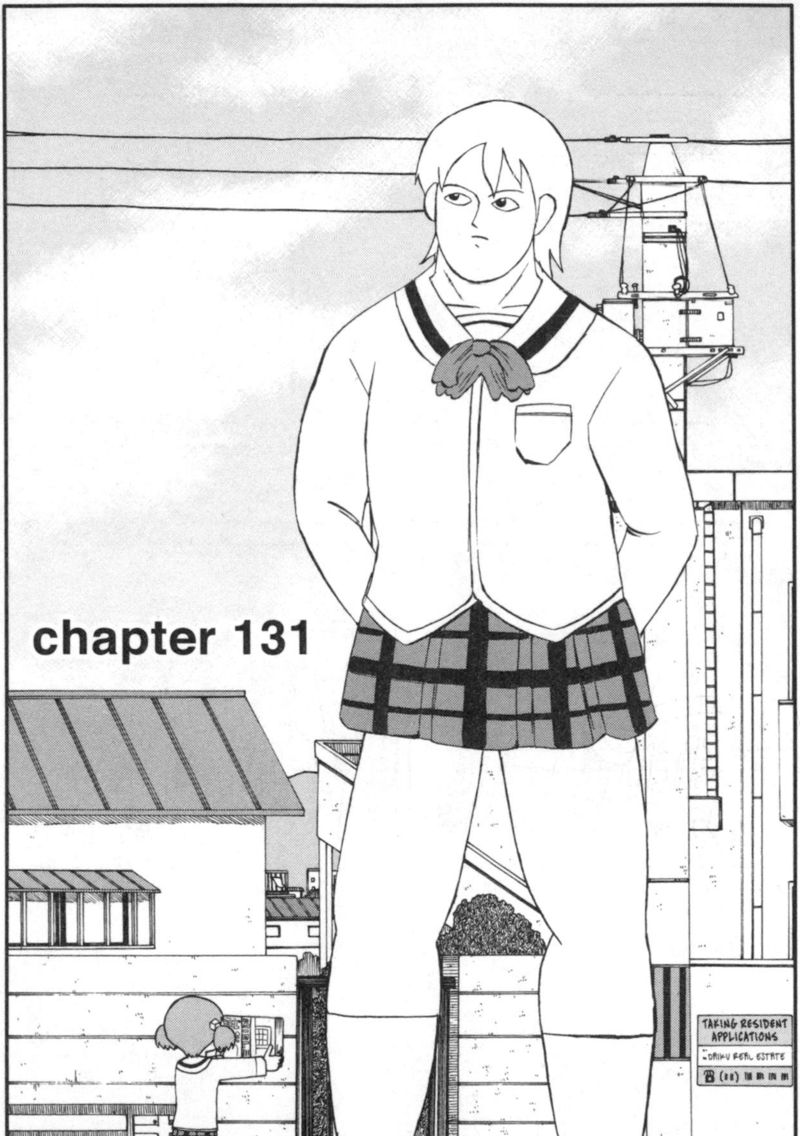
chapter 131
TAKING RESIDENT APPLICATIONS
DAIKU REAL ESTATE

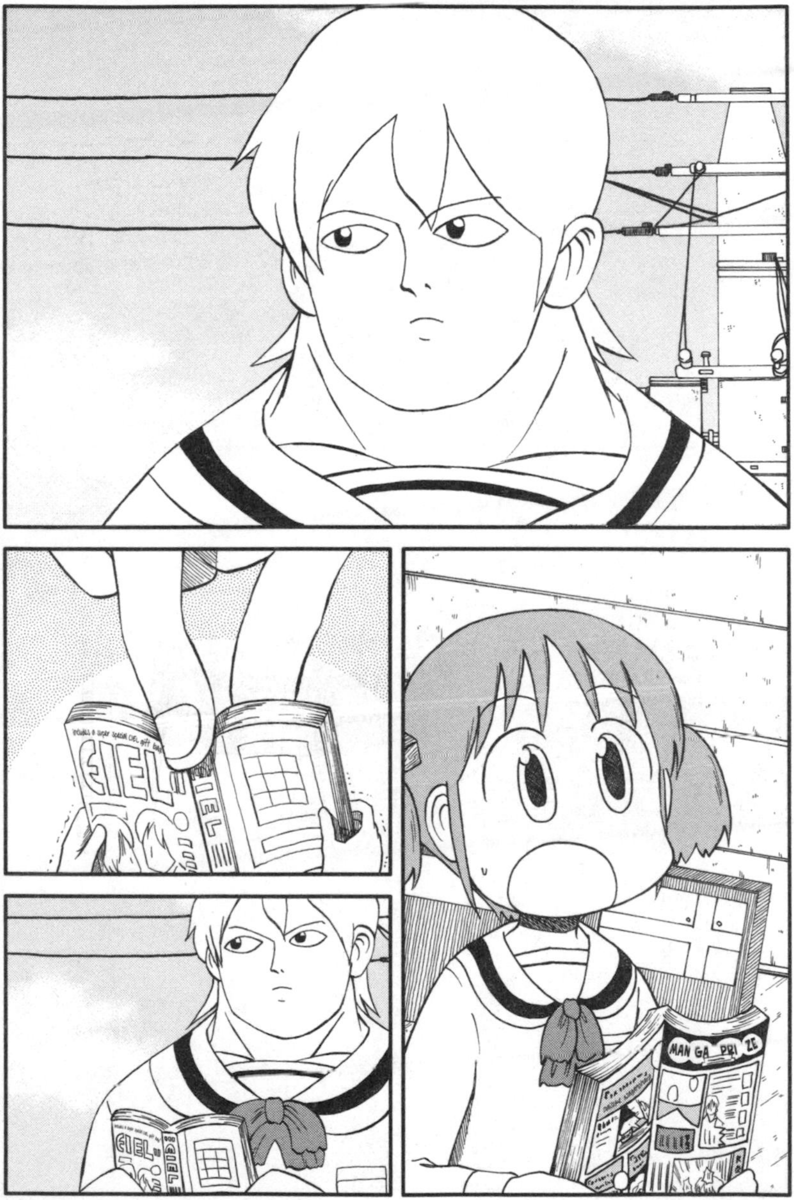
MANGA PRIZE
includes a super special CIEL gift
CIEL
CIEL

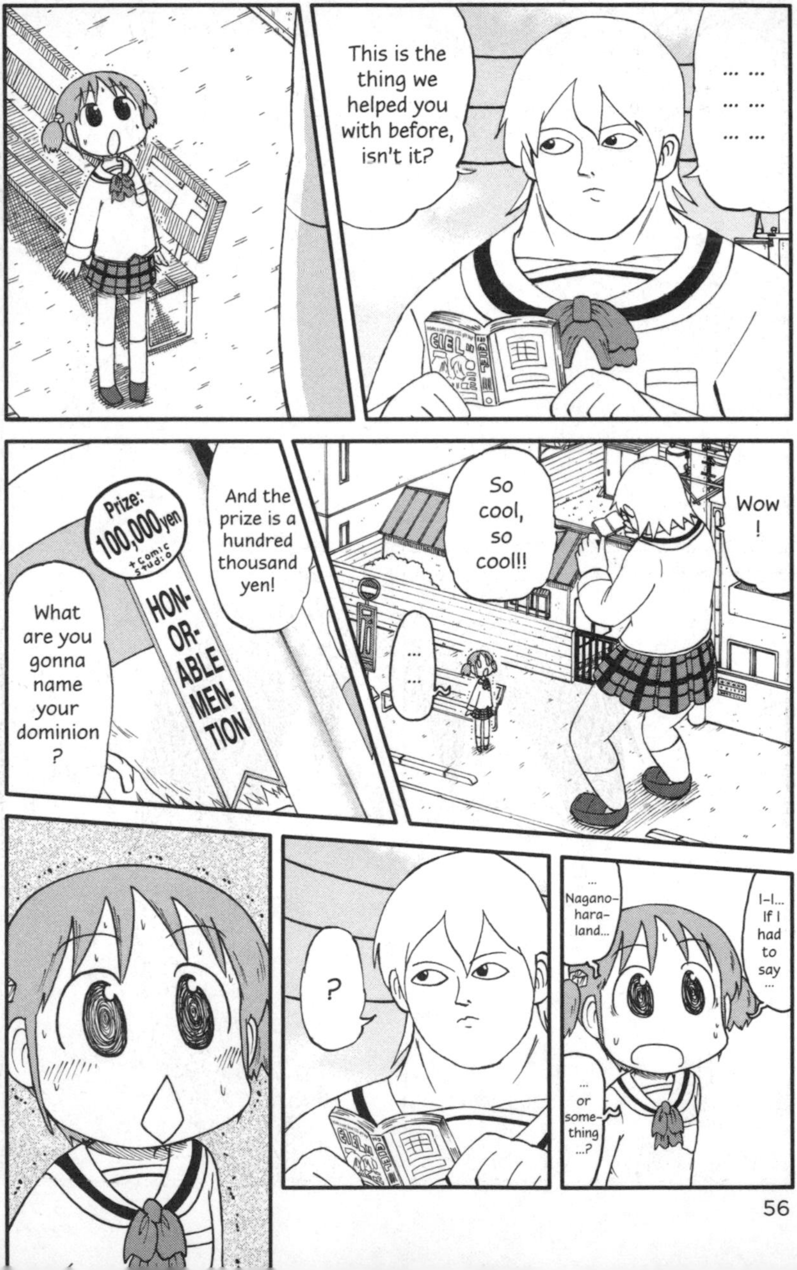
... ...
This is the thing we helped you with before, isn't it?
Wow!
So cool, so cool!!
... ...
And the prize is a hundred thousand yen!
Prize: 100,000yen +comic studio
HONORABLE MENTION
What are you gonna name your dominion?
I-I... If I had to say...
... Naganohara-land...
... or something...?
?

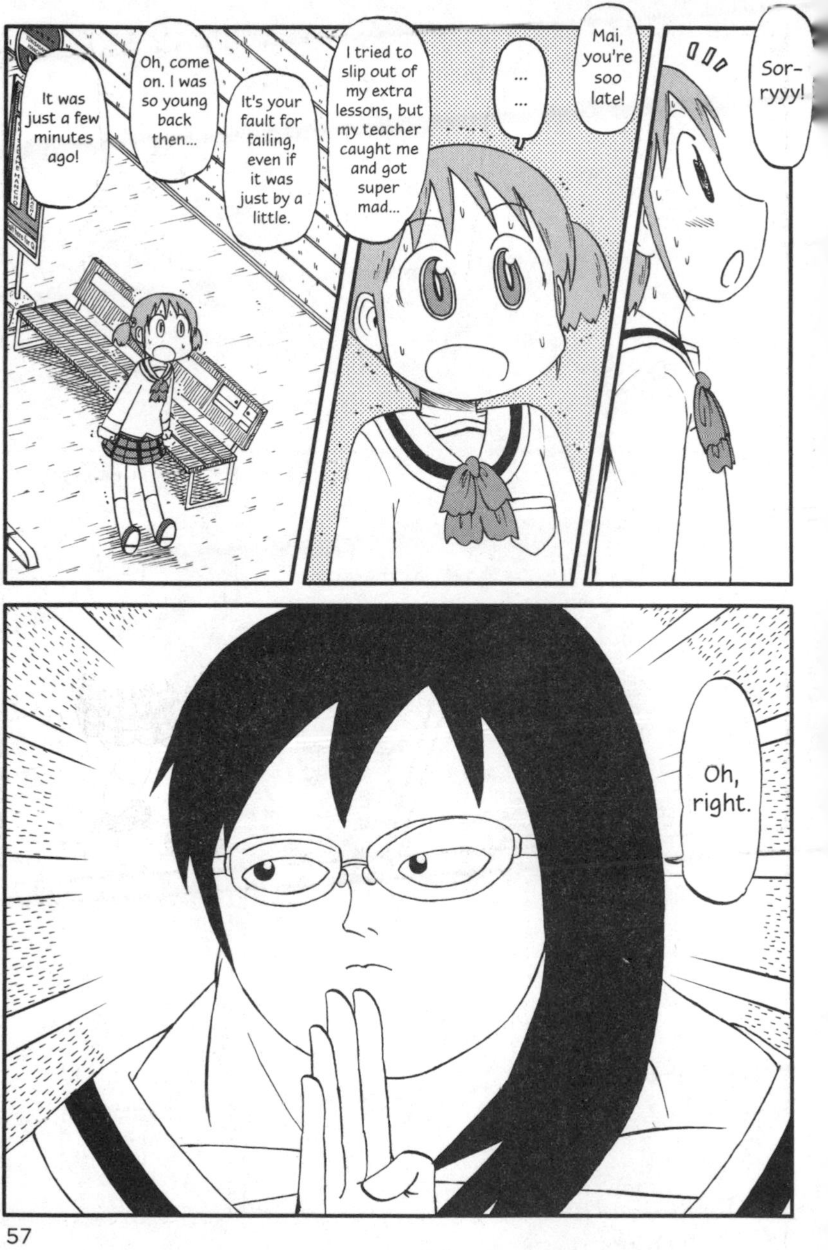
Sor-ryyy!
Mai, you're soo late!
... ...
I tried to slip out of my extra lessons, but my teacher caught me and got super mad...
It's your fault for failing, even if it was just by a little.
Oh, come on. I was so young back then...
It was just a few minutes ago!
Oh, right.

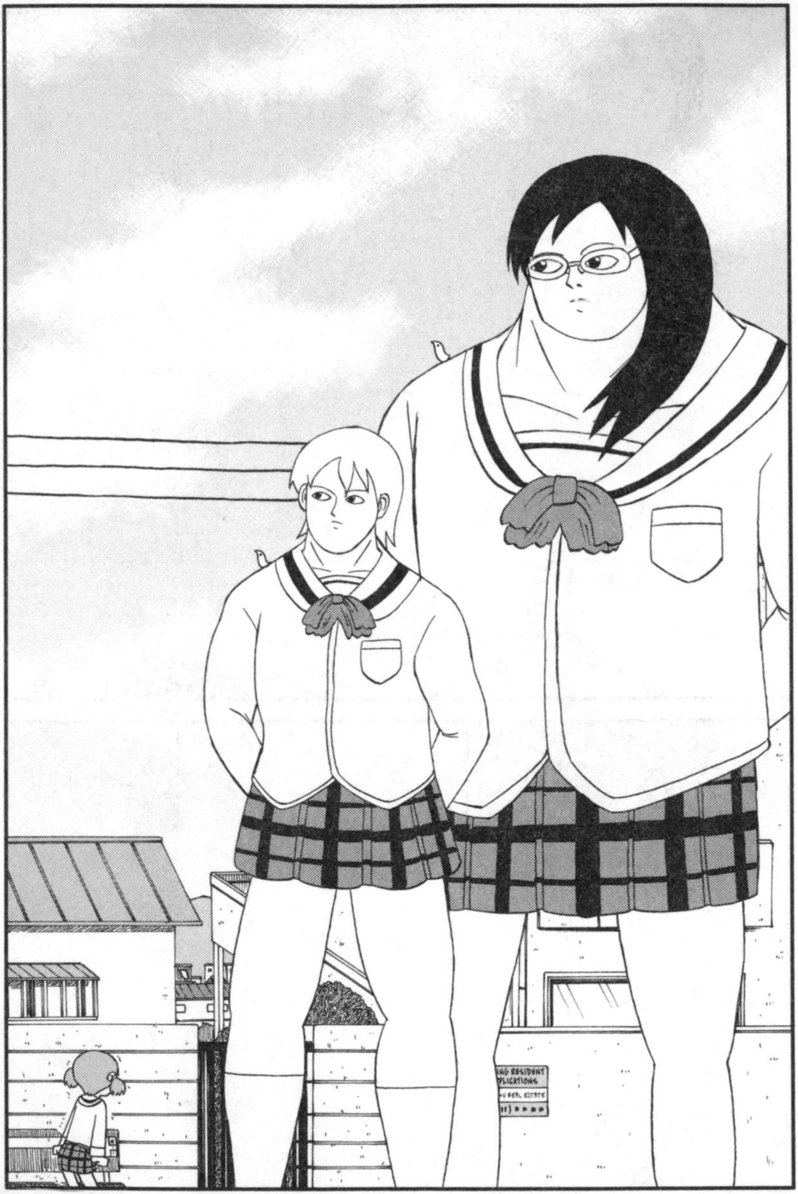
ING RESIDENT
PLICATIONS
REAL ESTATE

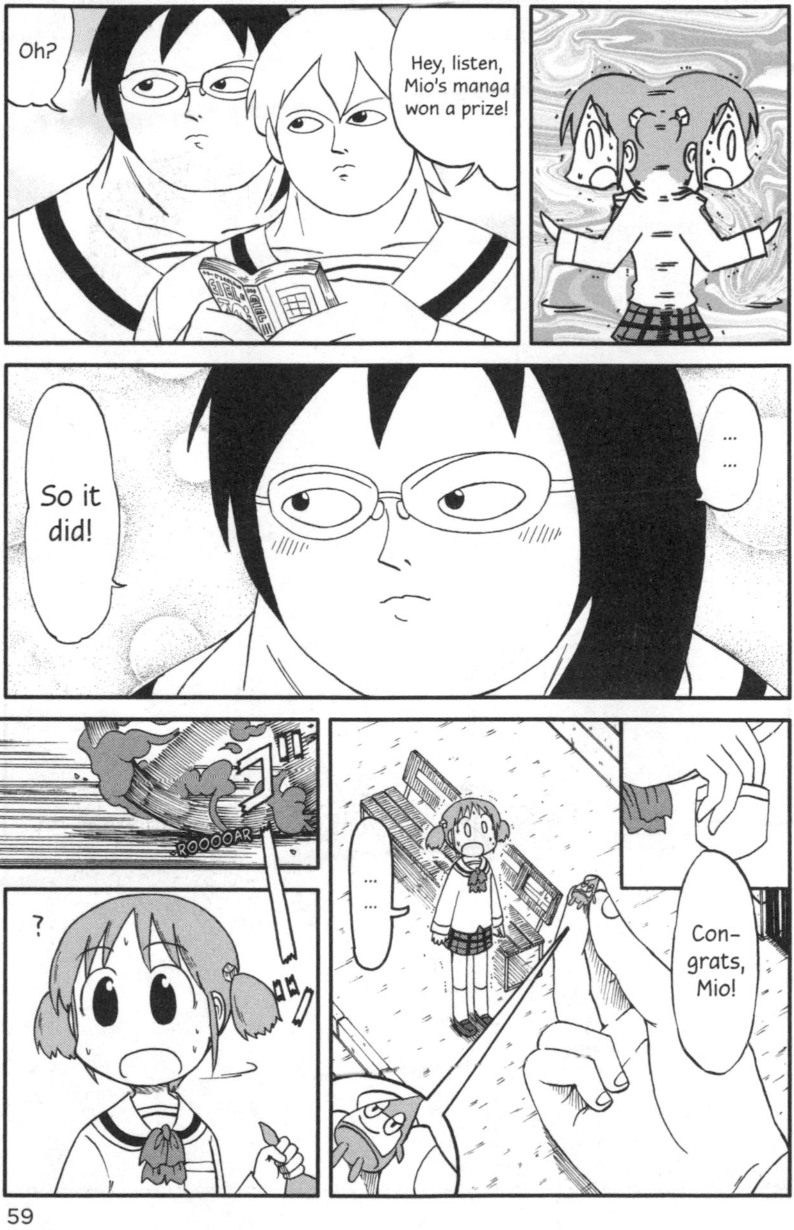
Hey, listen, Mio's manga won a prize!
Oh?
... ...
So it did!
Con-grats, Mio!
... ...
ROOOOAR
?

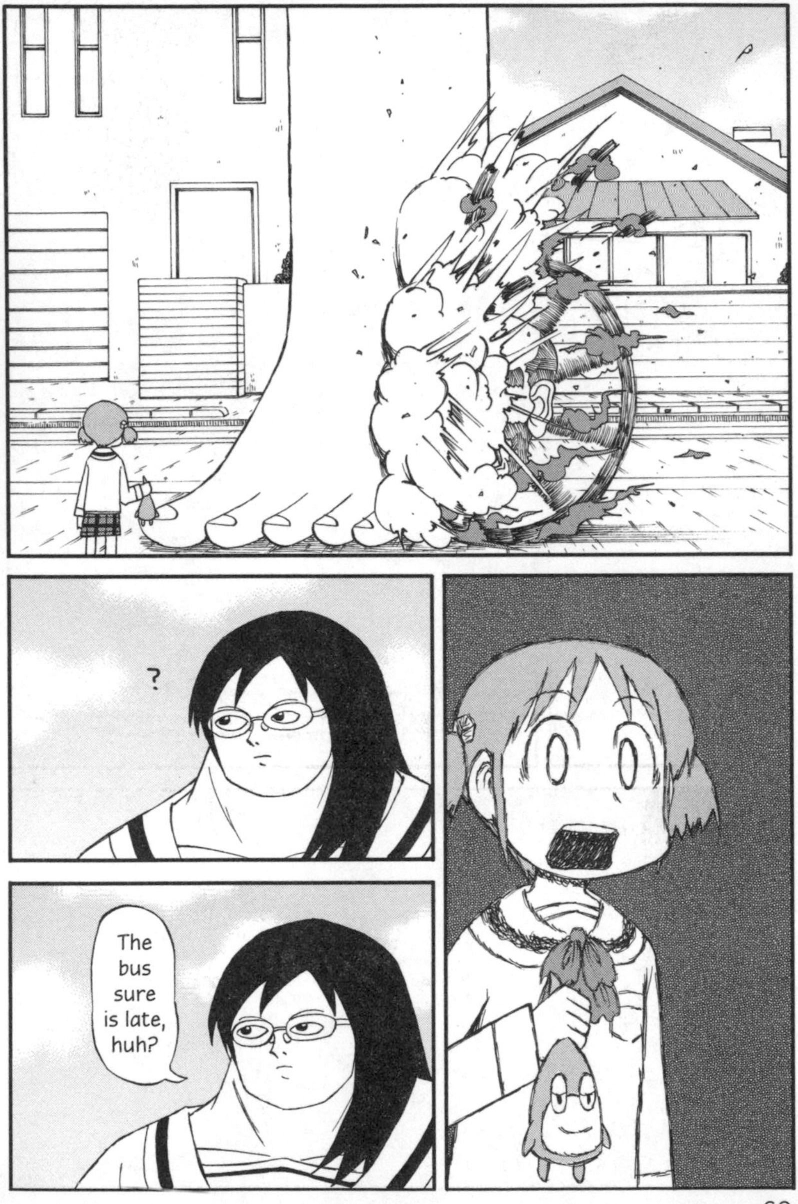
?
The bus sure is late, huh?

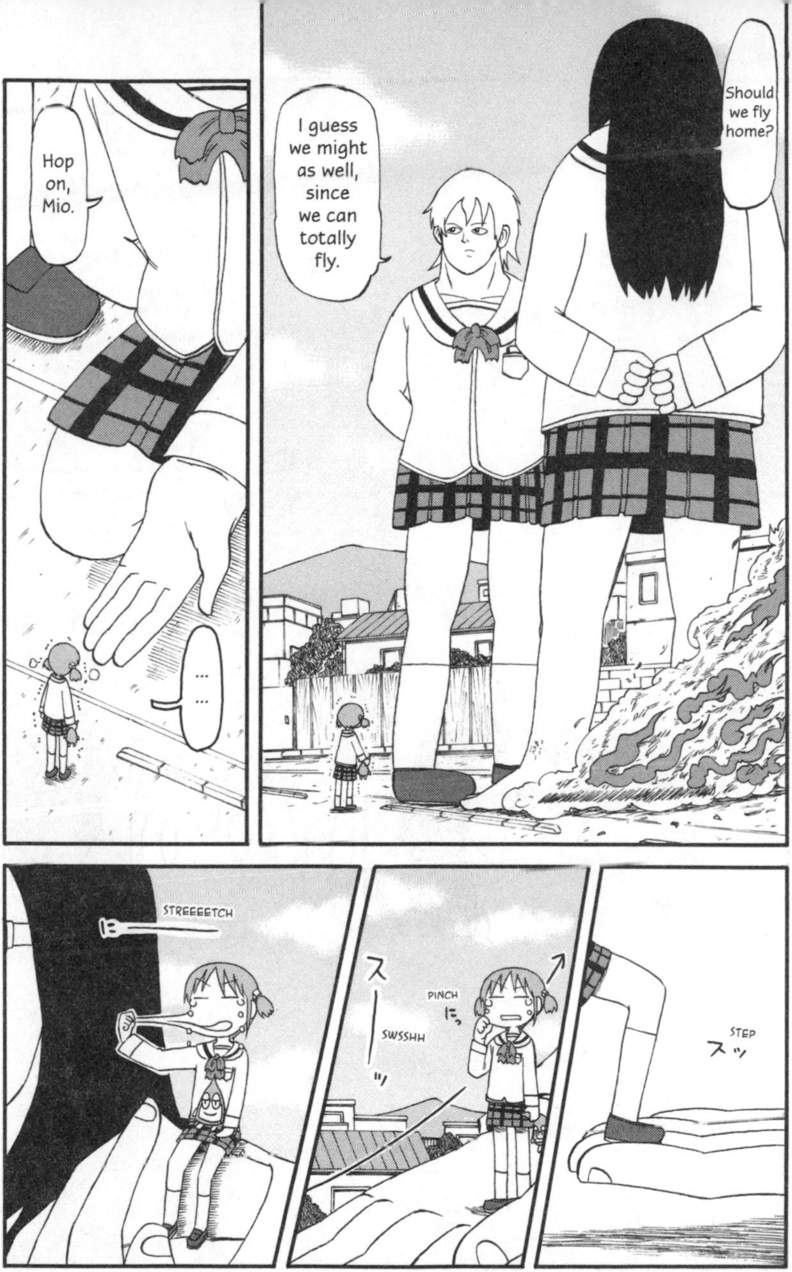

Should we fly home?
I guess we might as well, since we can totally fly.
Hop on, Mio.
... ...
STEP
スッ
PINCH
にっ
スーーッ
SWSSHH
STREEEETCH

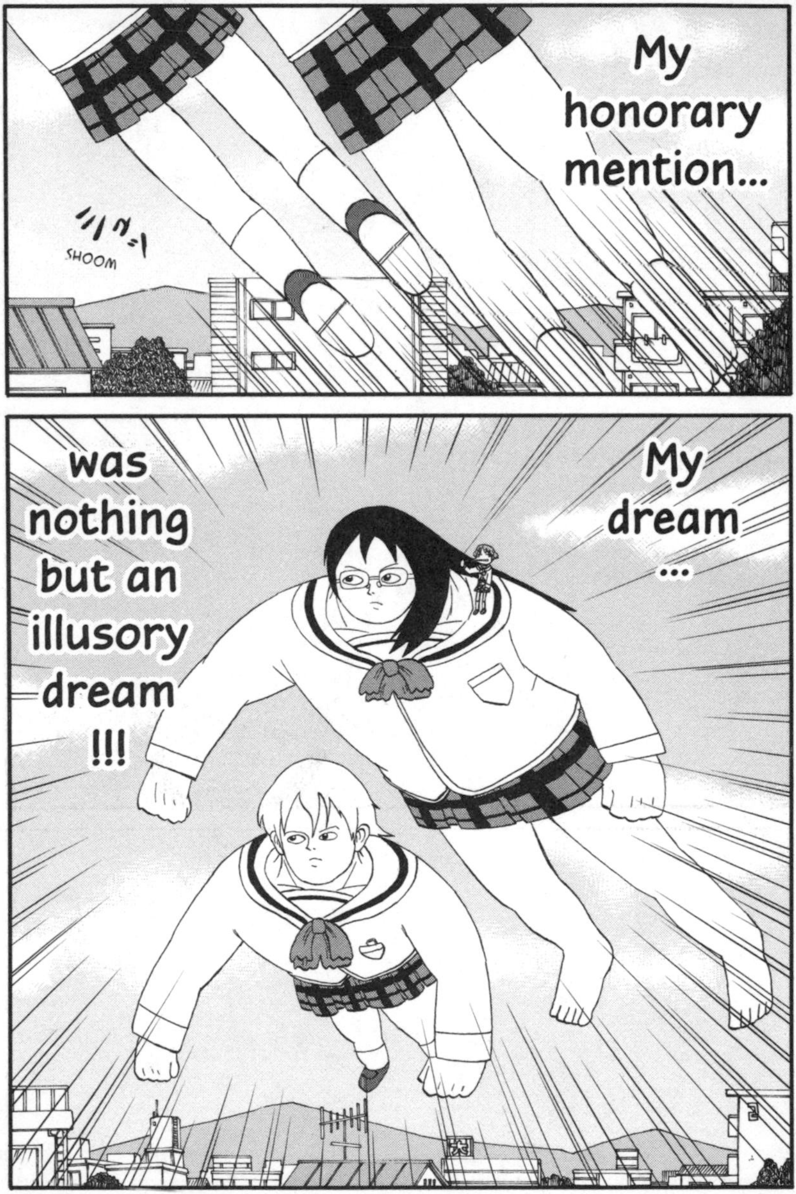
My honorary mention...
SHOOM
My dream ...
was nothing but an illusory dream !!!

chapter 131: end

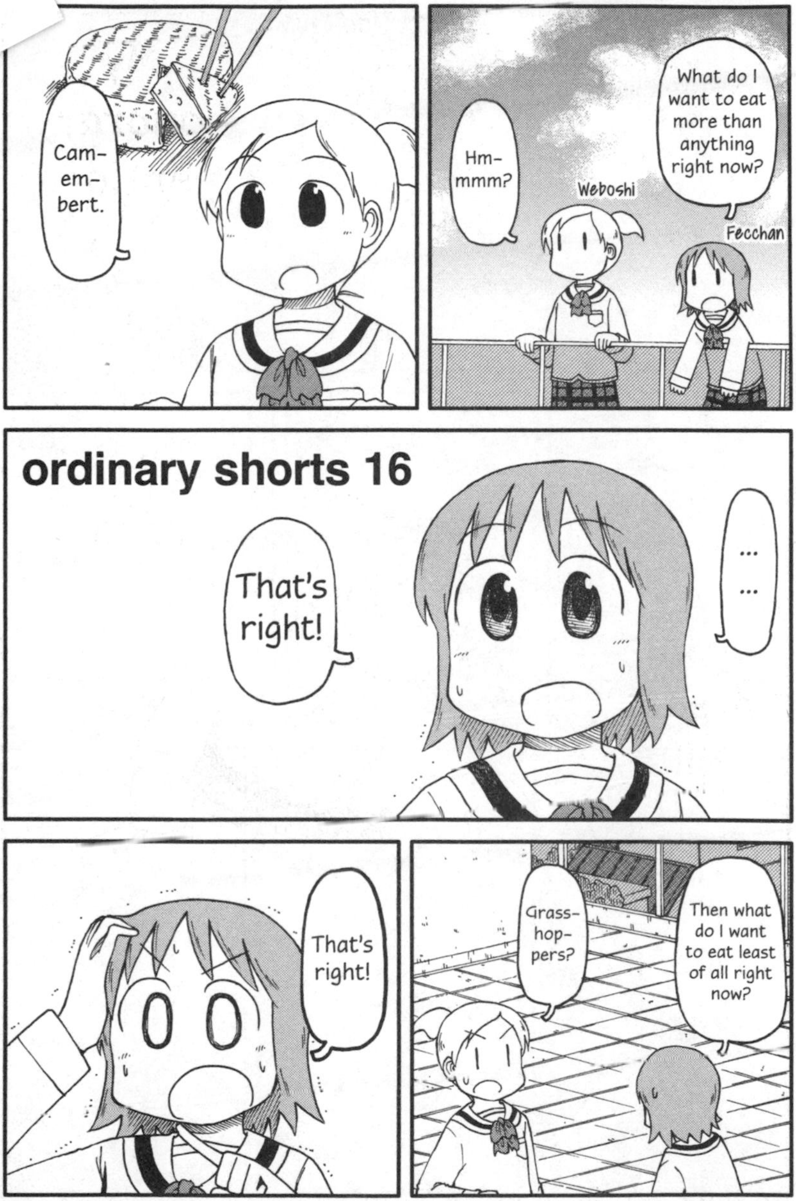
What do I want to eat more than anything right now?
Hm-mmm?
Weboshi
Fecchan
Cam-em-bert.
ordinary shorts 16
……
That's right!
Then what do I want to eat least of all right now?
Grass-hoppers?
That's right!

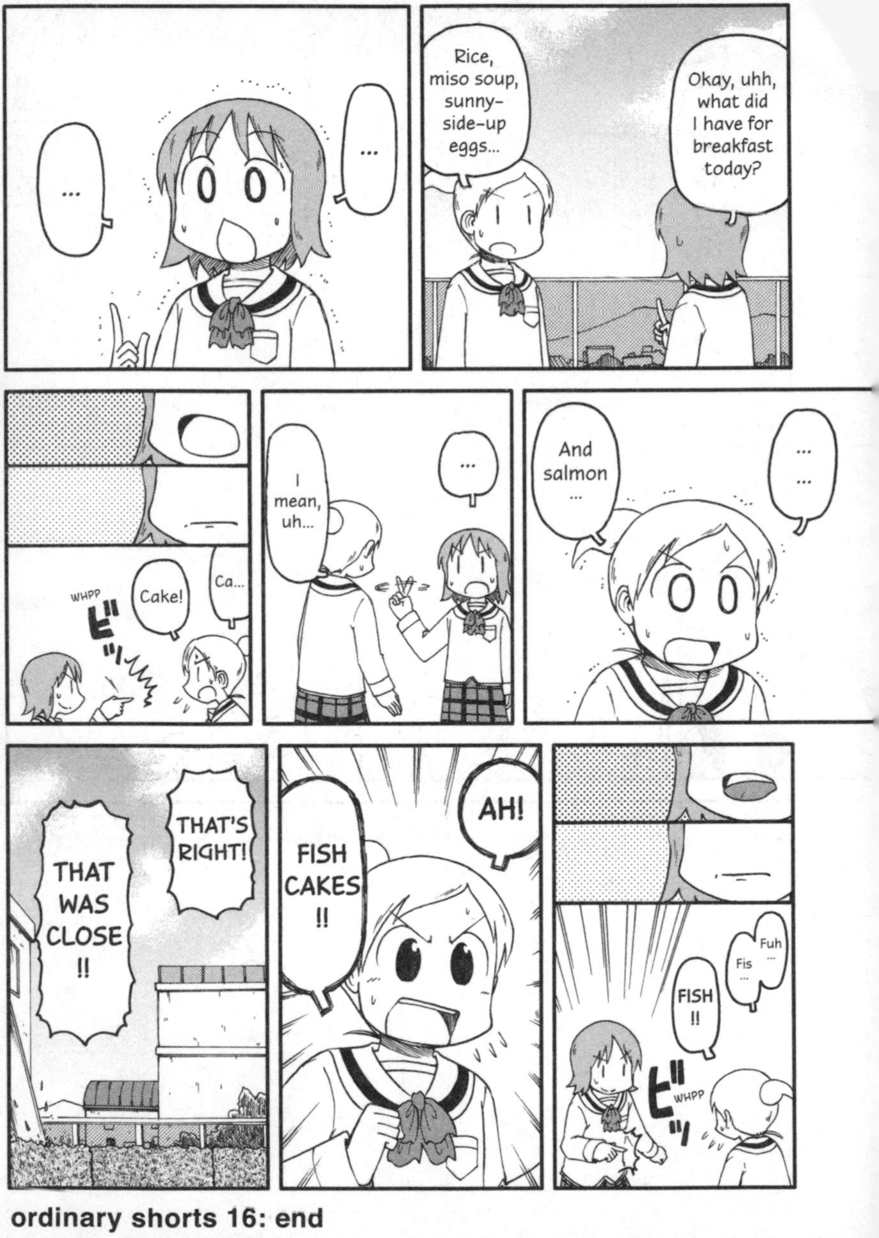
Okay, uhh, what did I have for breakfast today?
Rice, miso soup, sunny-side-up eggs...
...
...
...
...
And salmon ...
...
I mean, uh...
Ca...
Cake!
WHPP
Fuh ...
Fis ...
FISH !!
WHPP
AH!
FISH CAKES !!
THAT'S RIGHT!
THAT WAS CLOSE !!

ordinary shorts 16: end

chapter 132

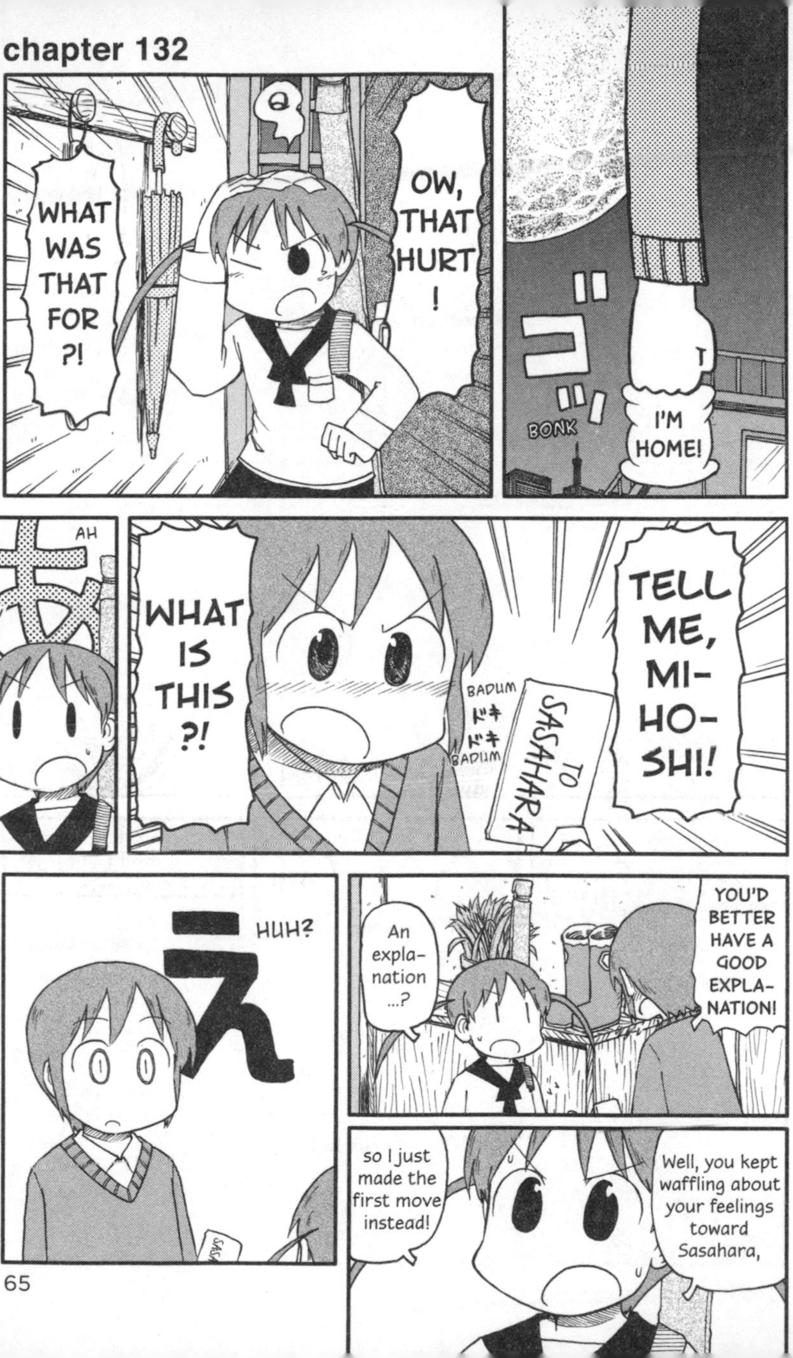
I'M HOME!
BONK
OW, THAT HURT!
WHAT WAS THAT FOR?!
TELL ME, MI-HO-SHI!
TO SASAHARA
BADUM ドキ ドキ BADUM
WHAT IS THIS?!
AH
How did she know that was me?!
YOU'D BETTER HAVE A GOOD EXPLA-NATION!
An expla-nation ...?
Well, you kept waffling about your feelings toward Sasahara,
so I just made the first move instead!
HUH?

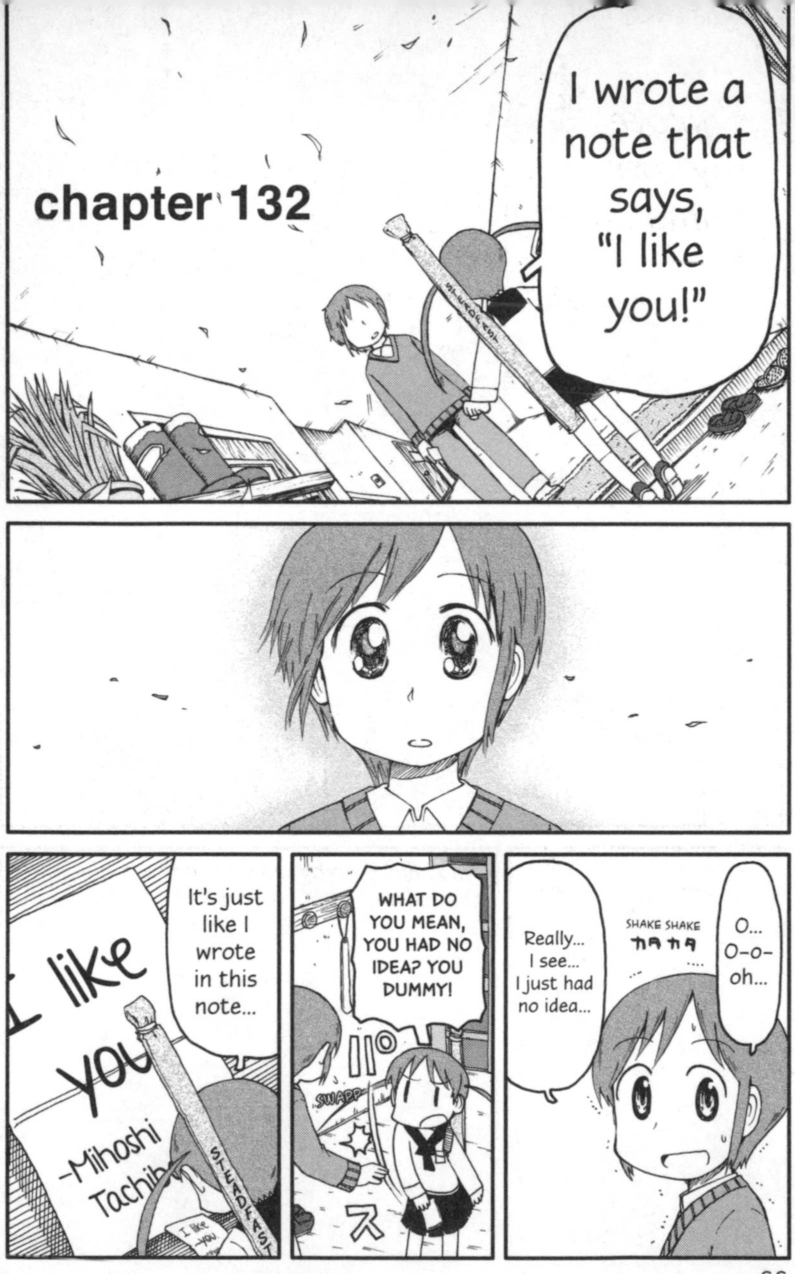
chapter 132
I wrote a note that says, "I like you!"
O... O-o-oh...
SHAKE SHAKE
カタカタ
Really... I see... I just had no idea...
WHAT DO YOU MEAN, YOU HAD NO IDEA? YOU DUMMY!
SWAPP
ス
It's just like I wrote in this note...
I like YOU
-Mihoshi Tachib
STEADFAST
I like you.

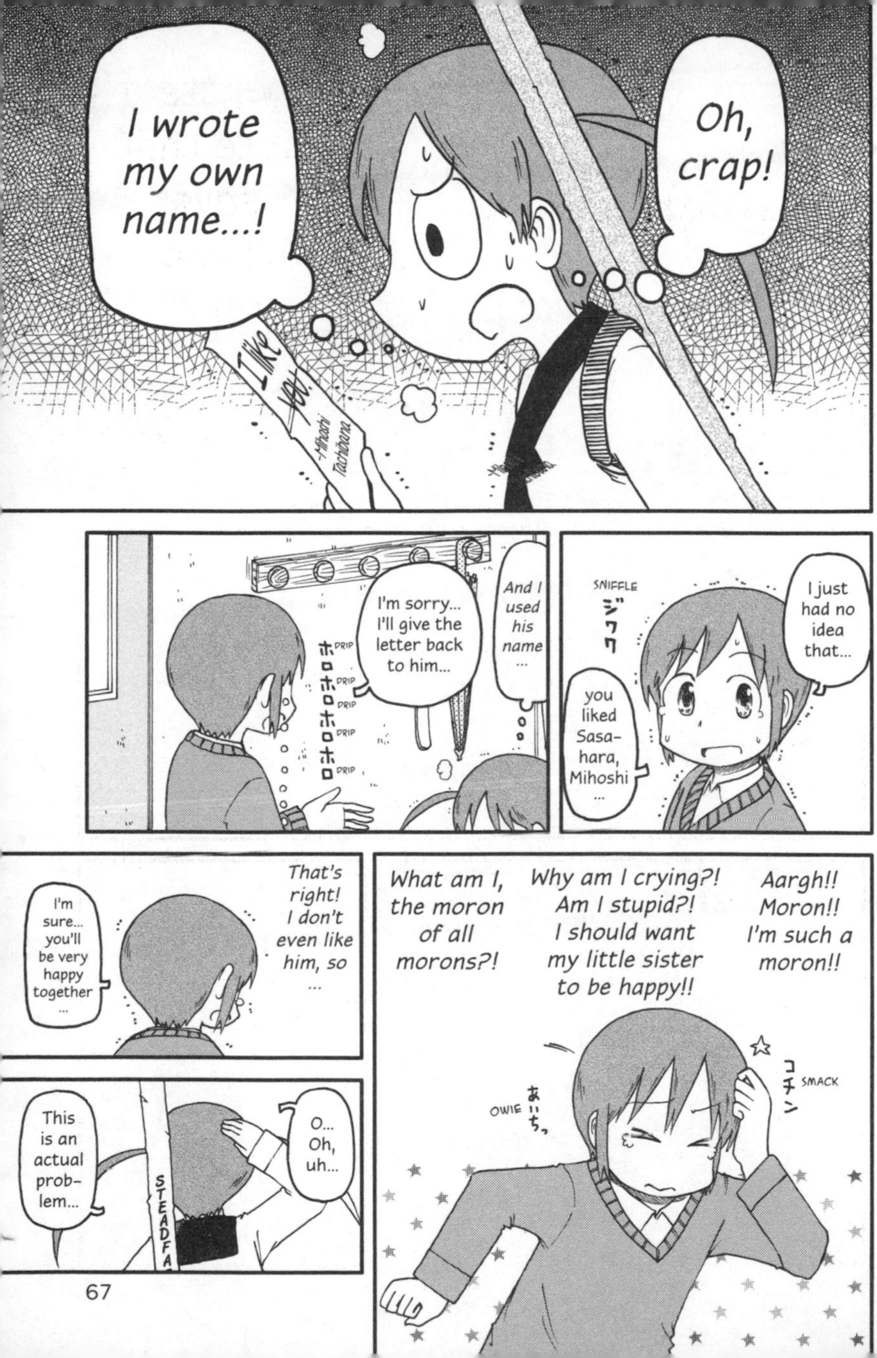

Oh, crap!
I wrote my own name...!
I like you.
-Mihoshi Tachibana
I just had no idea that...
SNIFFLE
ジワワ
you liked Sasa-hara, Mihoshi...
And I used his name...
I'm sorry... I'll give the letter back to him...
ホロホロホロホロ DRIP DRIP DRIP DRIP DRIP
Aargh!! Moron!! I'm such a moron!!
Why am I crying?! Am I stupid?! I should want my little sister to be happy!!
What am I, the moron of all morons?!
コチン SMACK
あいちっ OWIE
That's right! I don't even like him, so...
I'm sure... you'll be very happy together...
O... Oh, uh...
This is an actual prob-lem...
STEADFA

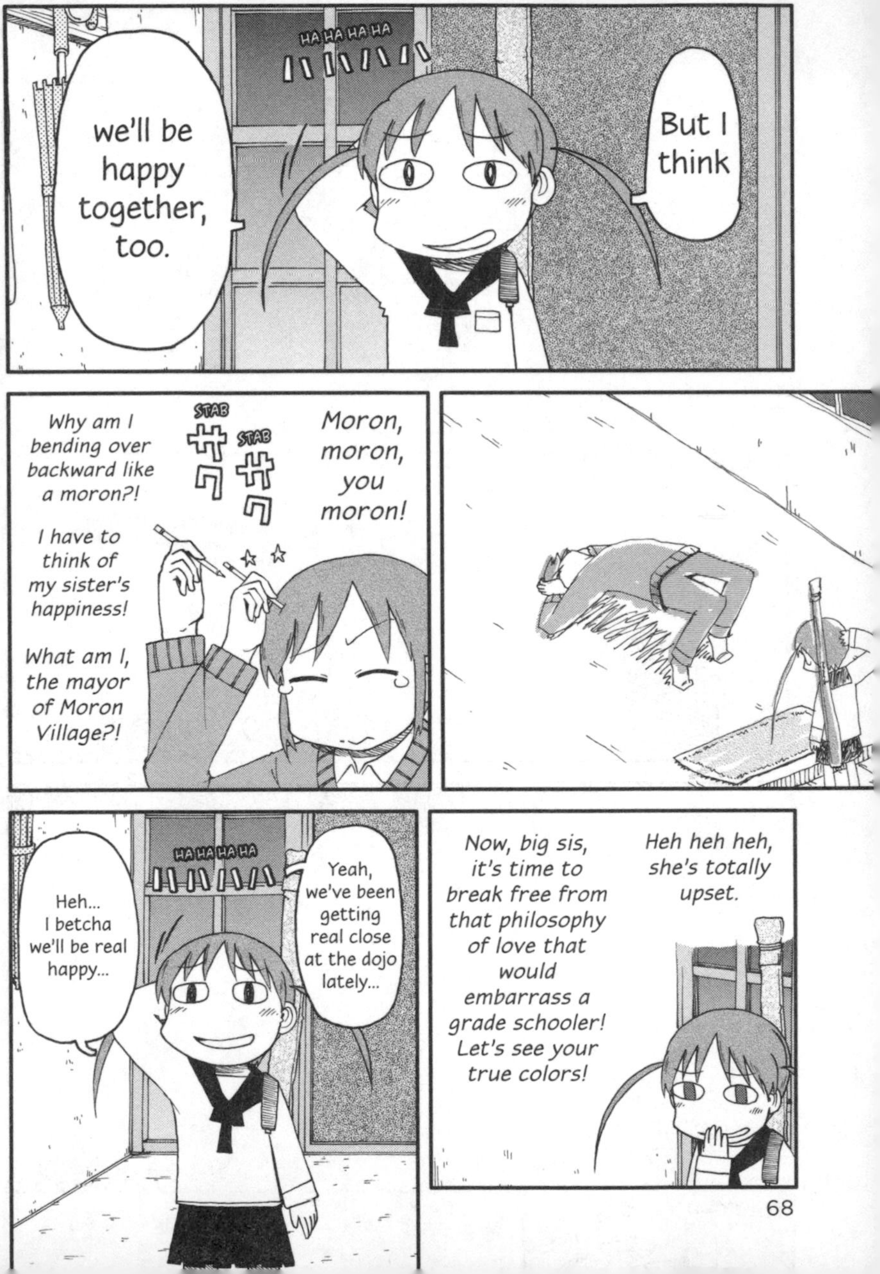

But I think
we'll be happy together, too.
HA HA HA HA
Moron, moron, you moron!
STAB
STAB
Why am I bending over backward like a moron?!
I have to think of my sister's happiness!
What am I, the mayor of Moron Village?!
Heh heh heh, she's totally upset.
Now, big sis, it's time to break free from that philosophy of love that would embarrass a grade schooler! Let's see your true colors!
Yeah, we've been getting real close at the dojo lately...
HA HA HA HA
Heh... I betcha we'll be real happy...

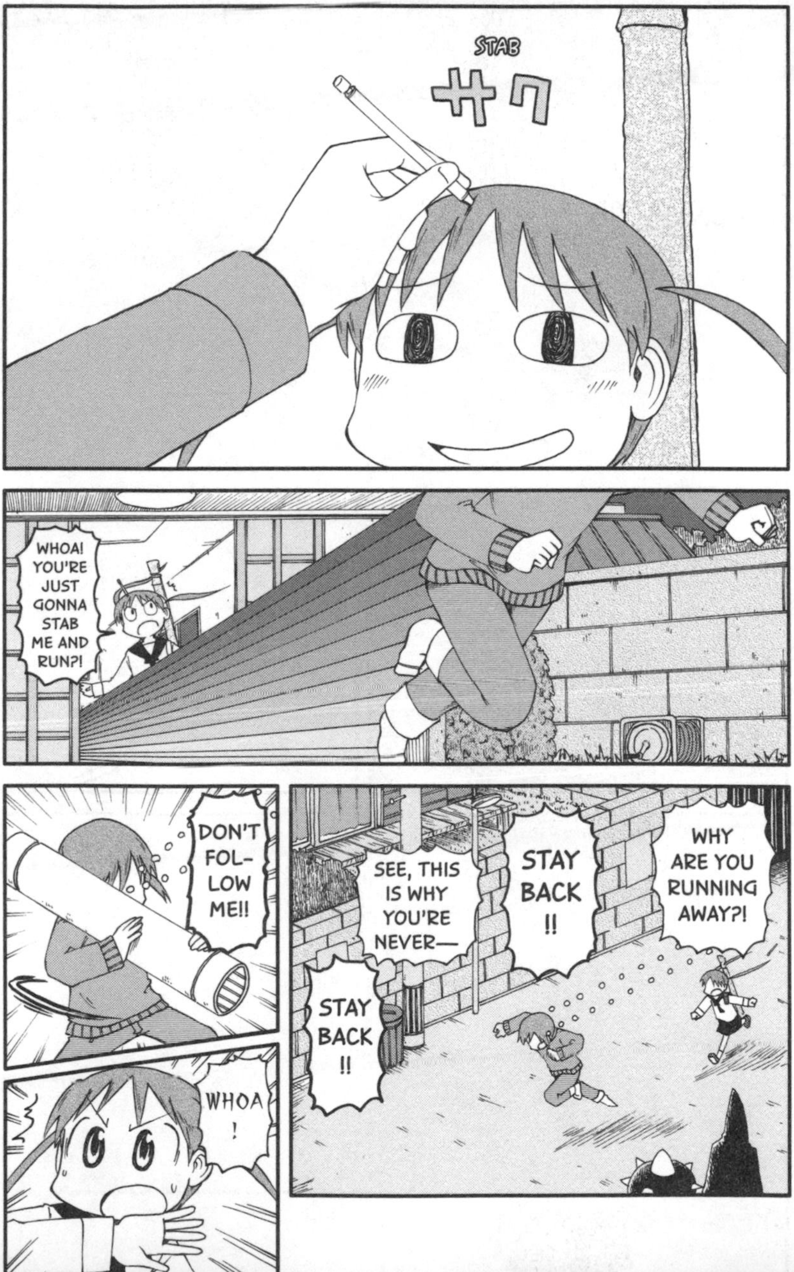
STAB
サク
WHOA! YOU'RE JUST GONNA STAB ME AND RUN?!
WHY ARE YOU RUNNING AWAY?!
STAY BACK !!
SEE, THIS IS WHY YOU'RE NEVER—
STAY BACK !!
DON'T FOL-LOW ME!!
WHOA !

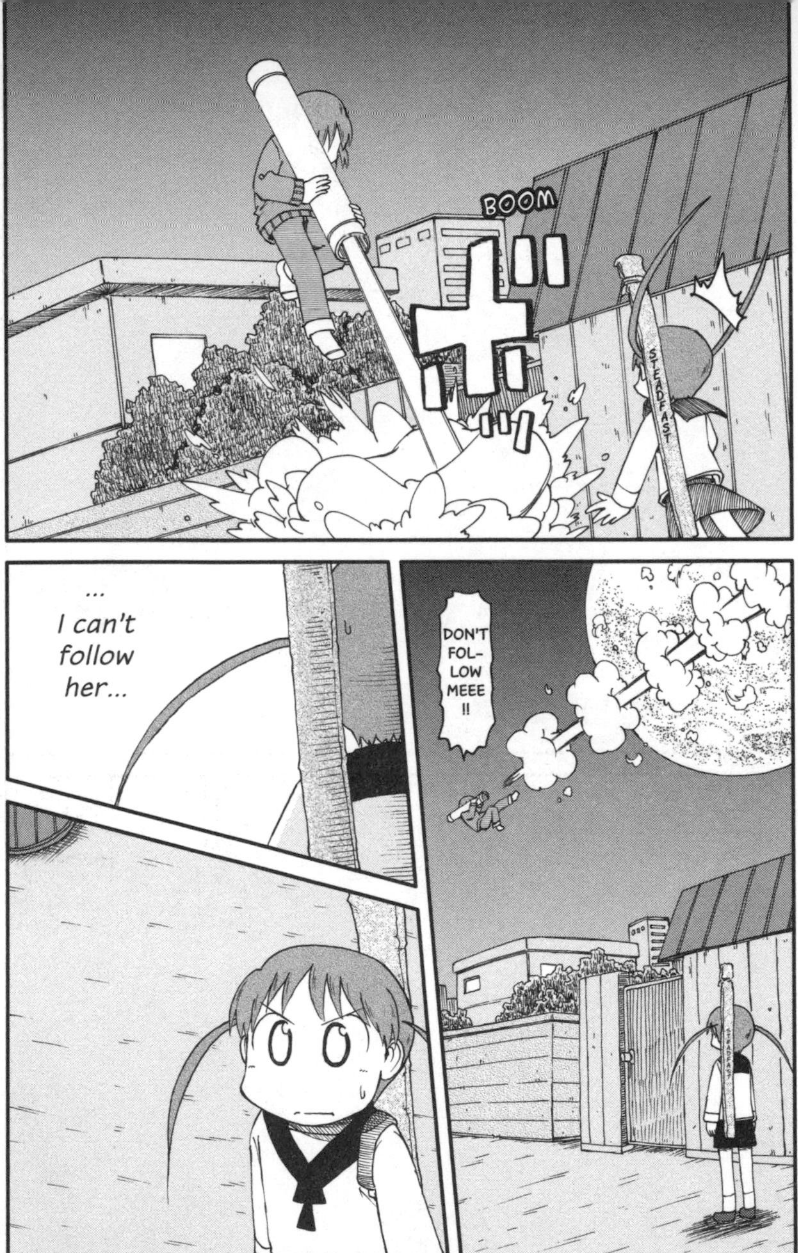
BOOM
STEADFAST
DON'T FOL- LOW MEEE !!
STEADFAST
... I can't follow her...

chapter 132: end

chapter 133

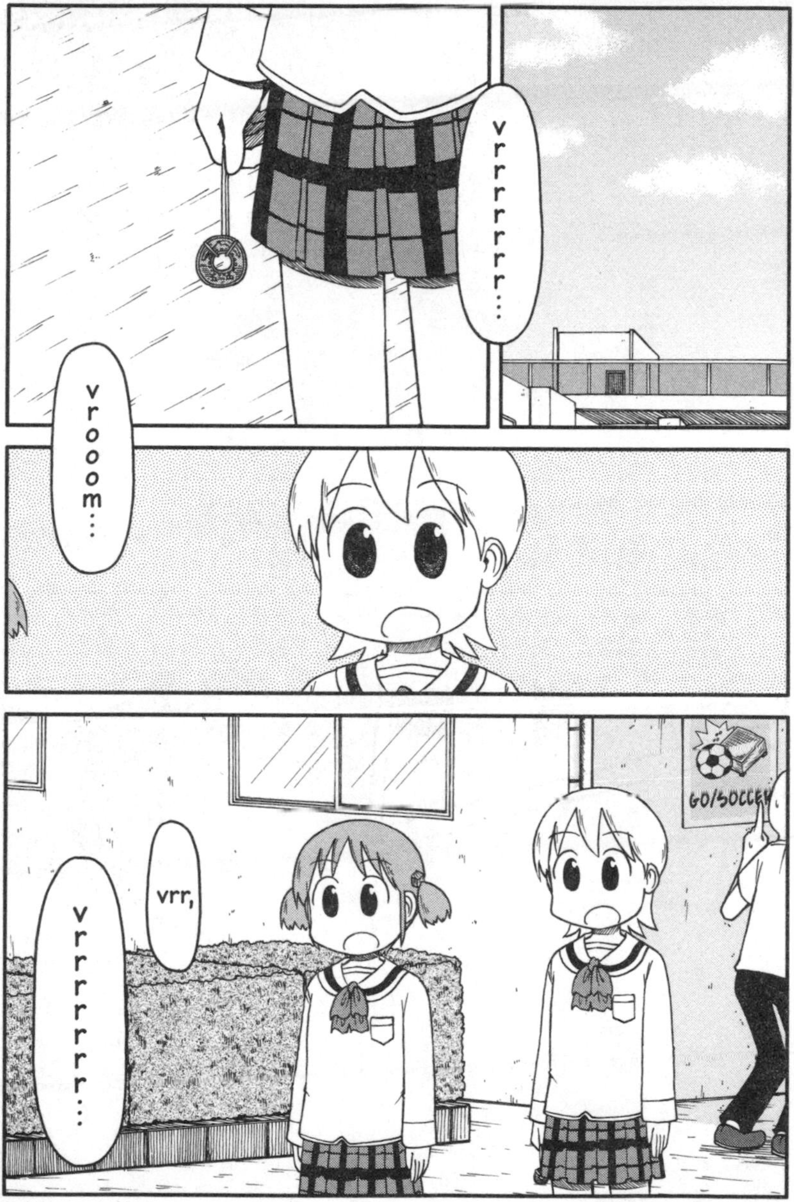
vrrrrrrr…
vroooom…
vrr,
vrrrrrrr…

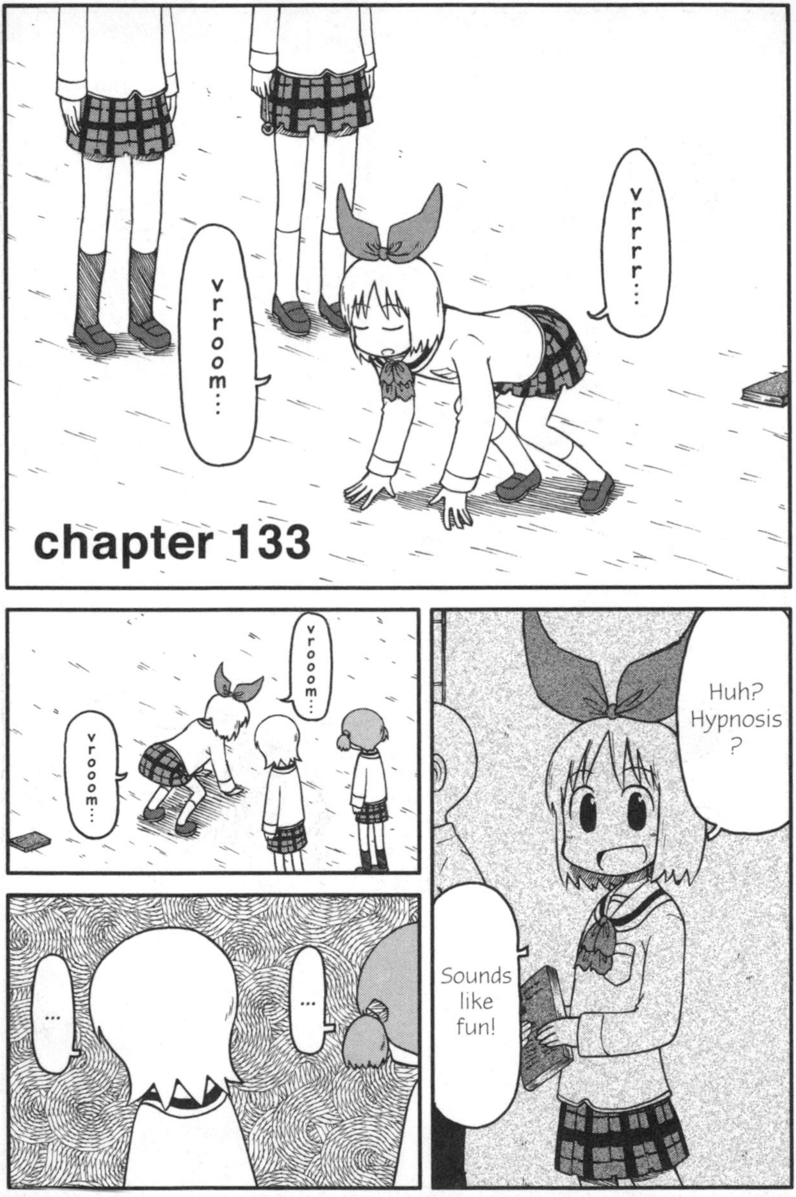
vrrrr…
vrroom…
chapter 133
Huh? Hypnosis?
Sounds like fun!
vrooom…
vrooom…
…
…

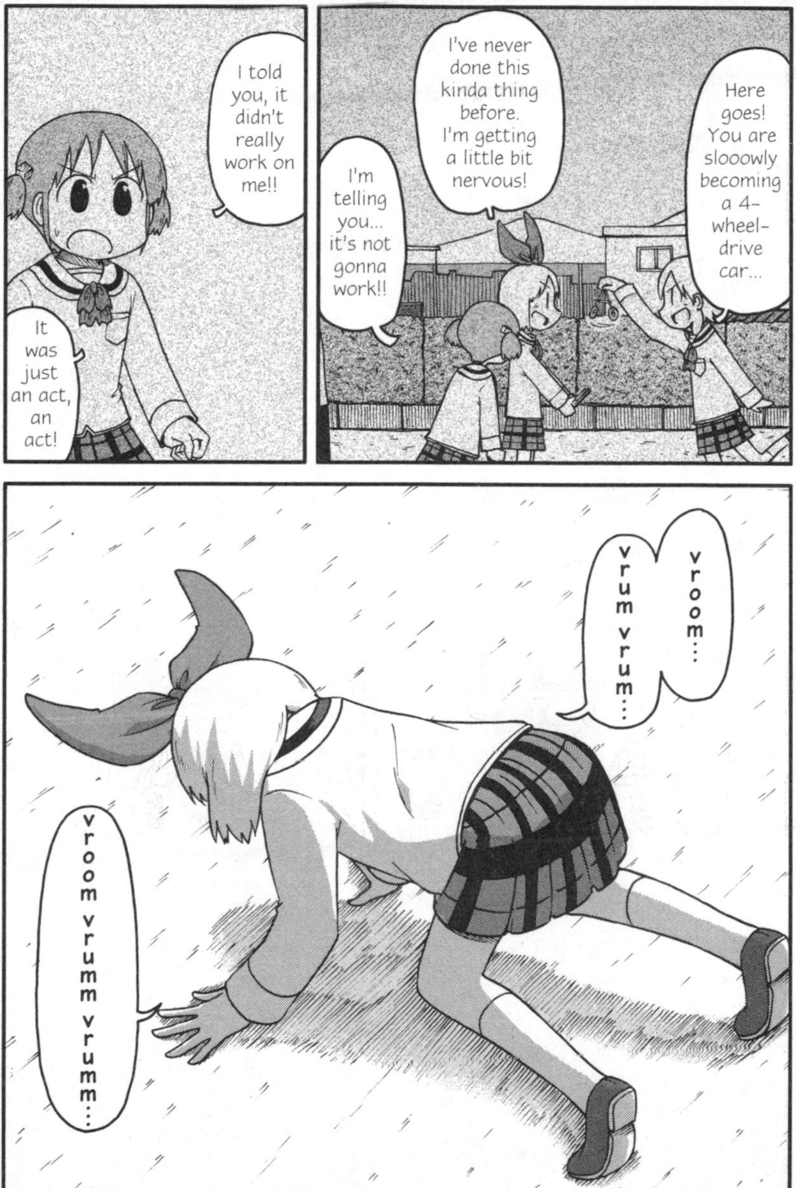
Here goes! You are slooowly becoming a 4-wheel-drive car...
I've never done this kinda thing before. I'm getting a little bit nervous!
I'm telling you... it's not gonna work!!
I told you, it didn't really work on me!!
It was just an act, an act!
vroom... vrum vrum...
vroom vrumm vrumm...

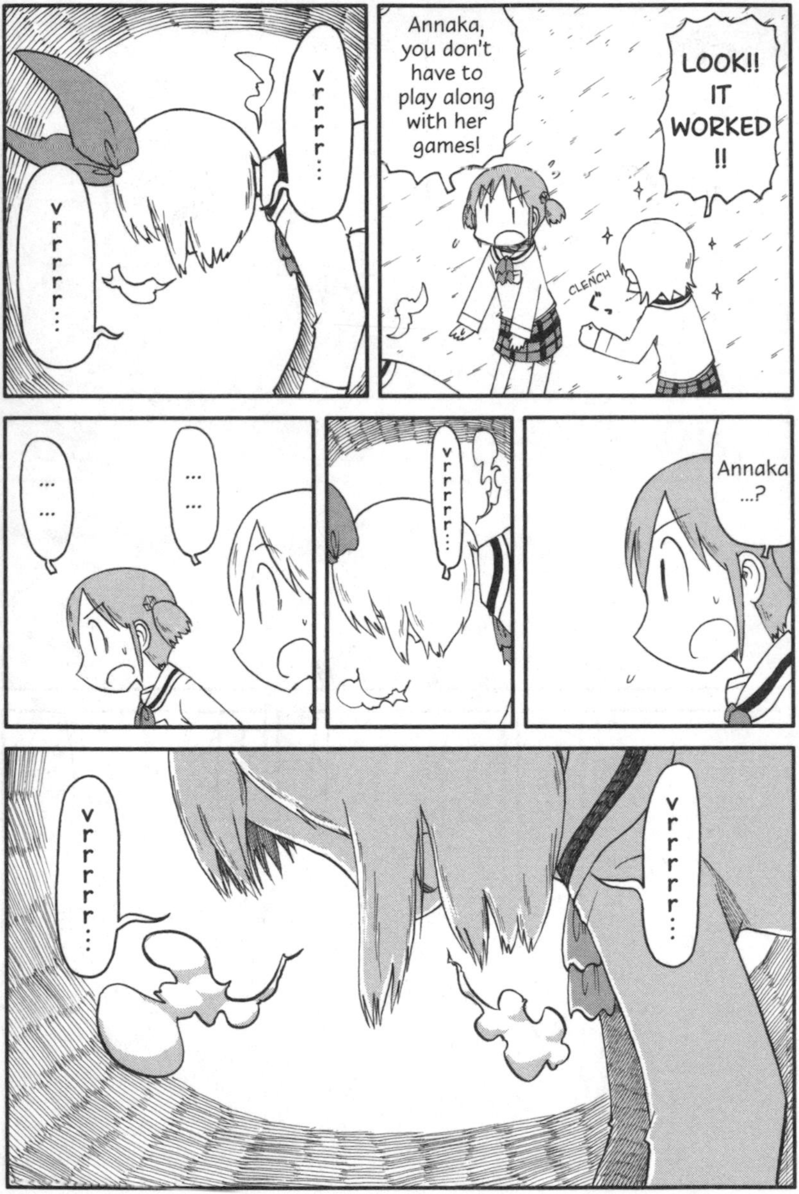
LOOK!! IT WORKED !!
Annaka, you don't have to play along with her games!
CLENCH
vrrrr…
vrrrrr…
Annaka …?
vrrrrr…
… …
… …
vrrrrr…
vrrrrr…

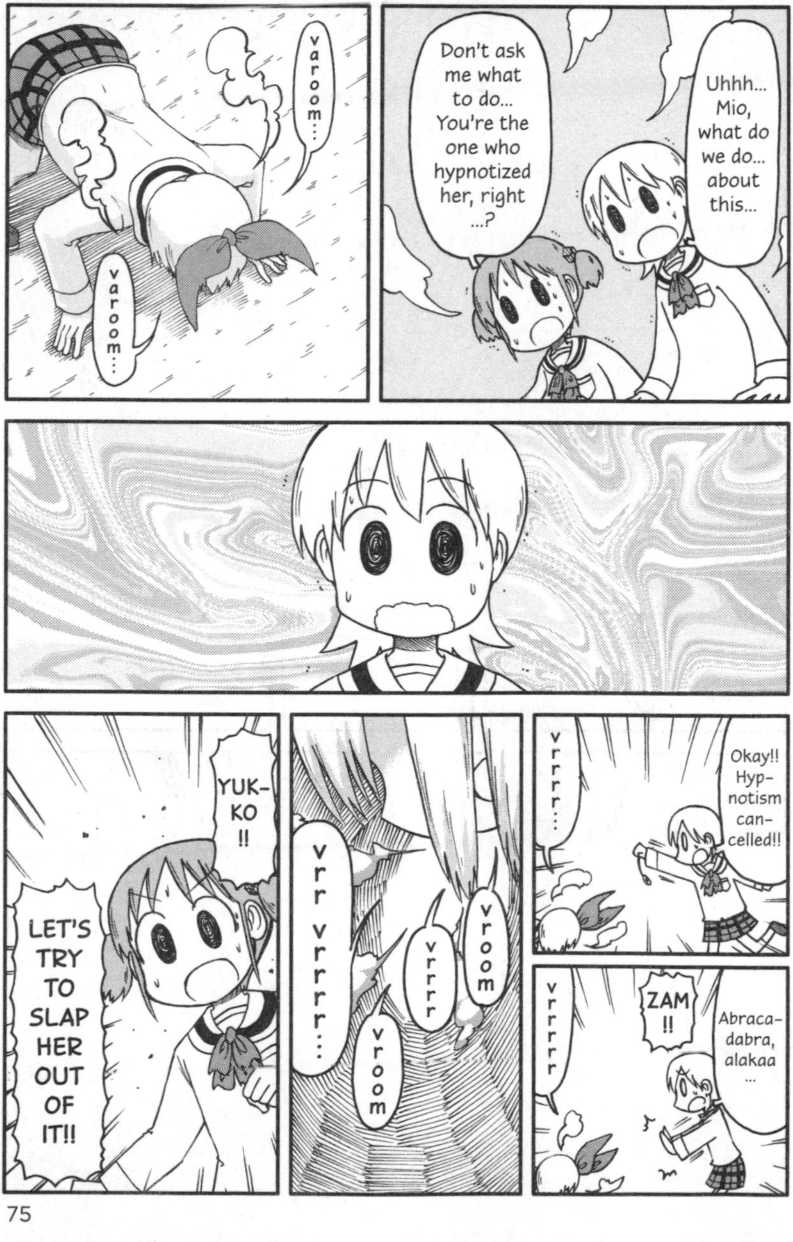
Uhhh... Mio, what do we do... about this...
Don't ask me what to do... You're the one who hypnotized her, right ...?
varoom...
varoom...
Okay!! Hypnotism cancelled!!
vrrrr...
Abracadabra, alakaa ...
ZAM !!
vrrrr
vroom
vrrr
vrr vrrrr...
vroom
YUKO !!
LET'S TRY TO SLAP HER OUT OF IT!!

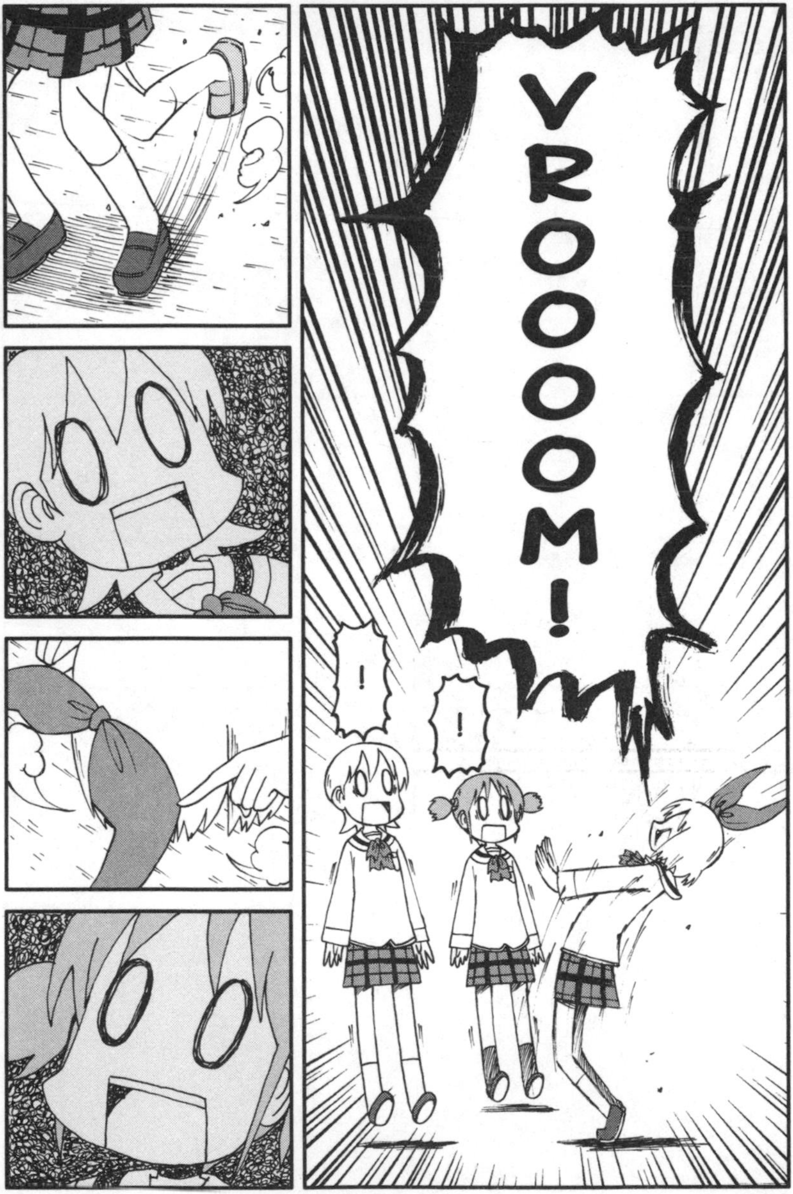
VROOOOOM!
!
!

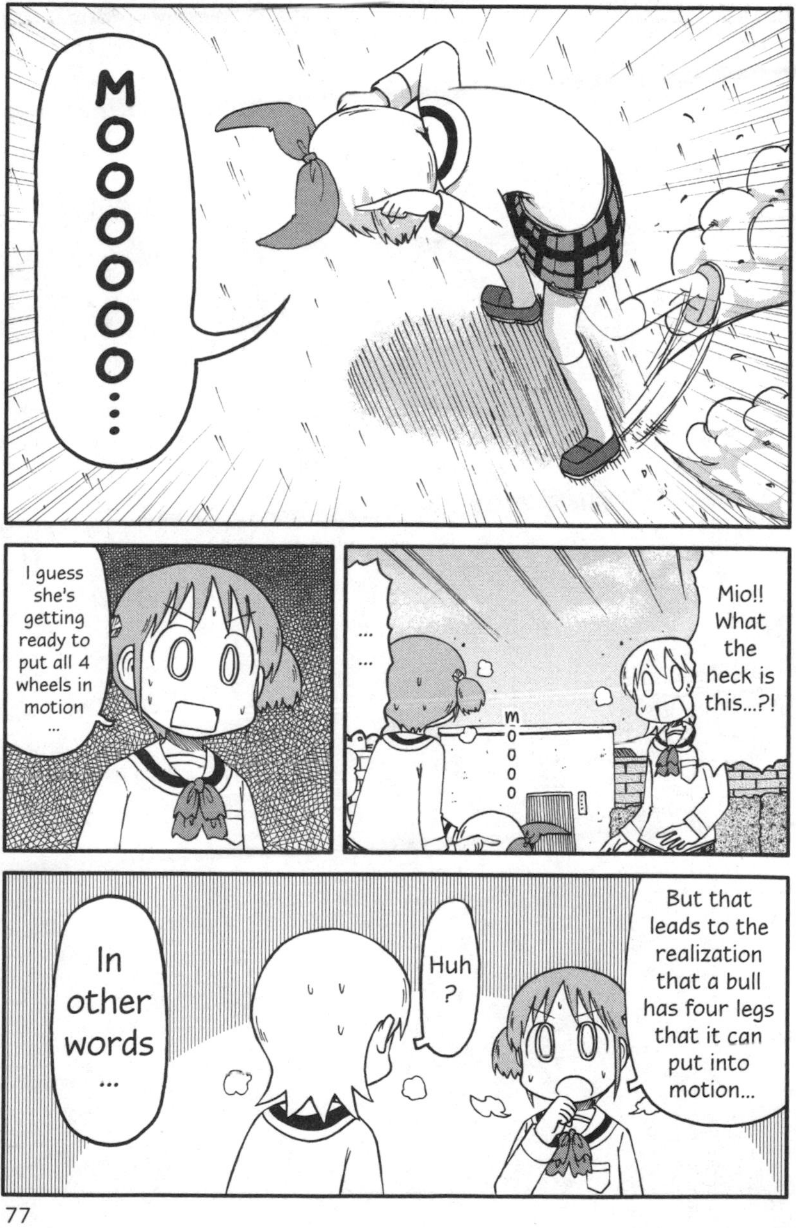
MOOOOOO...
Mio!! What the heck is this...?!
......
MOOOO
I guess she's getting ready to put all 4 wheels in motion ...
But that leads to the realization that a bull has four legs that it can put into motion...
Huh ?
In other words ...

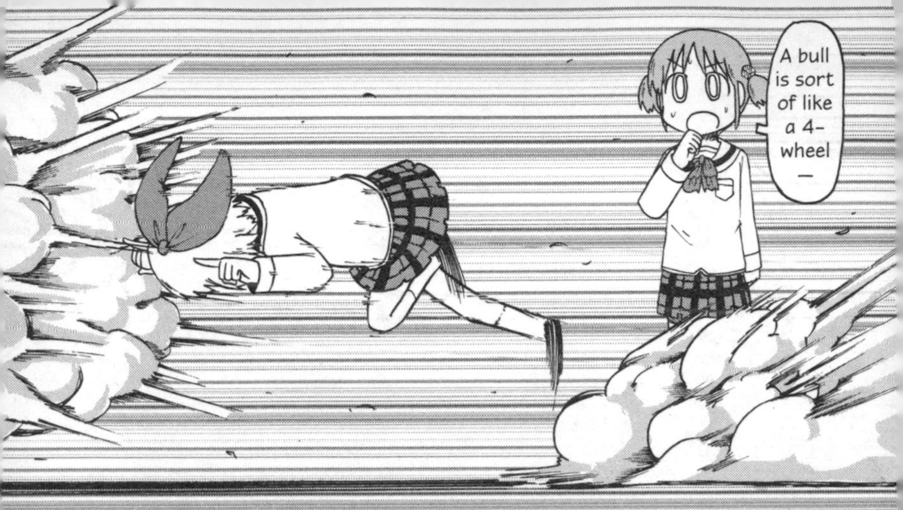
A bull is sort of like a 4-wheel —

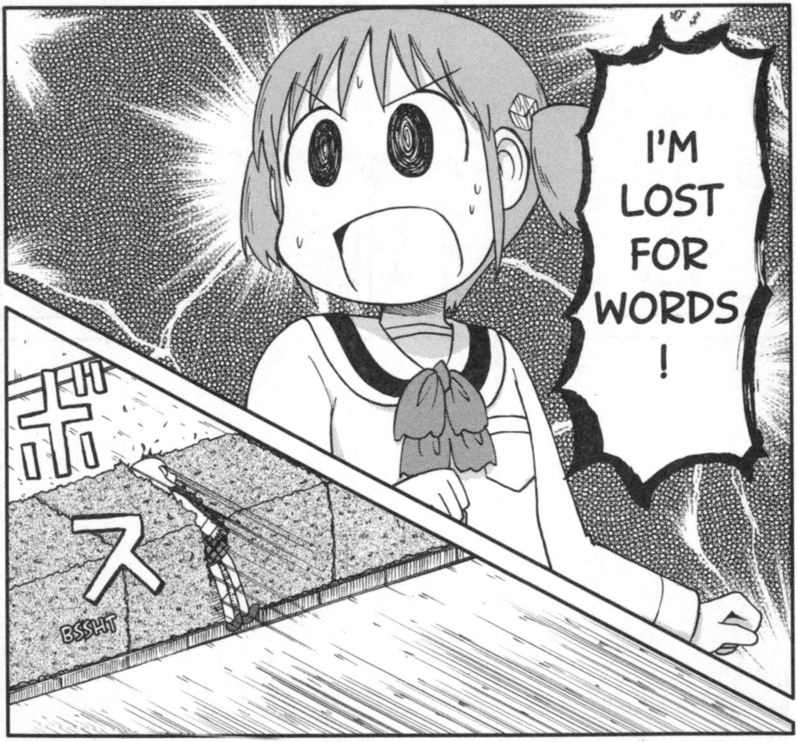
I'M LOST FOR WORDS !
ボス
BSSHT

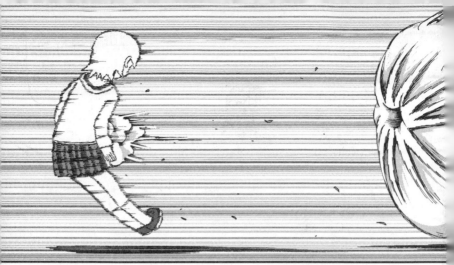

You are slooowly becoming a 4-wheel-drive car...
Huh? Are you trying to hypnotize me?
Isn't that just a trick that entertainers use?
I can't go along with something so unscientific.
C'mon, c'mon, see? You're becoming a 4-wheel-drive car...
Why 4-wheel drive, anyway?
Geez.
Don't make fun of science like that.

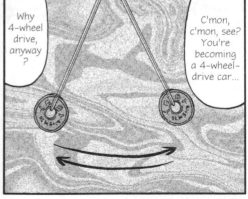

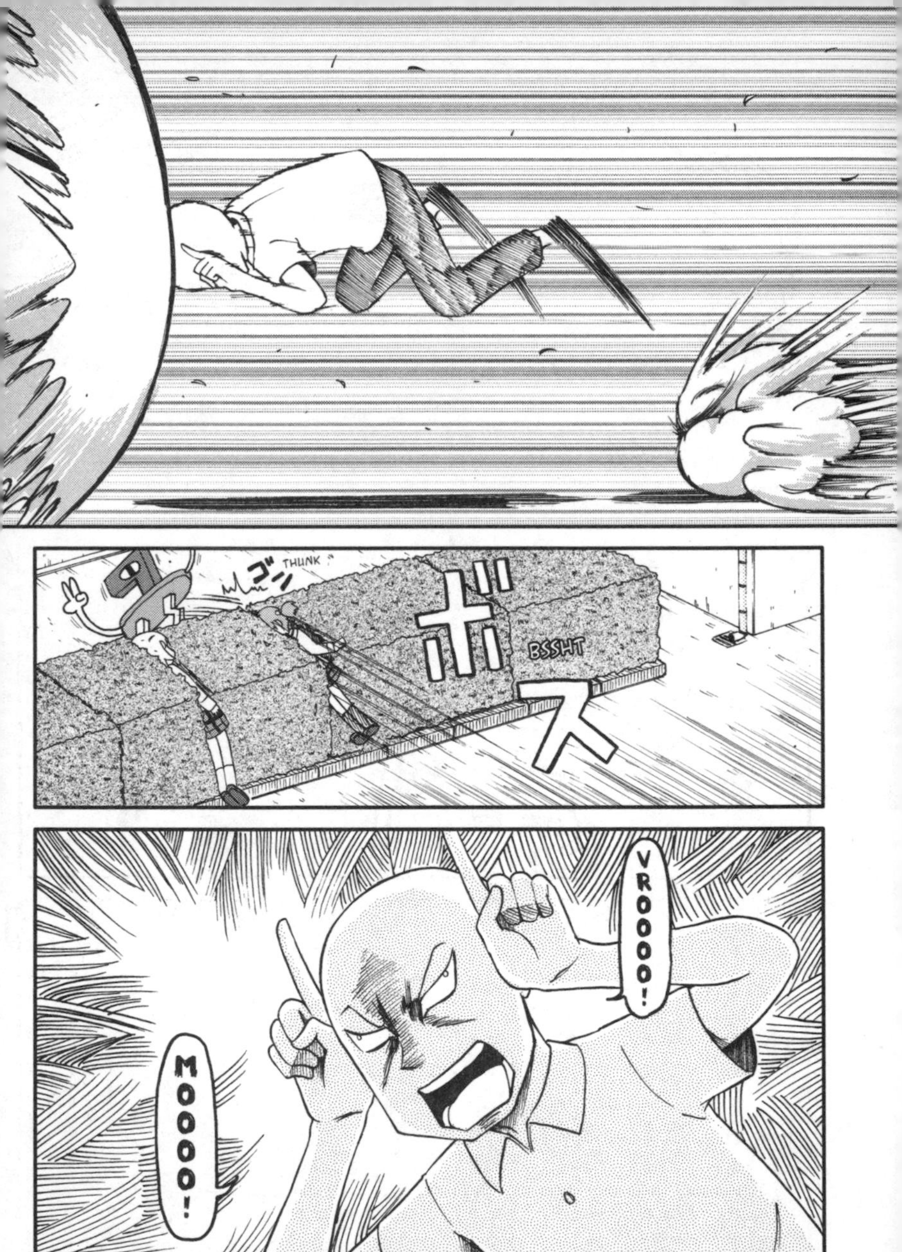
ゴン
THUNK
ボス
BSSHT
VROOOO!
MOOOO!

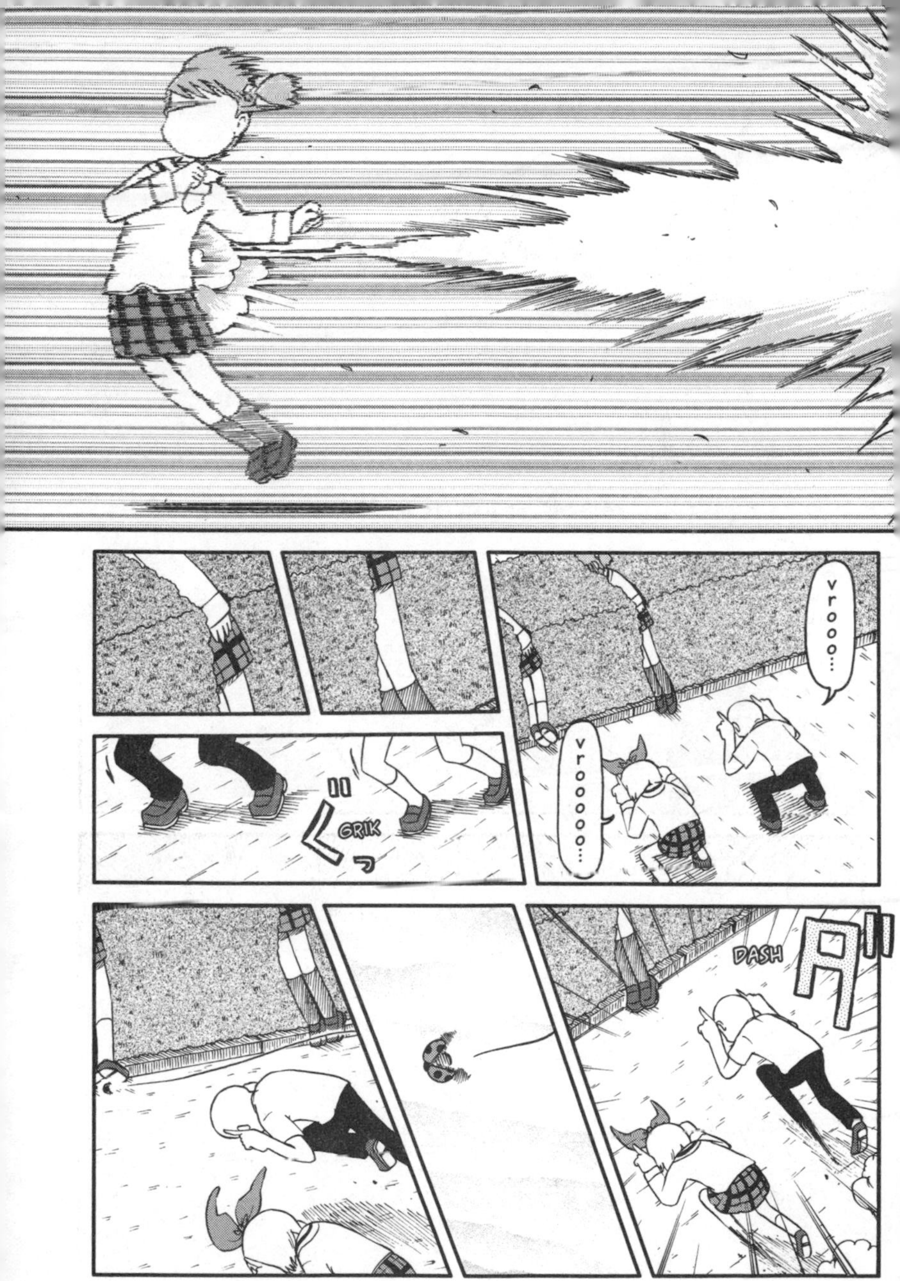
vrooo...
vroooooo...
GRIK
DASH

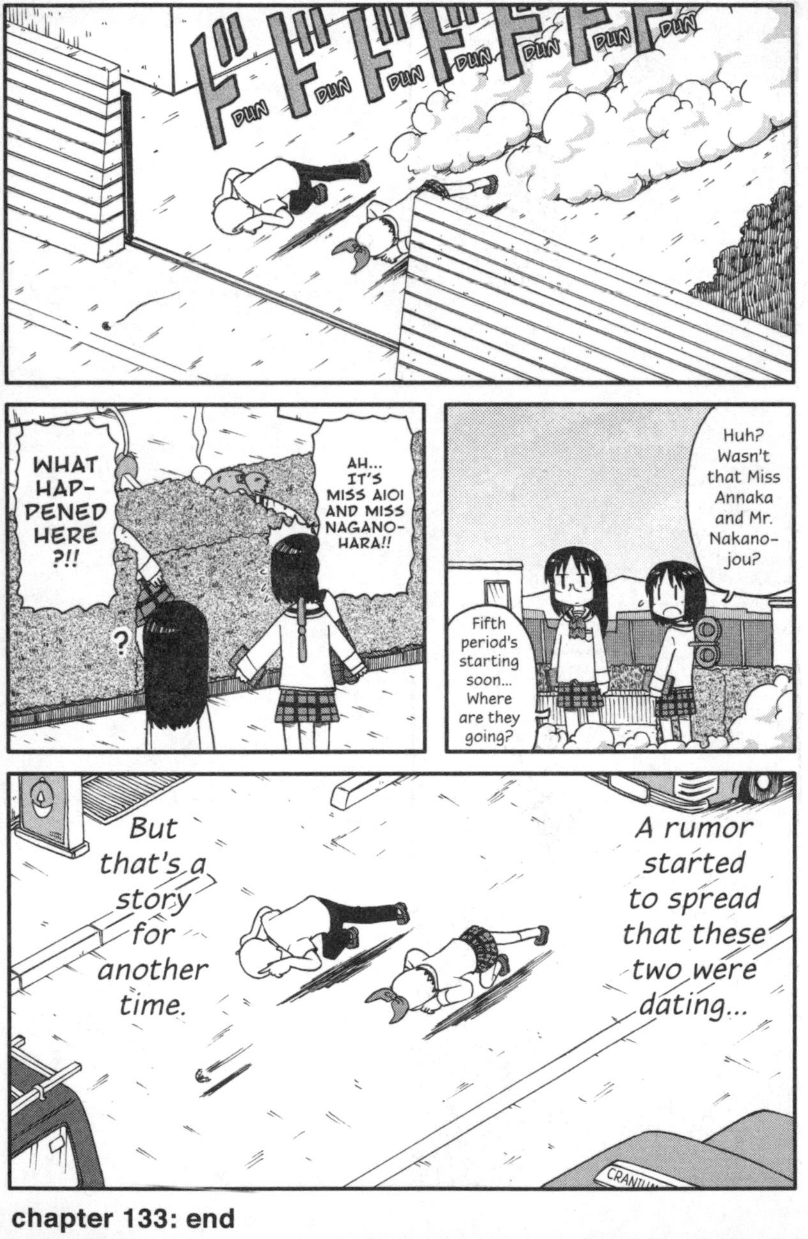
DUN DUN DUN DUN DUN DUN DUN
Huh? Wasn't that Miss Annaka and Mr. Nakano-jou?
Fifth period's starting soon... Where are they going?
AH... IT'S MISS AIOI AND MISS NAGANO-HARA!!
WHAT HAP-PENED HERE ?!!
?
A rumor started to spread that these two were dating...
But that's a story for another time.

chapter 133: end

chapter 134

FUJIOKA'S COMEBACK

first choke

This is Miss Minakami. She's transferring here from Alaska because of her father's job.
I'm Mai.
I'm single.
Minakami
I'm Yuuko Aioi! Must be tough transferring in 9th grade, huh?
You can ask me anything you don't know!!
You, too ...
Ask me anything you don't know...
HUH?
Okay ...
What part of Japan is Alaska in?
KRAKLE

break time

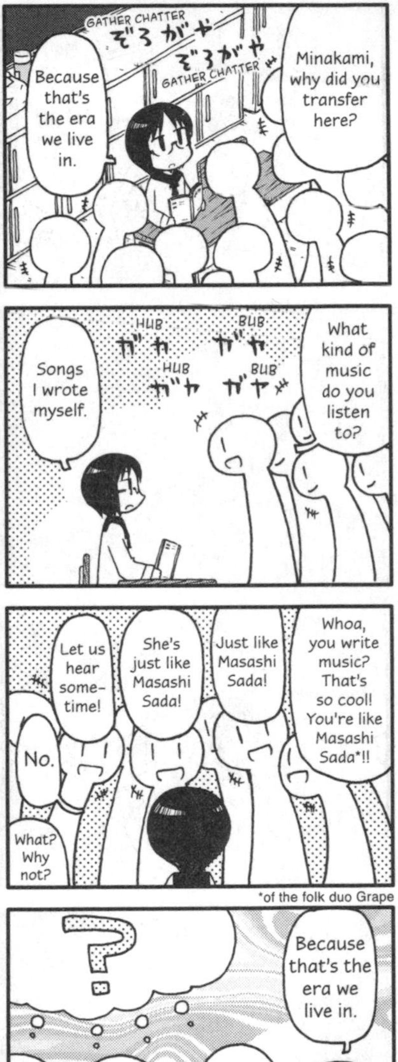
GATHER CHATTER
ぞろがや
ぞろがや
GATHER CHATTER
Minakami, why did you transfer here?
Because that's the era we live in.
HUB BUB
がや
HUB BUB
がや
What kind of music do you listen to?
Songs I wrote myself.
Whoa, you write music? That's so cool! You're like Masashi Sada*!!
Just like Masashi Sada!
She's just like Masashi Sada!
Let us hear some-time!
No.
What? Why not?
?
Because that's the era we live in.

*of the folk duo Grape

break time 2

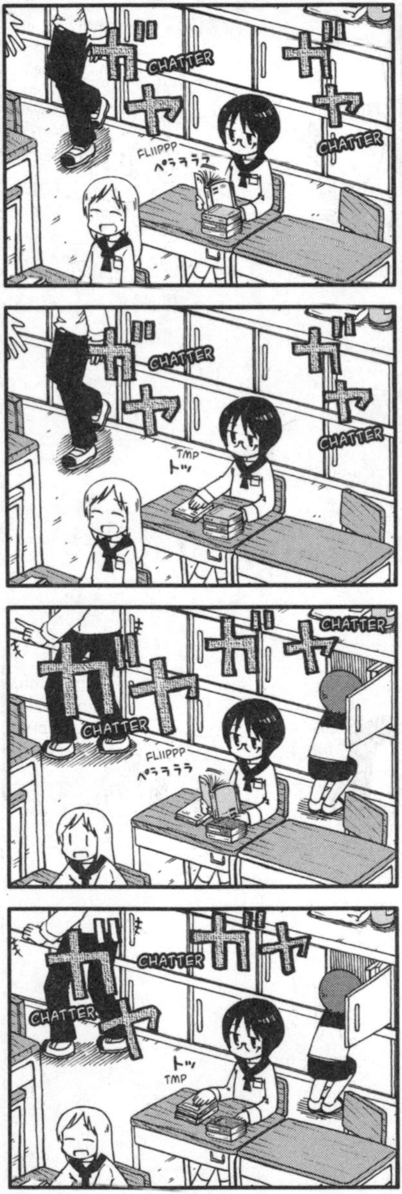
CHATTER
CHATTER
FLIIPPP
ペラララ
CHATTER
CHATTER
TMP
トッ
CHATTER
CHATTER
FLIIPPP
ペラララ
CHATTER
CHATTER
トッ
TMP

new record

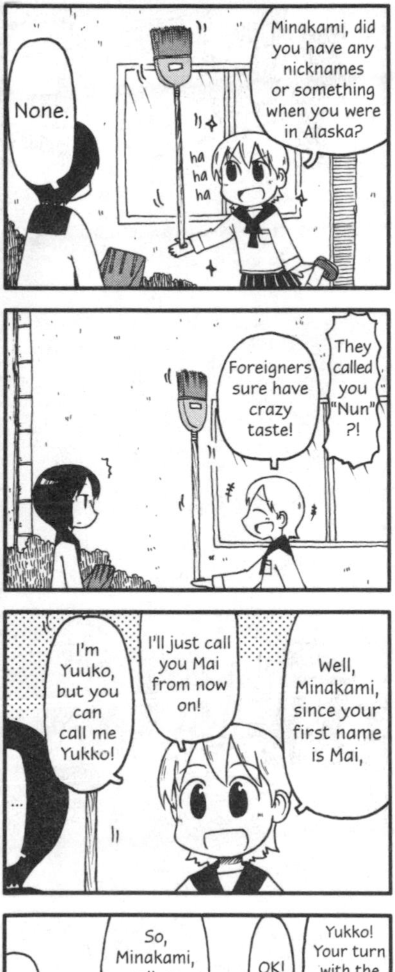
Minakami, did you have any nicknames or something when you were in Alaska?
ha ha ha
None.
They called you "Nun"?!
Foreigners sure have crazy taste!
Well, Minakami, since your first name is Mai,
I'll just call you Mai from now on!
I'm Yuuko, but you can call me Yukko!
...
Yukko! Your turn with the guidance counselor!
OK!
So, Minakami, call me Yukko from now on!
...

break time 3

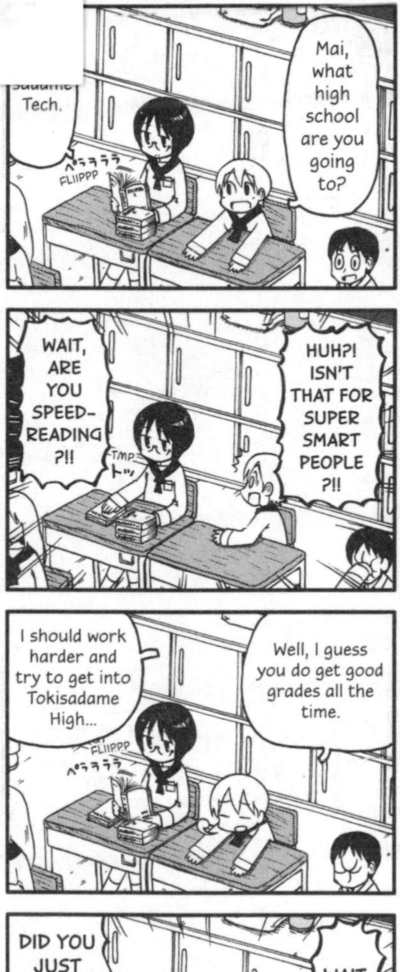
Mai, what high school are you going to?
ペラララ FLIIPPP
sadame Tech.
HUH?! ISN'T THAT FOR SUPER SMART PEOPLE?!!
TMP トッ
WAIT, ARE YOU SPEED-READING?!!
Well, I guess you do get good grades all the time.
I should work harder and try to get into Tokisadame High...
FLIIPPP ペラララ
WAIT A SEC!!
TMP トッ
DID YOU JUST READ THAT ONE BACKWARDS?!

steam

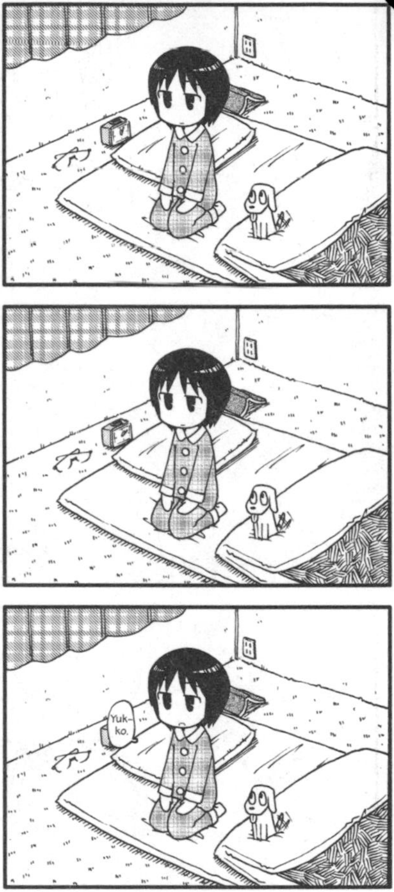
Yuk-ko.

untitled

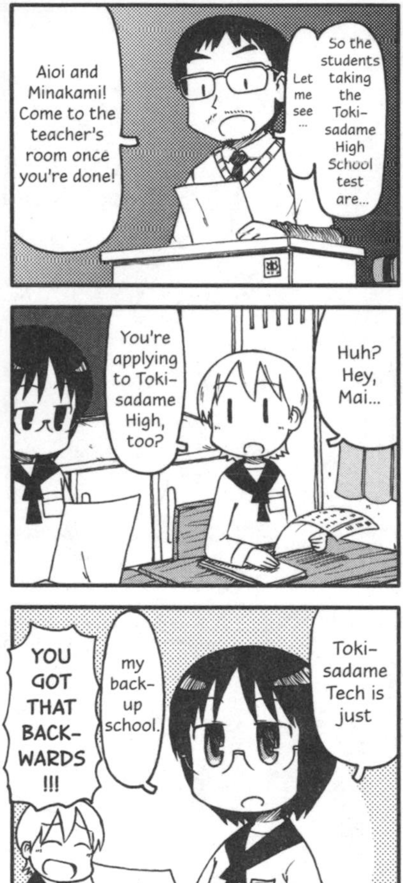
So the students taking the Toki-sadame High School test are...
Let me see ...
Aioi and Minakami! Come to the teacher's room once you're done!
Huh? Hey, Mai...
You're applying to Toki-sadame High, too?
Toki-sadame Tech is just
my back-up school.
YOU GOT THAT BACK-WARDS !!!
Well, but...
It'd be nice if we got to go to the same school.

chapter 134: end

chapter 135

FALCON'S SIDE-JOB COLLECTION

heavy clouds

Let's walk home together!
Okay!
Naganon, you're going to Tokisadame High, right? To be honest, I thought you'd aim for something a little higher.
Vera, are you going to Tokisadame Tech?
Yep! It'll be lonely, though...
I can't believe you're going to Tokisadame High just 'cause the person you like is going there!
Huh?
Your big sister mentioned it the other day.
Sis !!

praying to the gods

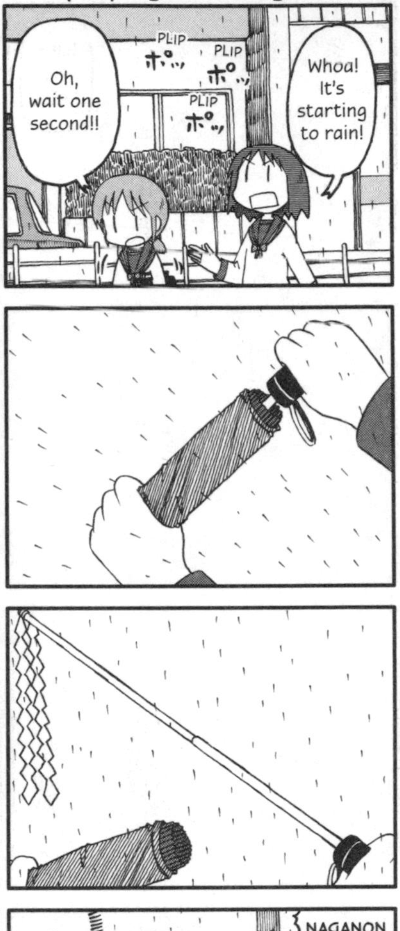
Whoa! It's starting to rain!
PLIP
PLIP
PLIP
Oh, wait one second!!
NAGANON, YOU BROUGHT A RAIN-MAKER?!
Sis !!

great escape

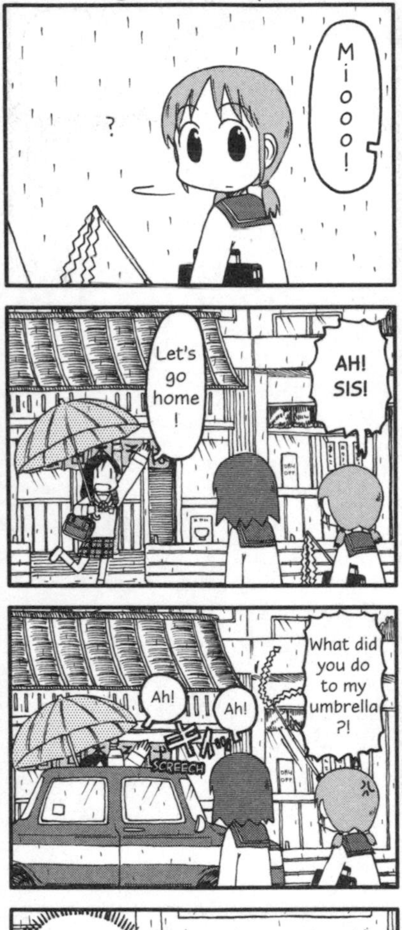
Miooo!
?
AH! SIS!
Let's go home!
What did you do to my umbrella?!
Ah!
Ah!
SCREECH
Take me home.
Sis?!!
VROOOOM

the ballad of the drizzle and the downpour

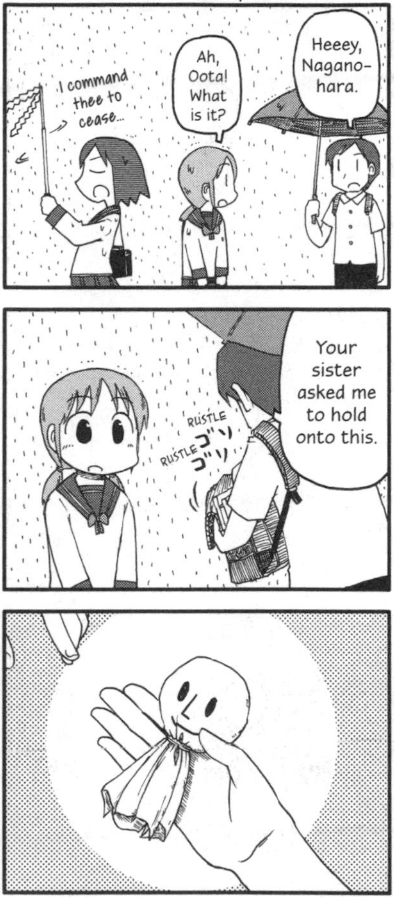
Heeey, Nagano-hara.
Ah, Oota! What is it?
I command thee to cease...
Your sister asked me to hold onto this.
RUSTLE
RUSTLE
ゴソゴソ
ピシャ
PSHAAP
A SUNNY DOLL?!

a soaked doll sings a melody by chopin

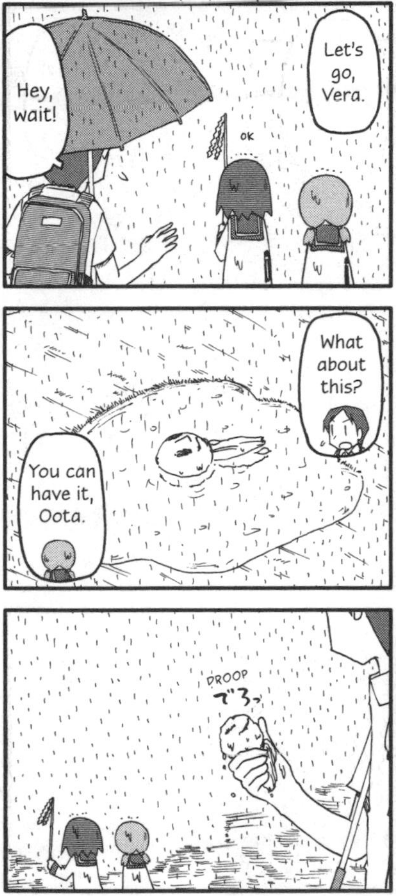
Let's go, Vera.
OK
Hey, wait!
What about this?
You can have it, Oota.
DROOP
でろっ

sis

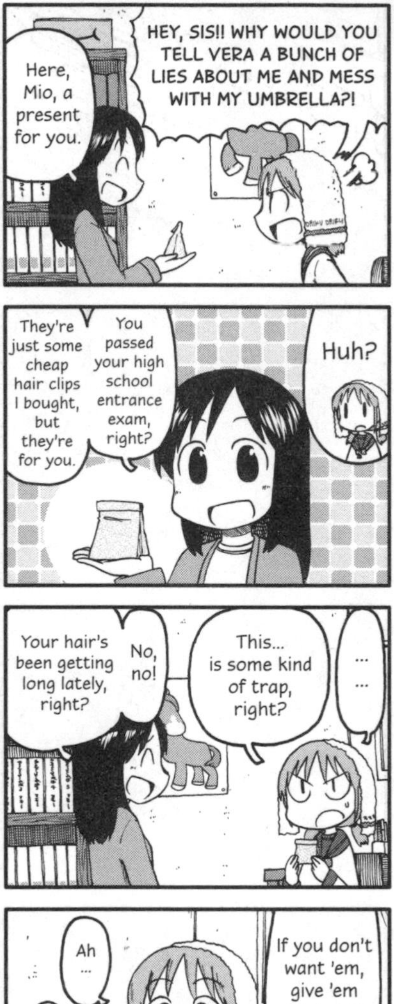
HEY, SIS!! WHY WOULD YOU TELL VERA A BUNCH OF LIES ABOUT ME AND MESS WITH MY UMBRELLA?!
Here, Mio, a present for you.
Huh?
You passed your high school entrance exam, right?
They're just some cheap hair clips I bought, but they're for you.
... ...
This... is some kind of trap, right?
No, no!
Your hair's been getting long lately, right?
If you don't want 'em, give 'em back and I'll use 'em.
Ah ...
Okay ...

sis

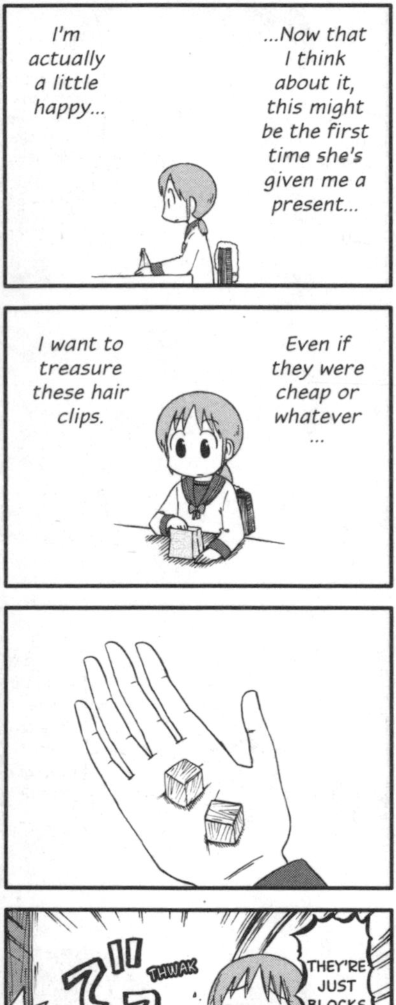
...Now that I think about it, this might be the first time she's given me a present...
I'm actually a little happy...
Even if they were cheap or whatever ...
I want to treasure these hair clips.
THEY'RE JUST BLOCKS OF WOOD !!
THWAK

word about this spreads, the gum company will rake in profits

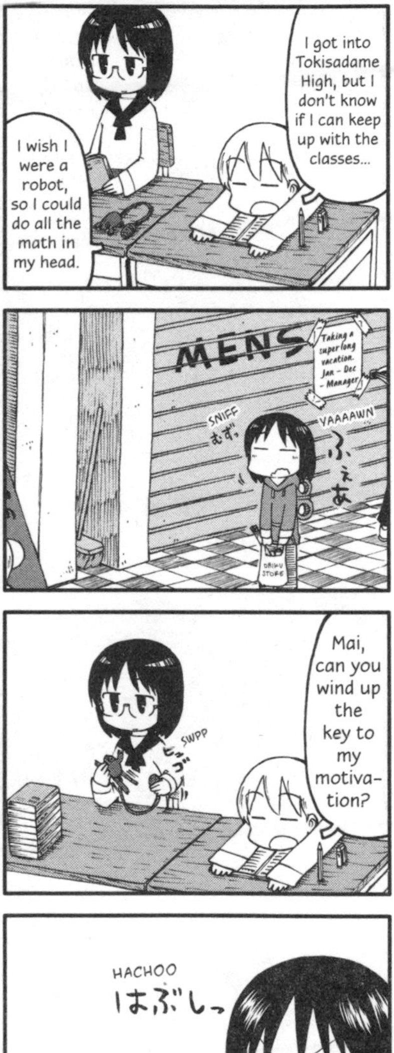
I got into Tokisadame High, but I don't know if I can keep up with the classes...
I wish I were a robot, so I could do all the math in my head.
MENS
Taking a super long vacation. Jan – Dec – Manager
SNIFF
むず
YAAAAWN
SWPP
Mai, can you wind up the key to my motivation?
HACHOO
はぶしっ

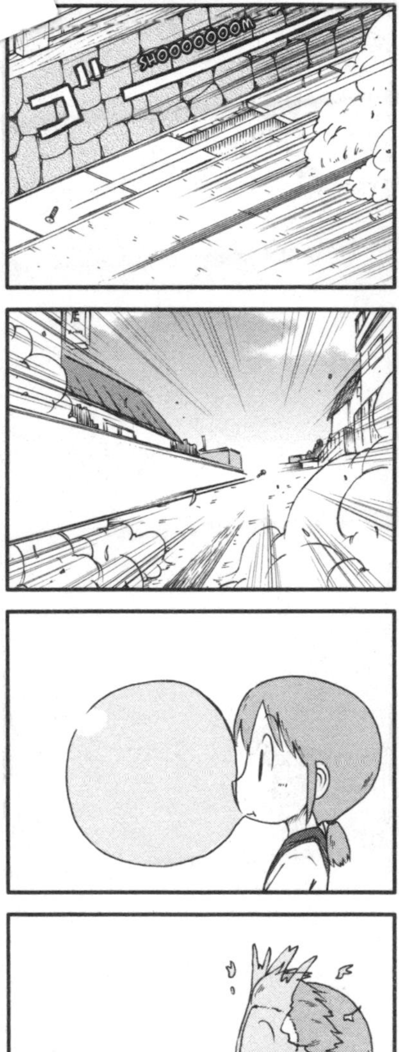
SHOOOOOOOM
ゴッ

sis

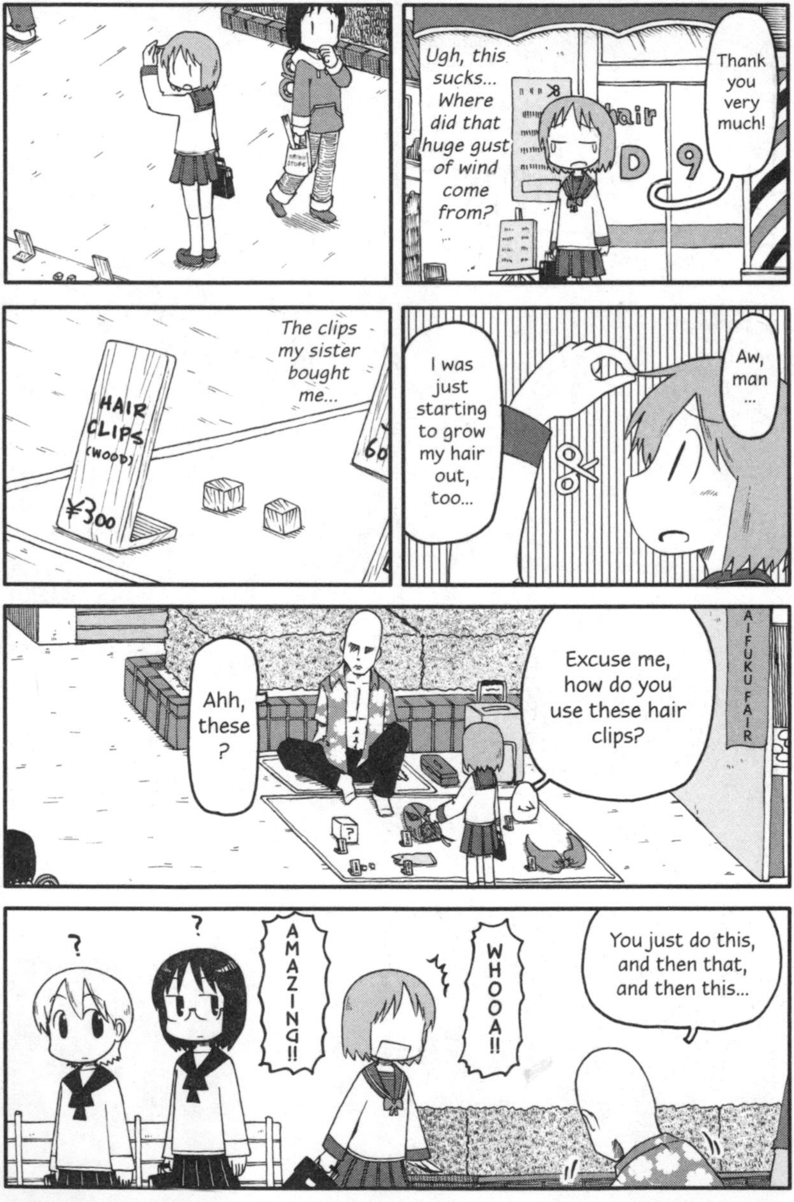
Thank you very much!
Ugh, this sucks... Where did that huge gust of wind come from?
hair
D9
Aw, man ...
I was just starting to grow my hair out, too...
The clips my sister bought me...
HAIR CLIPS (WOOD)
¥300
60
AIFUKU FAIR
Excuse me, how do you use these hair clips?
Ahh, these?
You just do this, and then that, and then this...
WHOOA!!
AMAZING!!
?
?

chapter 135: end

chapter 136

IT'S US!

TANABO, SUMIKA, AND MIHOSHI'S

MIDDLE SCHOOL DIARY!

enthusiasm

Mihoshi, Sumika, can you guys listen to the new traditional comedy that I wrote?
Ooh!
Sure!
Just a sec-ond.
upsie
Up-sie.
Up-sie.
TANABO

all set

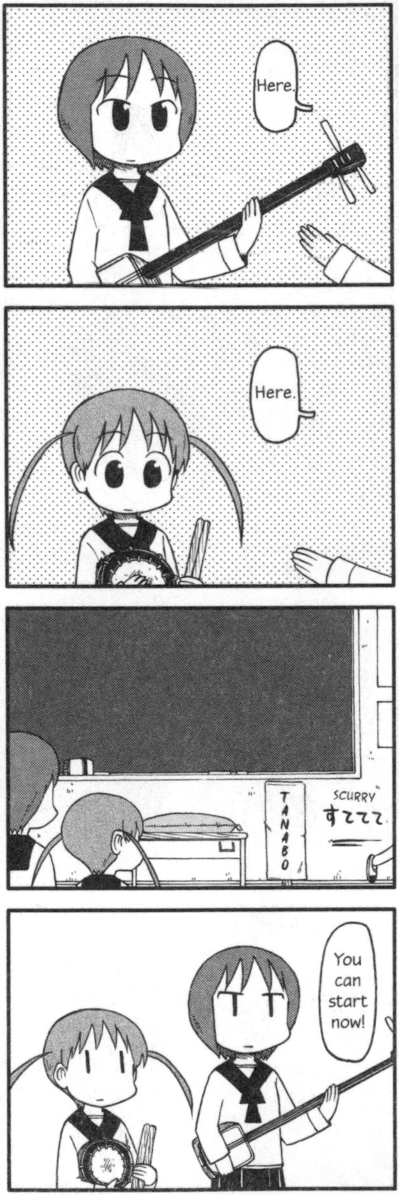
Here.
Here.
SCURRY
すててて
TANABO
You can start now!

breakdown

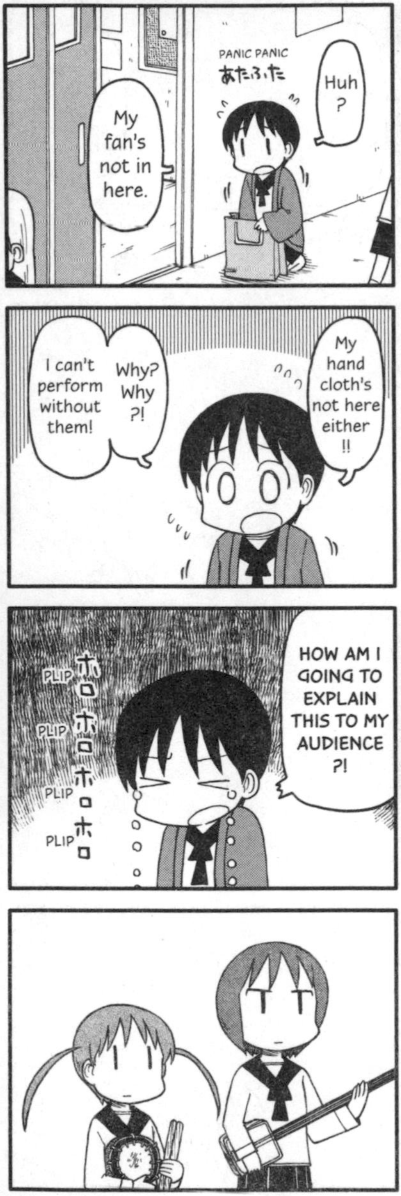
PANIC PANIC
あたふた
Huh?
My fan's not in here.
My hand cloth's not here either !!
Why? Why ?!
I can't perform without them!
HOW AM I GOING TO EXPLAIN THIS TO MY AUDIENCE ?!
PLIP PLIP PLIP PLIP
ホロホロホロホロ

natural

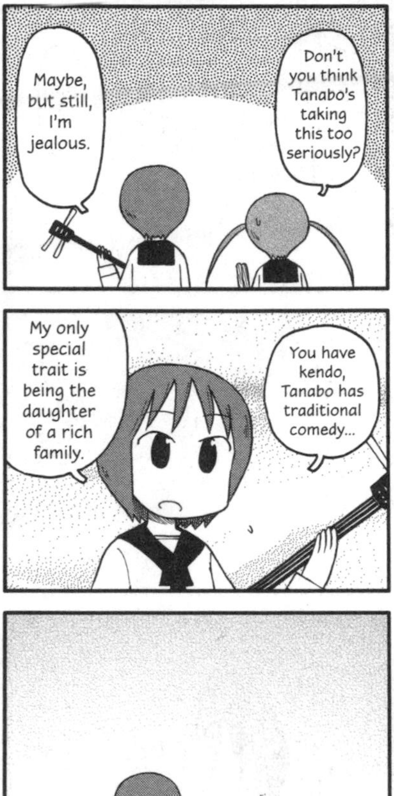
Don't you think Tanabo's taking this too seriously?
Maybe, but still, I'm jealous.
You have kendo, Tanabo has traditional comedy...
My only special trait is being the daughter of a rich family.
I'm jealous ...

more than jealous

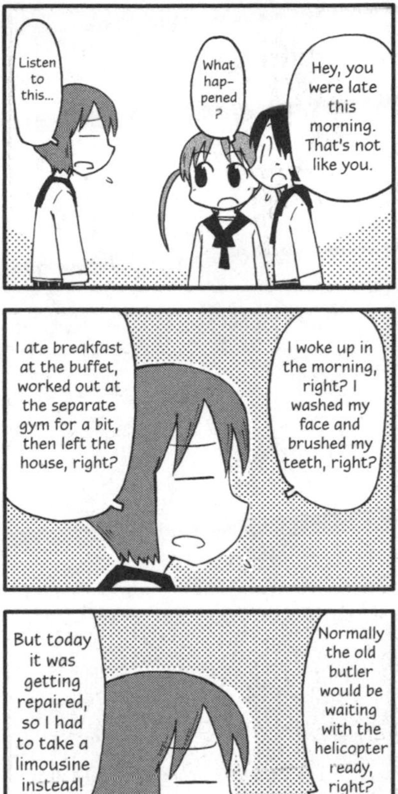
Hey, you were late this morning. That's not like you.
What hap-pened?
Listen to this...
I woke up in the morning, right? I washed my face and brushed my teeth, right?
I ate breakfast at the buffet, worked out at the separate gym for a bit, then left the house, right?
Normally the old butler would be waiting with the helicopter ready, right?
But today it was getting repaired, so I had to take a limousine instead!

growing distance

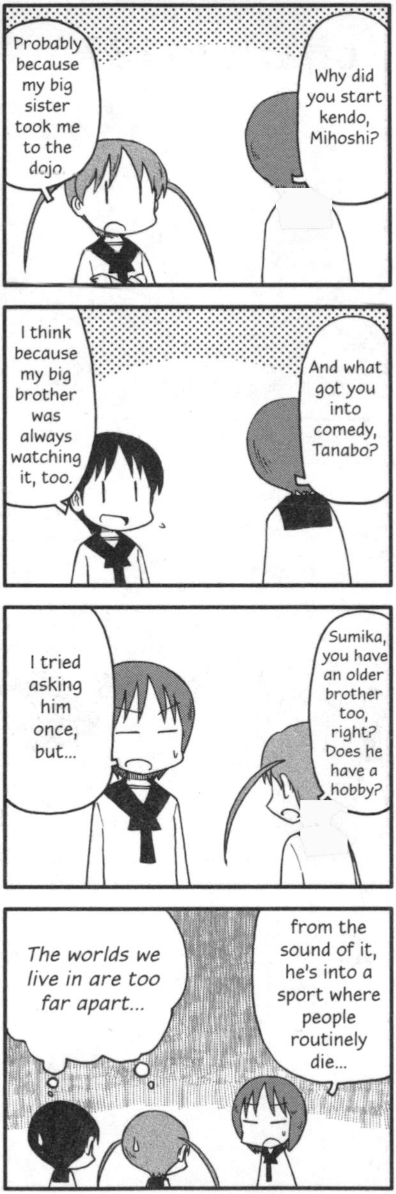
Why did you start kendo, Mihoshi?
Probably because my big sister took me to the dojo.
And what got you into comedy, Tanabo?
I think because my big brother was always watching it, too.
Sumika, you have an older brother too, right? Does he have a hobby?
I tried asking him once, but...
from the sound of it, he's into a sport where people routinely die...
The worlds we live in are too far apart...

quickly closing the gap

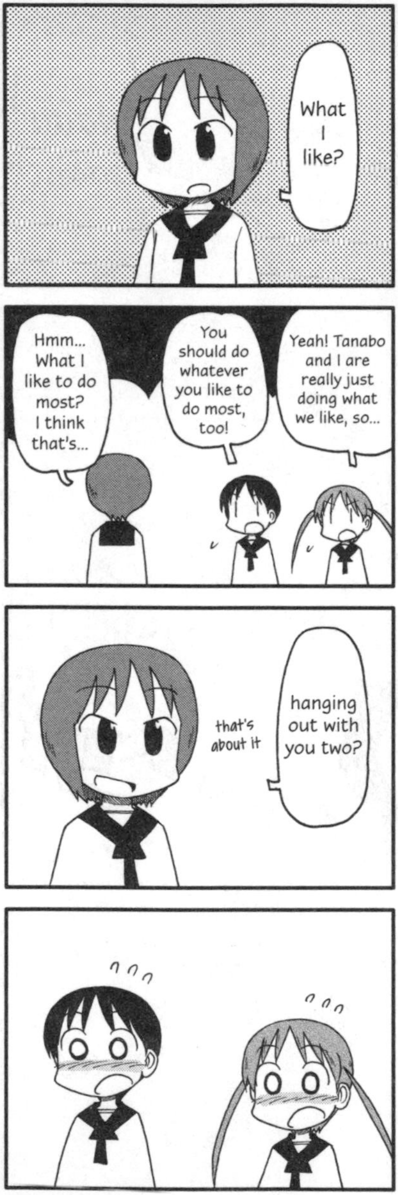
What I like?
Yeah! Tanabo and I are really just doing what we like, so...
You should do whatever you like to do most, too!
Hmm... What I like to do most? I think that's...
hanging out with you two?
that's about it

chapter 136: end

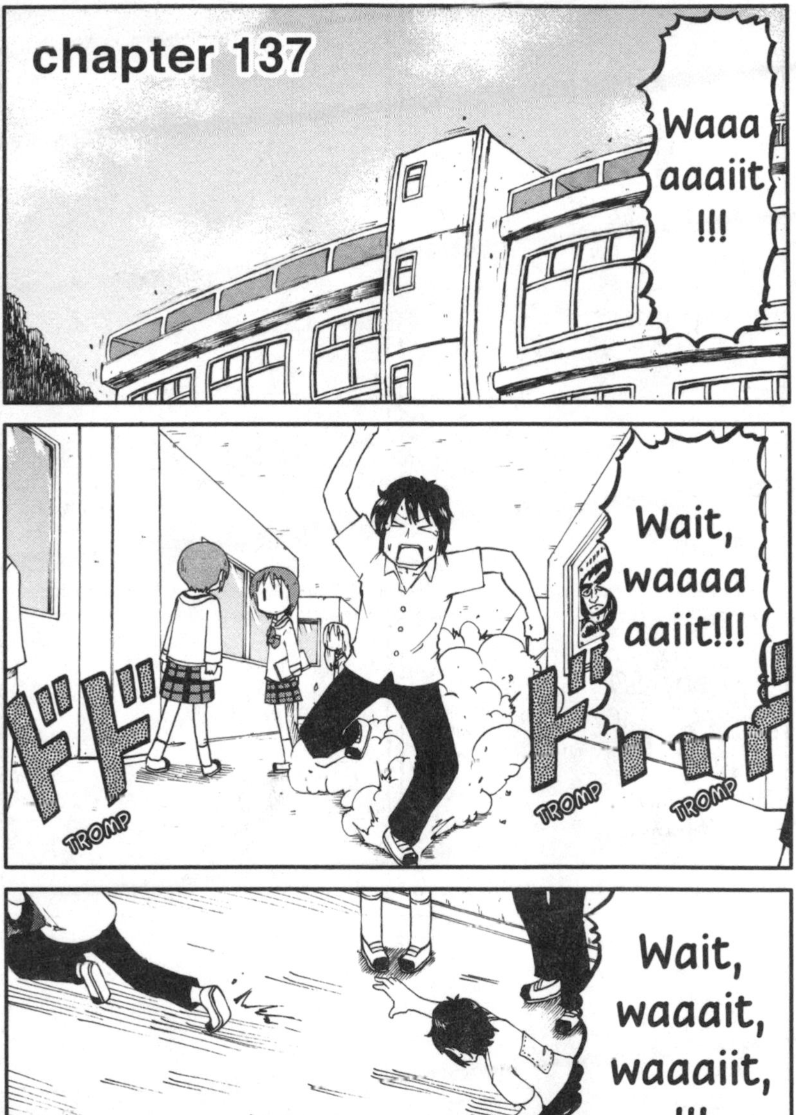
chapter 137
Waaa aaaiit !!!
Wait, waaaa aaiit!!!
ドドドドド
TROMP
TROMP
TROMP
Wait, waaait, waaaiit, !!!

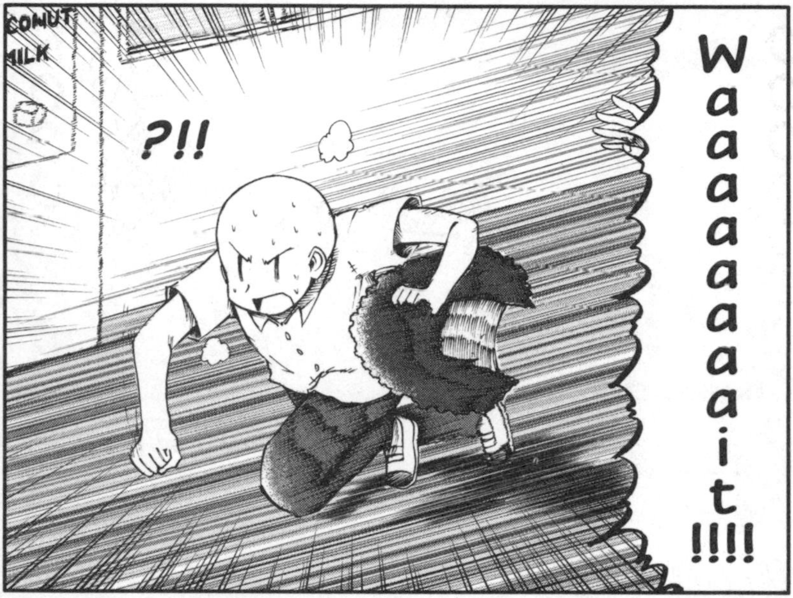
Waaaaaaaait!!!!
?!!

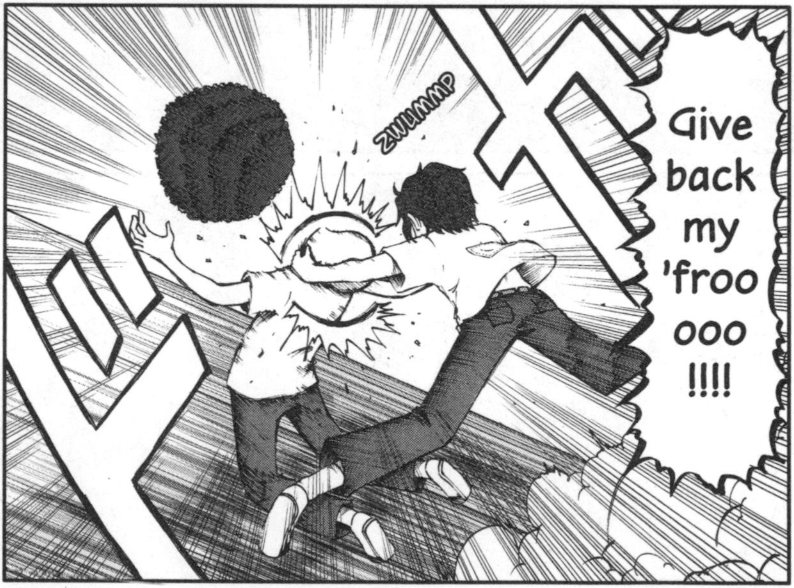
Give back my 'froo ooo !!!!
ZWUMMP

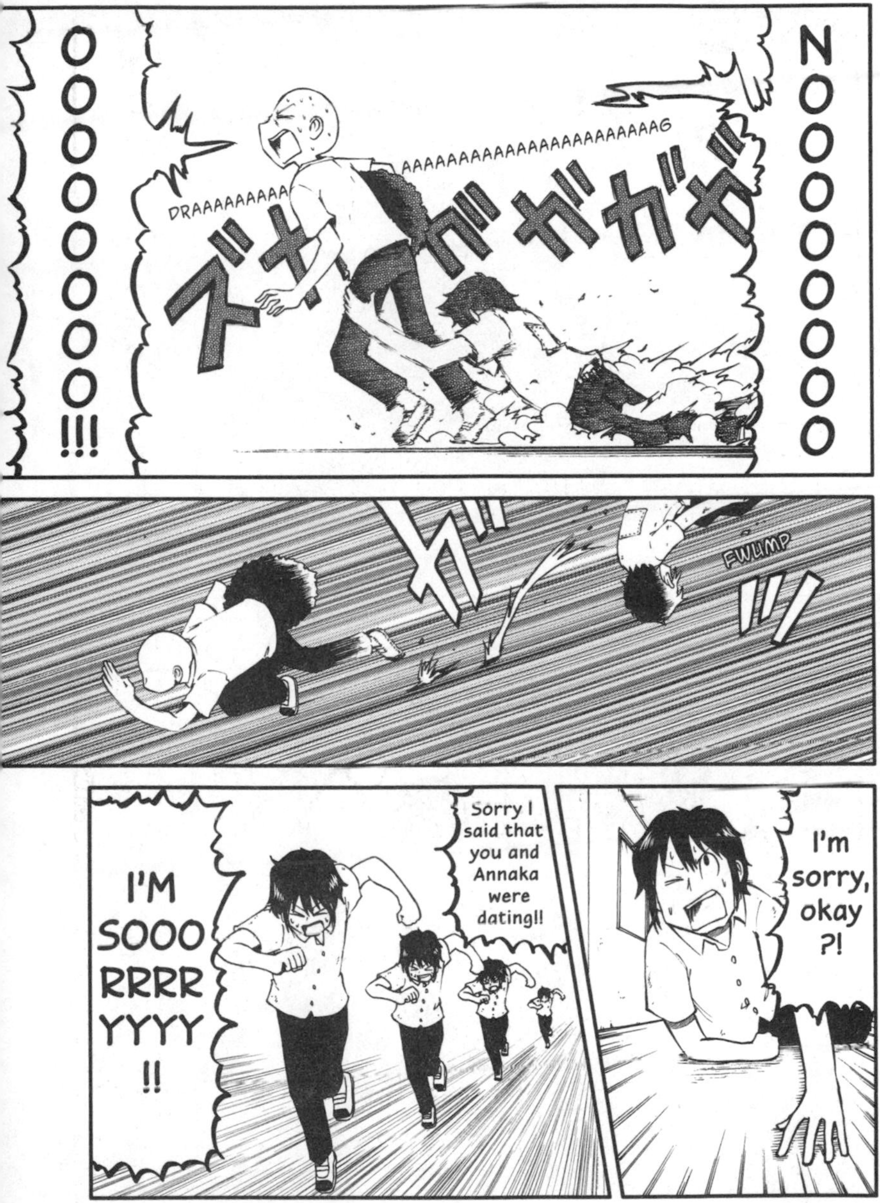
NOOOOOOOOOOO
DRAAAAAAAAAA
AAAAAAAAAAAAAAAAAAAAAAAAG
OOOOOOOOOOO!!!
FWUMP
I'm sorry, okay?!
Sorry I said that you and Annaka were dating!!
I'M SOOORRRRYYYY!!

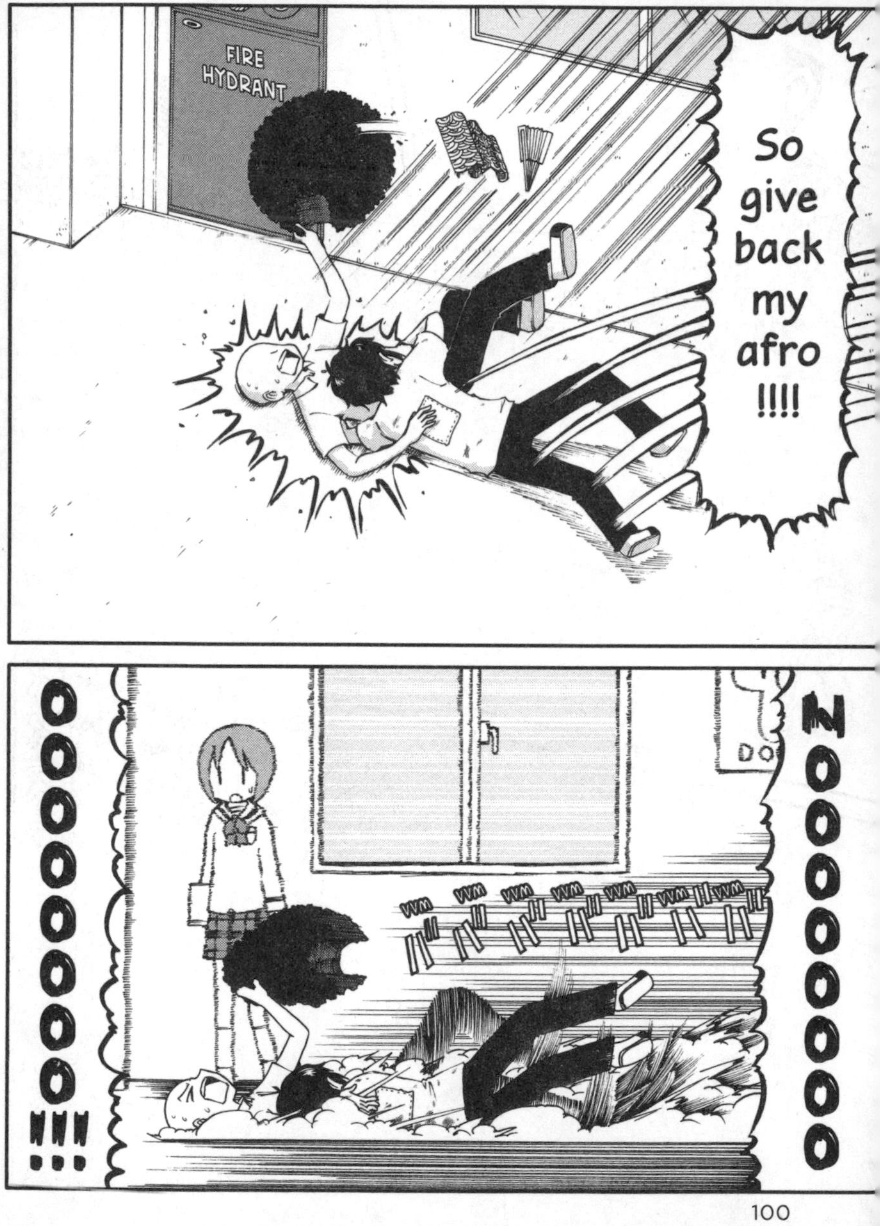
FIRE HYDRANT
So give back my afro !!!!
NOOOOOOOOOOOO
OOOOOOOOOOOOO!!!!

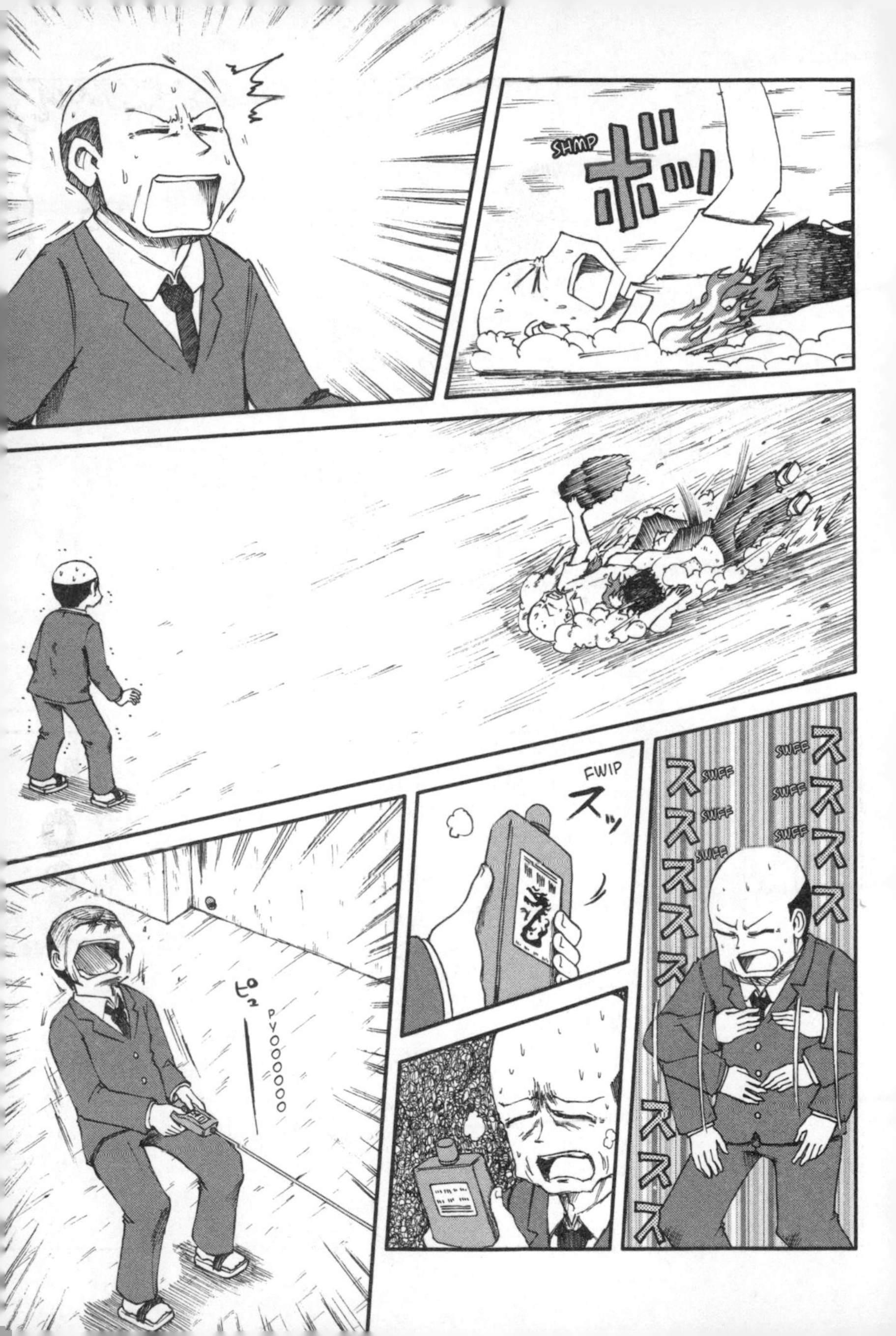
ボッ
SHMP
ススススススス
SWFF
SWFF
SWFF
SWFF
SWFF
スッ
FWIP
ピュ
PYOOOOOO

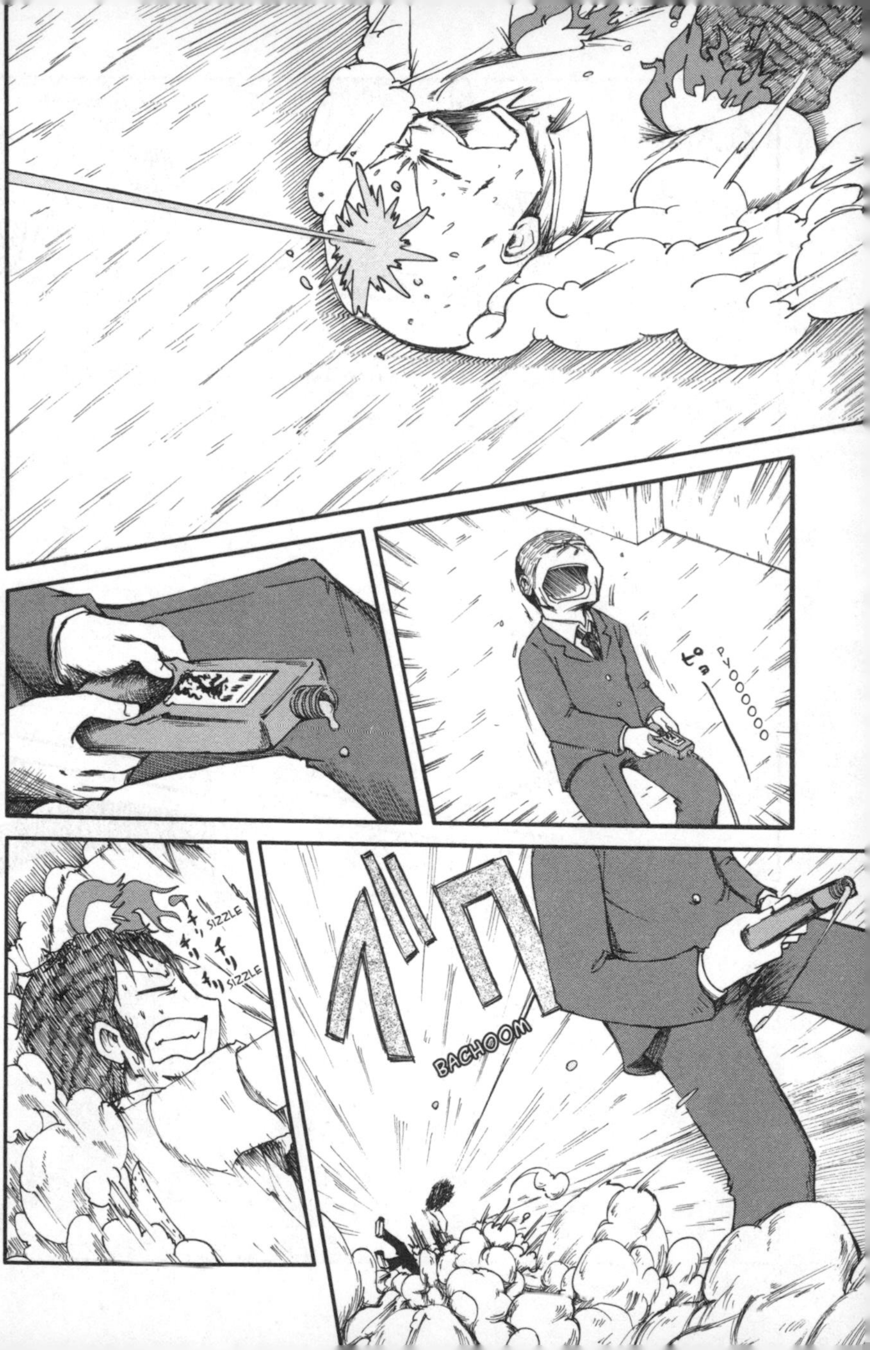

PYOOOOOOO
BACHOOM
チリ SIZZLE
チリ
チリ SIZZLE

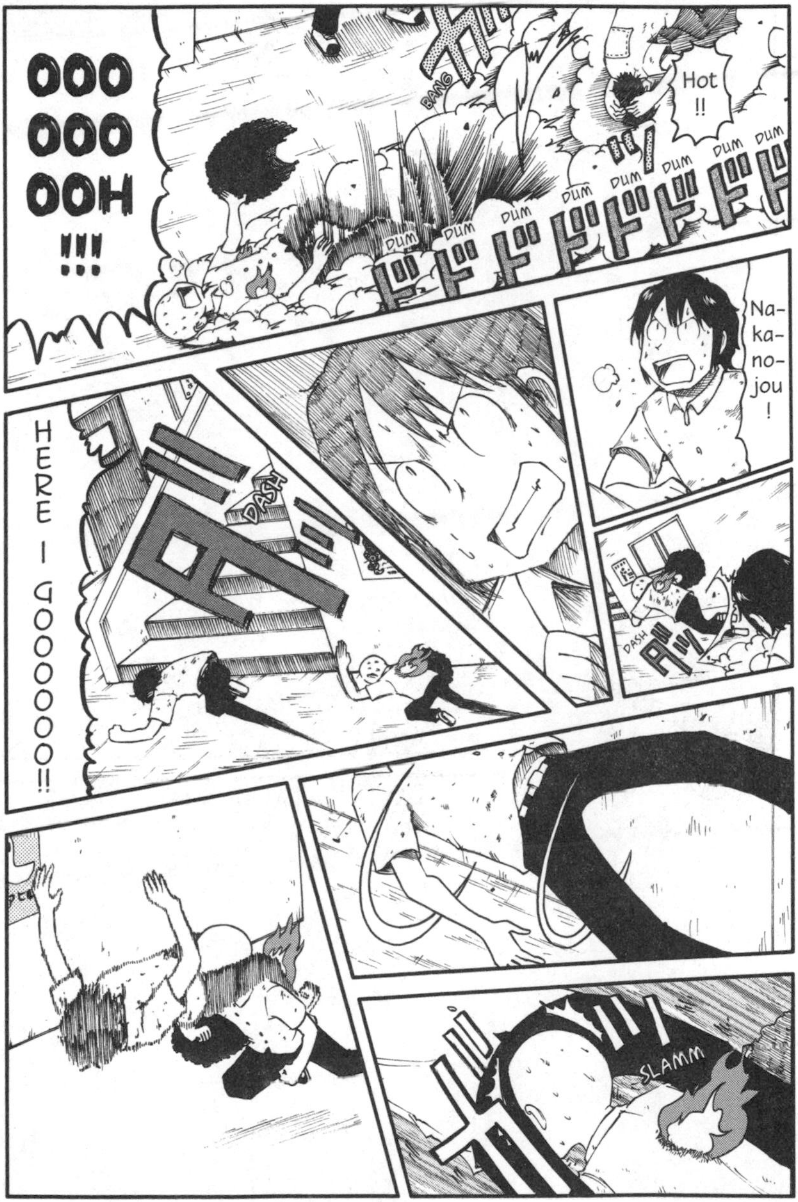
Hot !!
BANG
DUM
DUM
DUM
DUM
DUM
DUM
DUM
DUM
DUM
OOO OOO OOH !!!!
Na-ka-no-jou !
DASH
DASH
HERE I GOOOOOOO!!
SLAMM

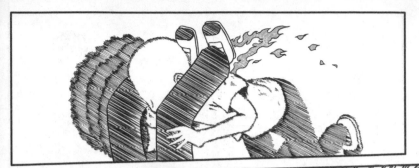

WHAMM

Heee
yaaah
!

PEEP

PEEP

PEEP

PEEP

PEEP

PEEP

What
on
earth
was
that
all...

SMOLDER

SMOLDER

104

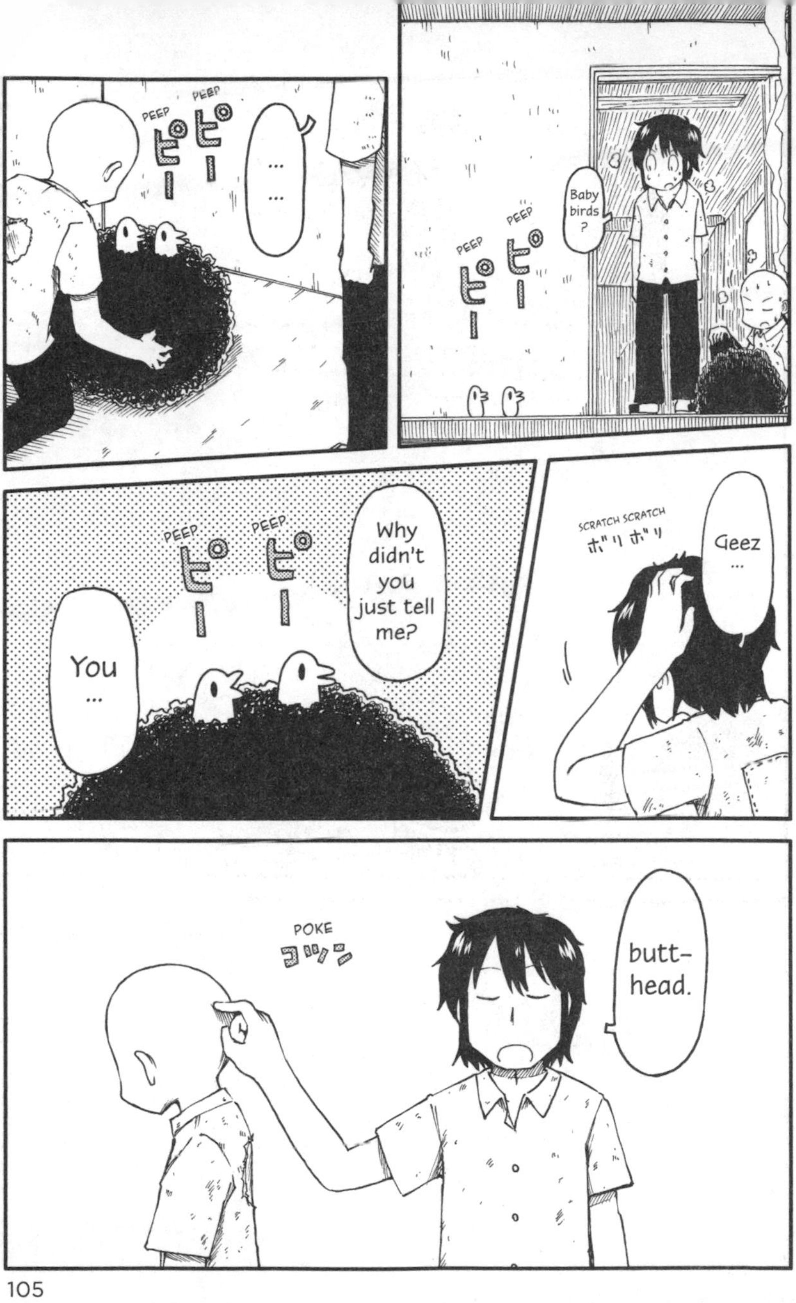

Baby birds ?
PEEP PEEP
ピーピー
PEEP PEEP
ピーピー
… …
SCRATCH SCRATCH
ボリボリ
Geez …
Why didn't you just tell me?
PEEP PEEP
ピーピー
You …
POKE
コツン
butt-head.

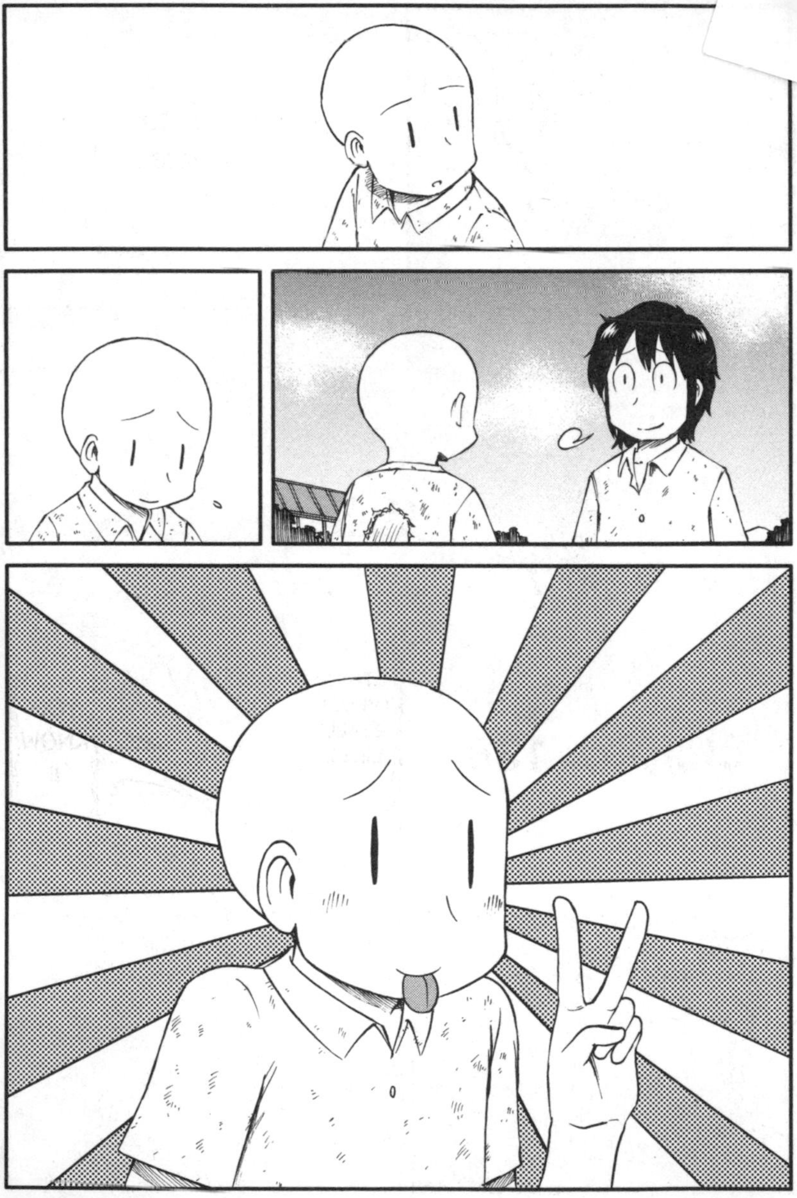

chapter 137: end

I have to apologize...

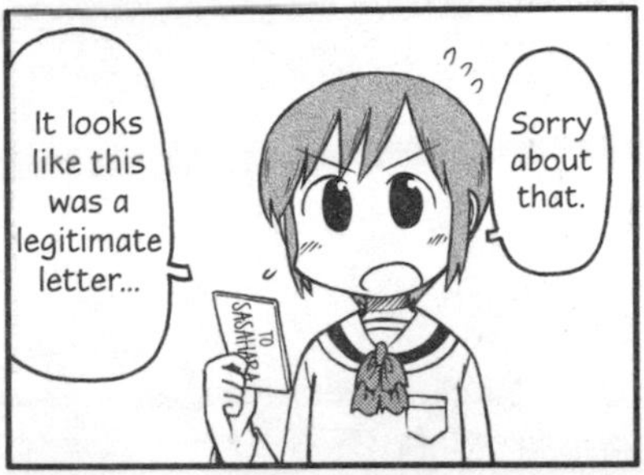
Sorry about that.
It looks like this was a legitimate letter...
TO SASAHARA

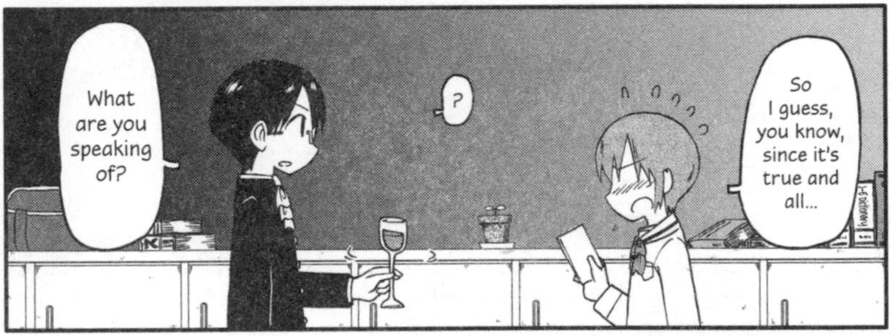
So I guess, you know, since it's true and all...
?
What are you speaking of?

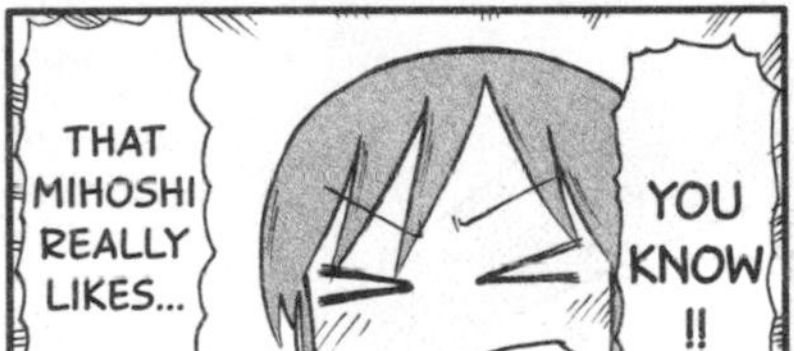
THAT MIHOSHI REALLY LIKES...
YOU KNOW!!

chapter 138

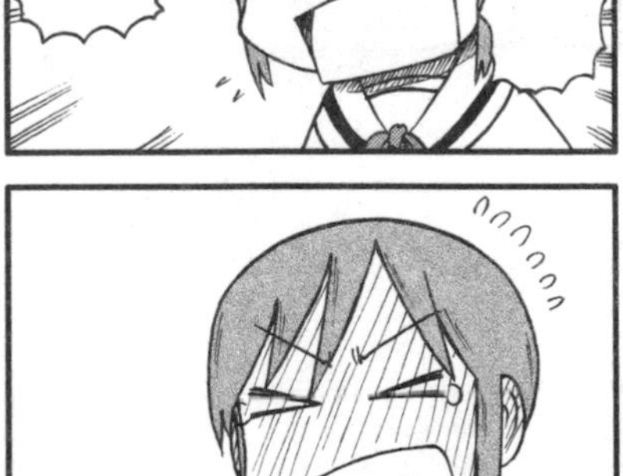

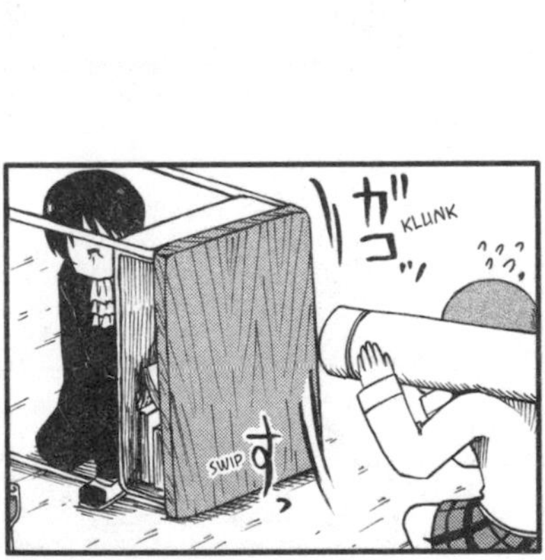
KLUNK
SWIP

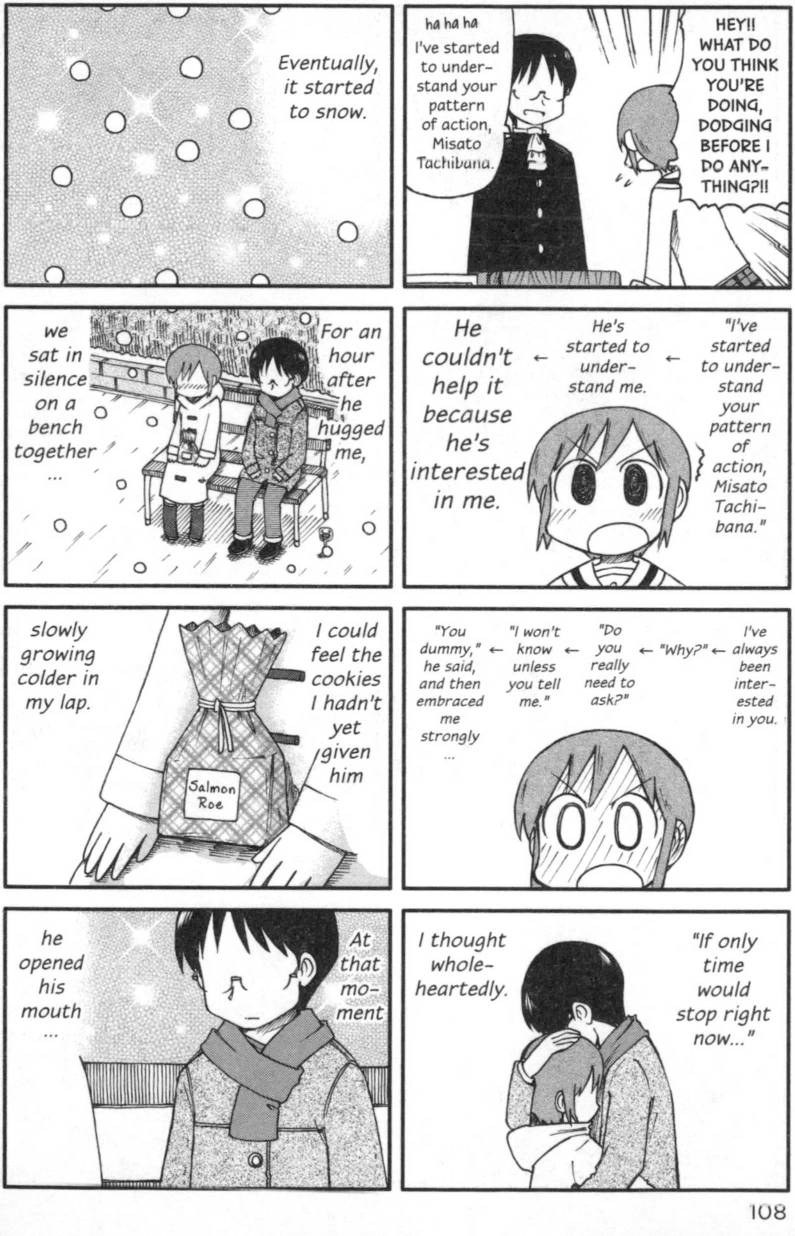
HEY!! WHAT DO YOU THINK YOU'RE DOING, DODGING BEFORE I DO ANYTHING?!!
ha ha ha
I've started to understand your pattern of action, Misato Tachibana.
Eventually, it started to snow.
"I've started to understand your pattern of action, Misato Tachibana."
←
He's started to understand me.
←
He couldn't help it because he's interested in me.
For an hour after he hugged me,
we sat in silence on a bench together...
I've always been interested in you.
←
"Why?"
←
"Do you really need to ask?"
←
"I won't know unless you tell me."
←
"You dummy," he said, and then embraced me strongly...
I could feel the cookies I hadn't yet given him
slowly growing colder in my lap.
Salmon Roe
"If only time would stop right now..."
I thought wholeheartedly.
At that moment
he opened his mouth...

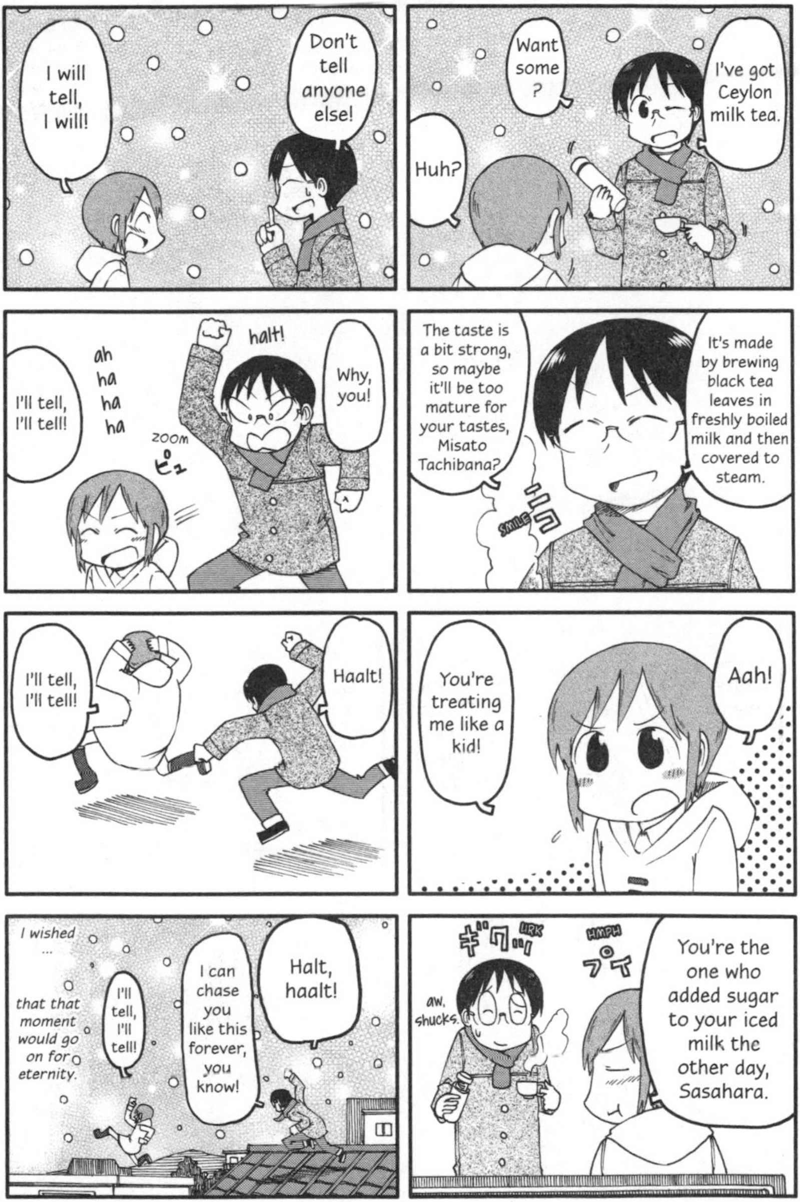
I've got Ceylon milk tea.
Want some?
Huh?
Don't tell anyone else!
I will tell, I will!
It's made by brewing black tea leaves in freshly boiled milk and then covered to steam.
The taste is a bit strong, so maybe it'll be too mature for your tastes, Misato Tachibana?
SMILE
ニコ
Why, you!
halt!
ah ha ha ha
ZOOM
ピュ
I'll tell, I'll tell!
Aah!
You're treating me like a kid!
Haalt!
I'll tell, I'll tell!
You're the one who added sugar to your iced milk the other day, Sasahara.
HMPH
プイ
URK
ギクッ
aw, shucks.
Halt, haalt!
I can chase you like this forever, you know!
I'll tell, I'll tell!
I wished ...
that that moment would go on for eternity.

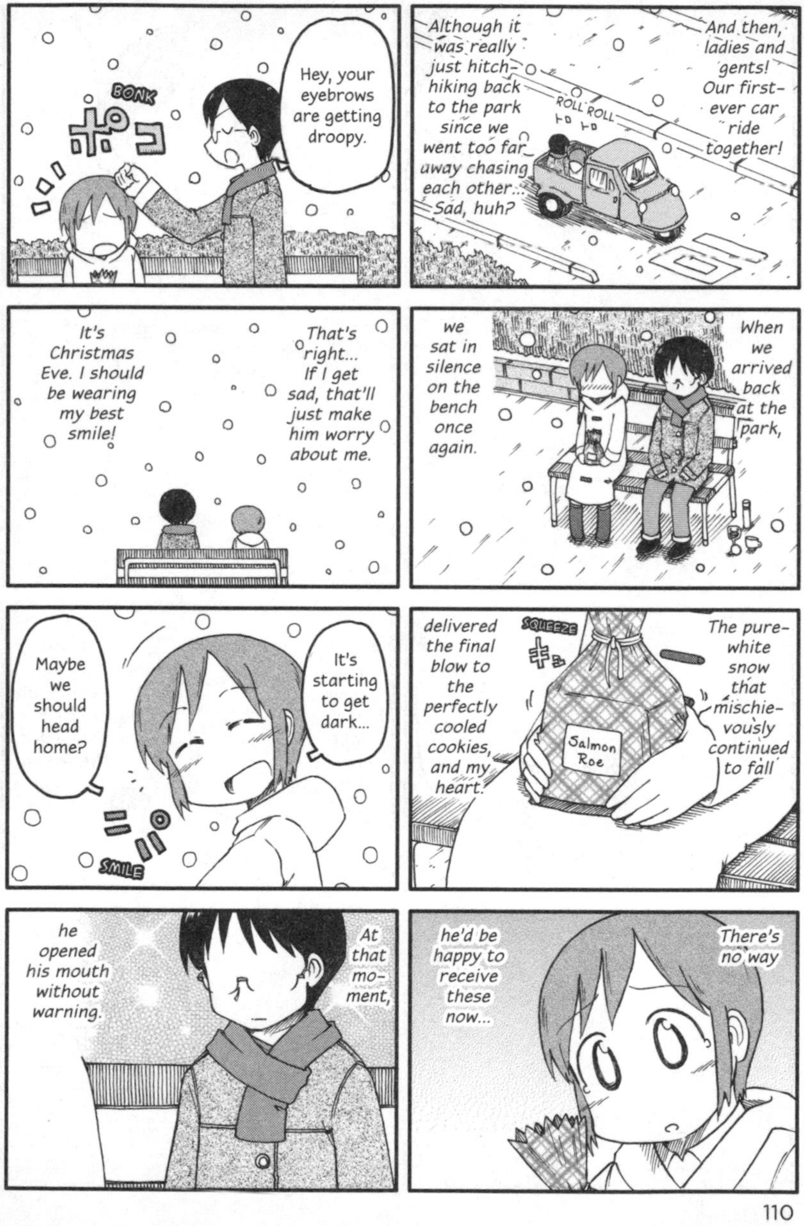
And then, ladies and gents! Our first-ever car ride together!
Although it was really just hitchhiking back to the park since we went too far away chasing each other... Sad, huh?
ROLL ROLL
Hey, your eyebrows are getting droopy.
BONK
When we arrived back at the park,
we sat in silence on the bench once again.
That's right... If I get sad, that'll just make him worry about me.
It's Christmas Eve. I should be wearing my best smile!
The pure-white snow that mischievously continued to fall
SQUEEZE
Salmon Roe
delivered the final blow to the perfectly cooled cookies, and my heart.
It's starting to get dark...
Maybe we should head home?
SMILE
There's no way
he'd be happy to receive these now...
At that moment,
he opened his mouth without warning.

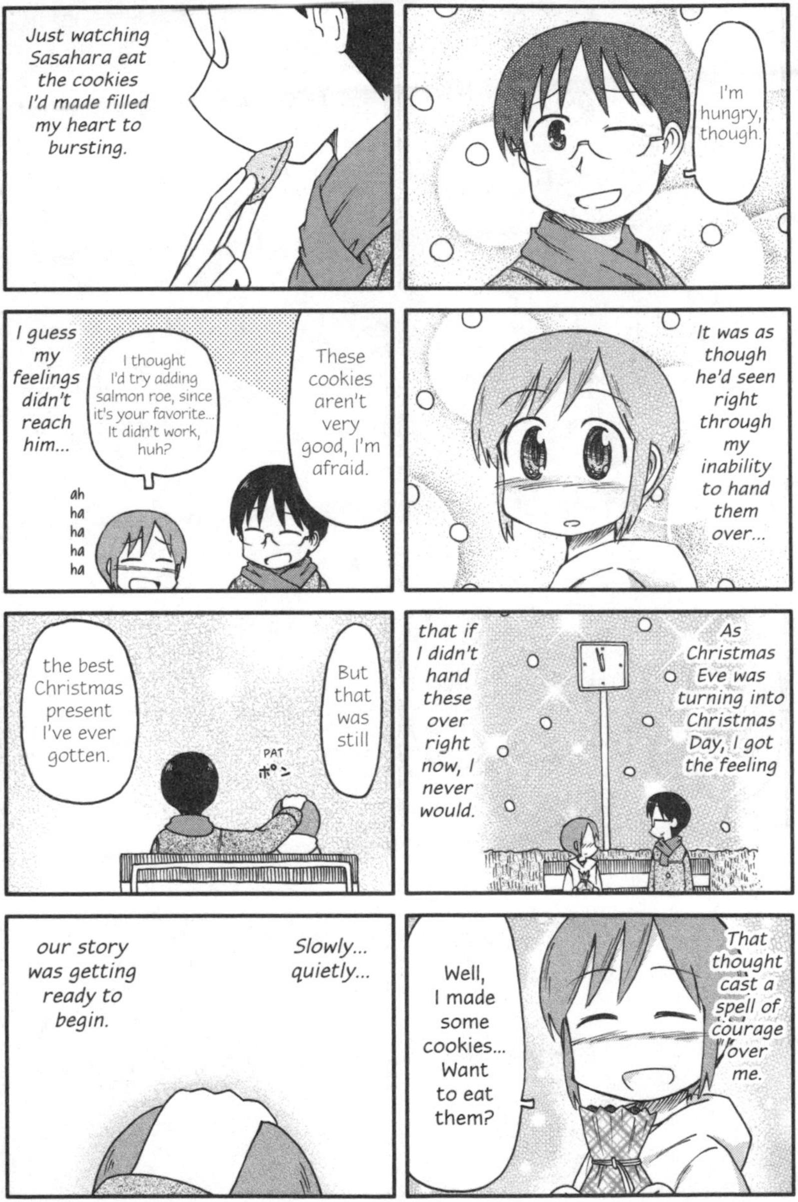

I'm hungry, though.
Just watching Sasahara eat the cookies I'd made filled my heart to bursting.
It was as though he'd seen right through my inability to hand them over...
These cookies aren't very good, I'm afraid.
I thought I'd try adding salmon roe, since it's your favorite... It didn't work, huh?
I guess my feelings didn't reach him...
ah ha ha ha ha
As Christmas Eve was turning into Christmas Day, I got the feeling
that if I didn't hand these over right now, I never would.
But that was still
PAT
ポン
the best Christmas present I've ever gotten.
That thought cast a spell of courage over me.
Well, I made some cookies... Want to eat them?
Slowly... quietly...
our story was getting ready to begin.

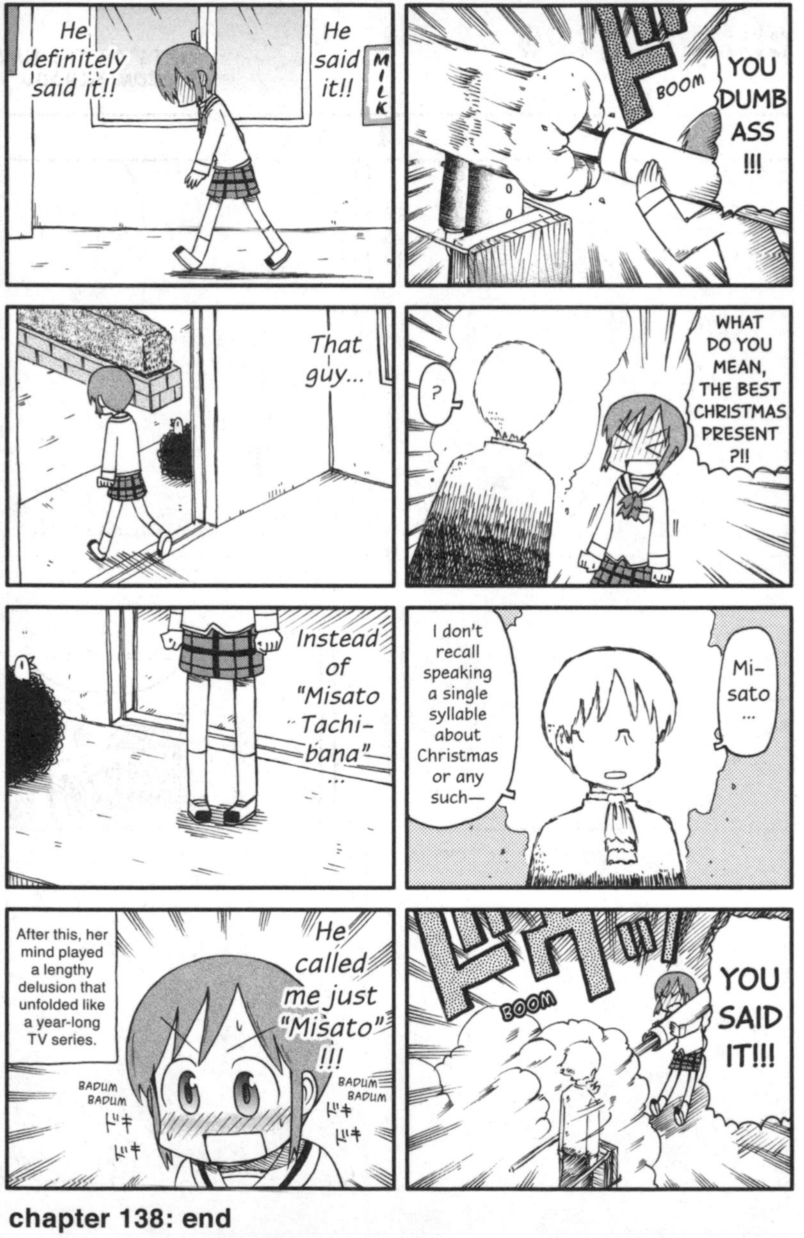
BOOM
YOU DUMB ASS !!!
He said it!!
MILK
He definitely said it!!
WHAT DO YOU MEAN, THE BEST CHRISTMAS PRESENT ?!!
?
That guy...
Mi-sato ...
I don't recall speaking a single syllable about Christmas or any such—
Instead of "Misato Tachi-bana" ...
YOU SAID IT!!!
BOOM
He called me just "Misato" !!!
BADUM BADUM
ドキ
ドキ
BADUM BADUM
ドキ
ドキ
After this, her mind played a lengthy delusion that unfolded like a year-long TV series.

chapter 138: end

chapter 139

CAREFUL ON YOUR WAY HOME!

MOMENTS ON THE WAY HOME FROM SCHOOL

1

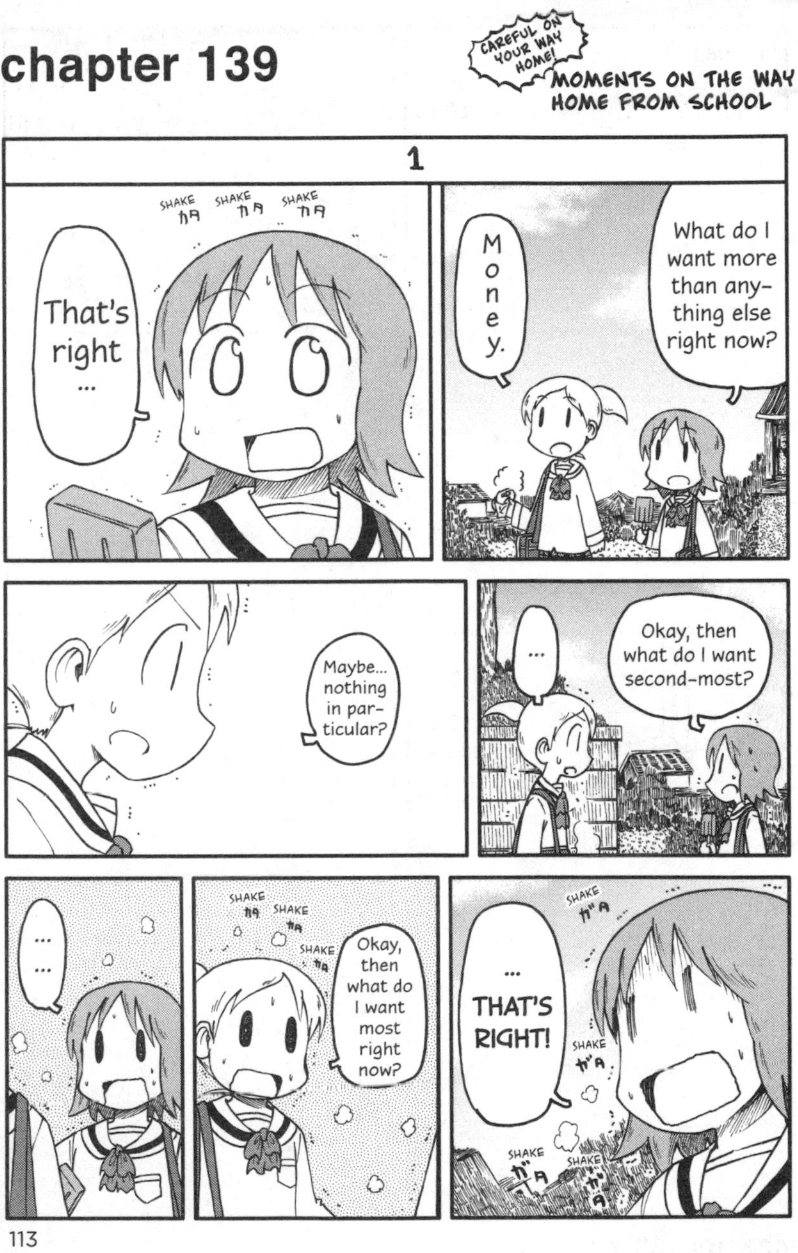
What do I want more than anything else right now?
Money.
SHAKE SHAKE SHAKE
That's right ...
Okay, then what do I want second-most?
...
Maybe... nothing in particular?
SHAKE
... THAT'S RIGHT!
SHAKE
SHAKE
SHAKE
SHAKE SHAKE SHAKE
Okay, then what do I want most right now?
... ...

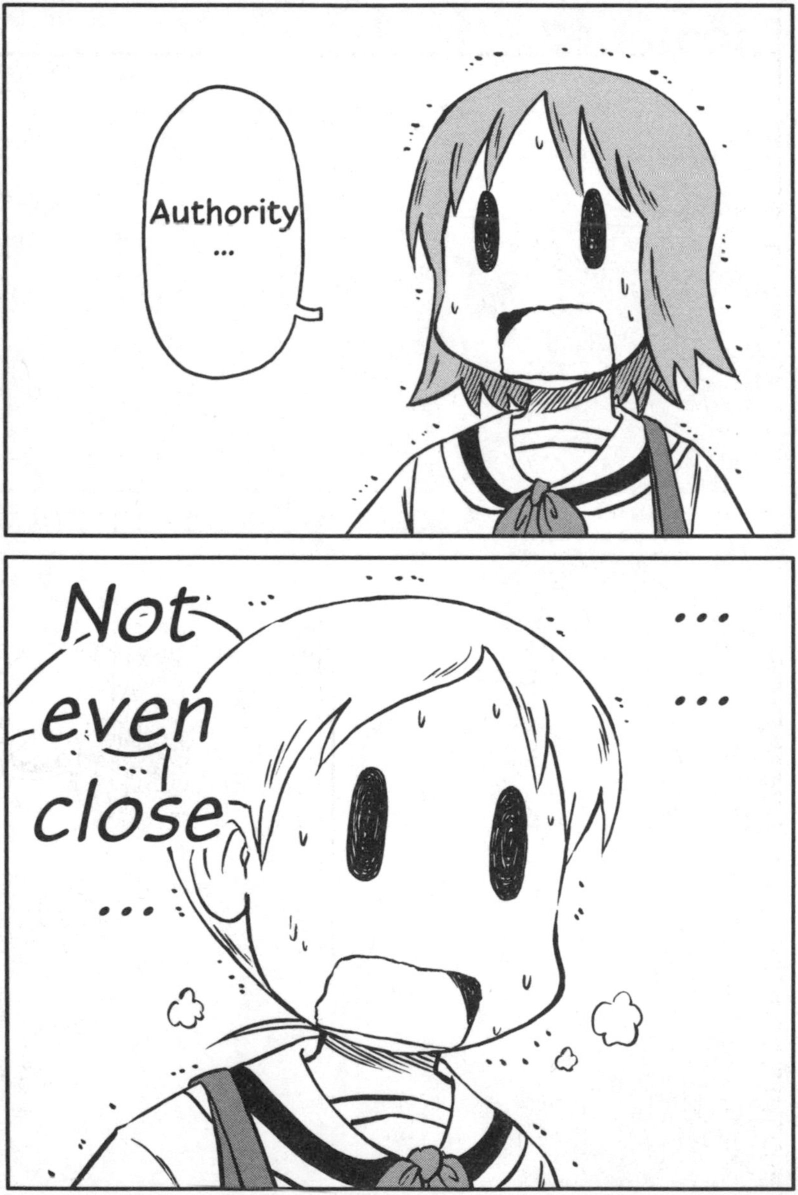
Authority ...
... ...
Not even close
...

2

キョロ GLANCE
キョロ GLANCE
EGGPLANT
¥100 EACH
TOKISADAME BATTING CENTER

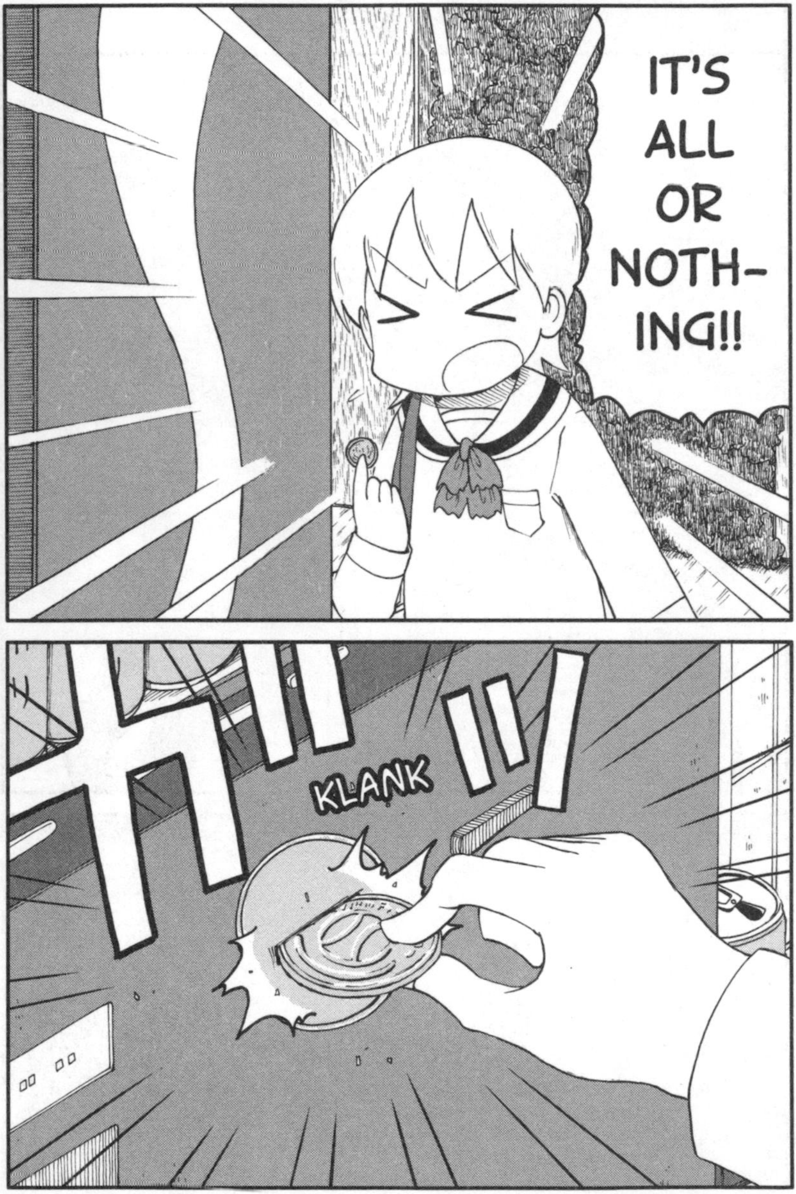
IT'S ALL OR NOTH-ING!!
KLANK

3
I finally got my hands on the illusory secret elixir "Dragon" ...
But even though I've been using it every day, my scalp hasn't responded a whit.
I bought that cart in the hopes that the intense exercise would raise my metabolism
I keep persevering, even though it appears to be totally pointless.
Just as I was down to my last bottle of the elixir,
I ended up using most of it to try to solve an emergency situation.
Even so, I placed all of my hopes in those last few drops.
But if I continue to wait, even though I've been duped...
Mr. Shino-nome.

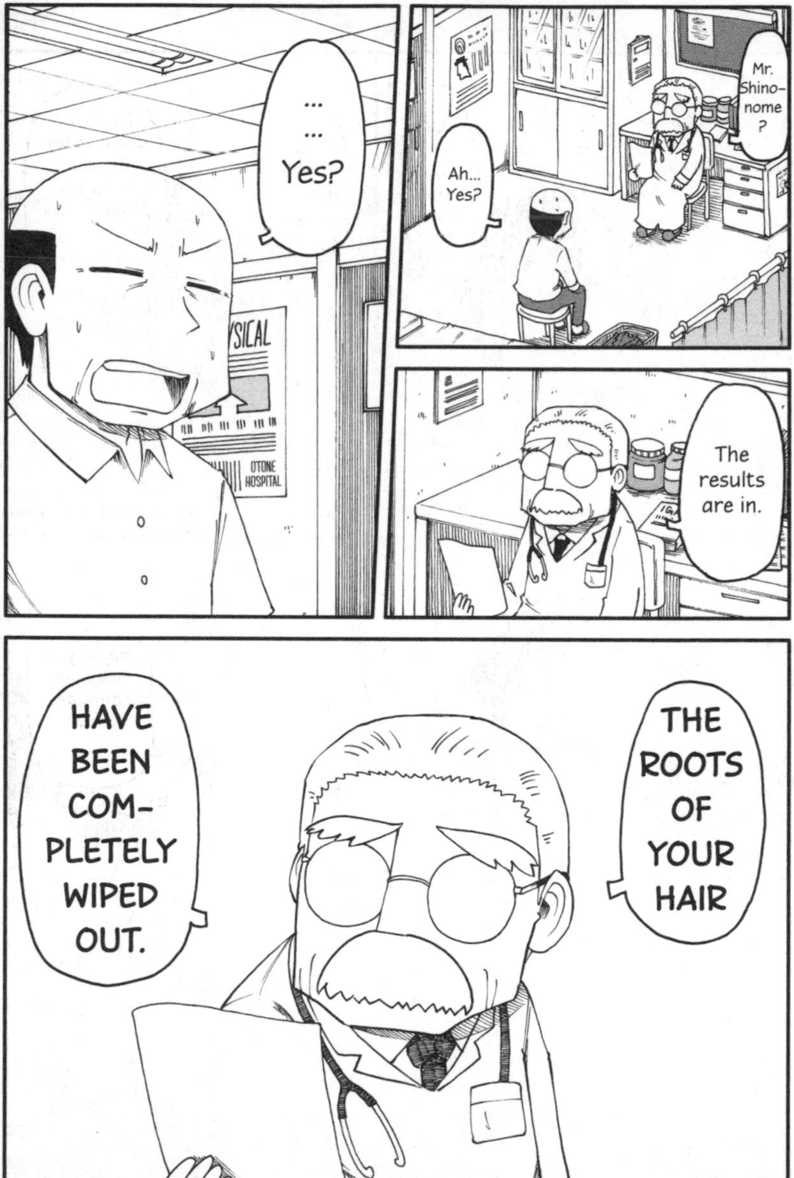
Mr. Shino-nome?
Ah... Yes?
The results are in.
... ... Yes?
YSICAL
OTONE HOSPITAL
THE ROOTS OF YOUR HAIR
HAVE BEEN COM-PLETELY WIPED OUT.

4
I'm sorry about today, Tanaka. I'll make a proper house for the chicks tomorrow.
I keep telling you, it's fine!
It's just, without that thing ...
that thing
I feel like I've got no individuality at all!
Then maybe you and I are comrades now?
'cause we both have no individuality?
You're not wrong there.

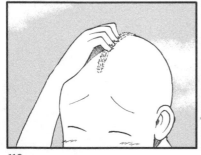

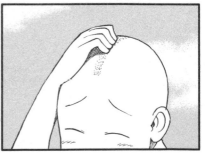

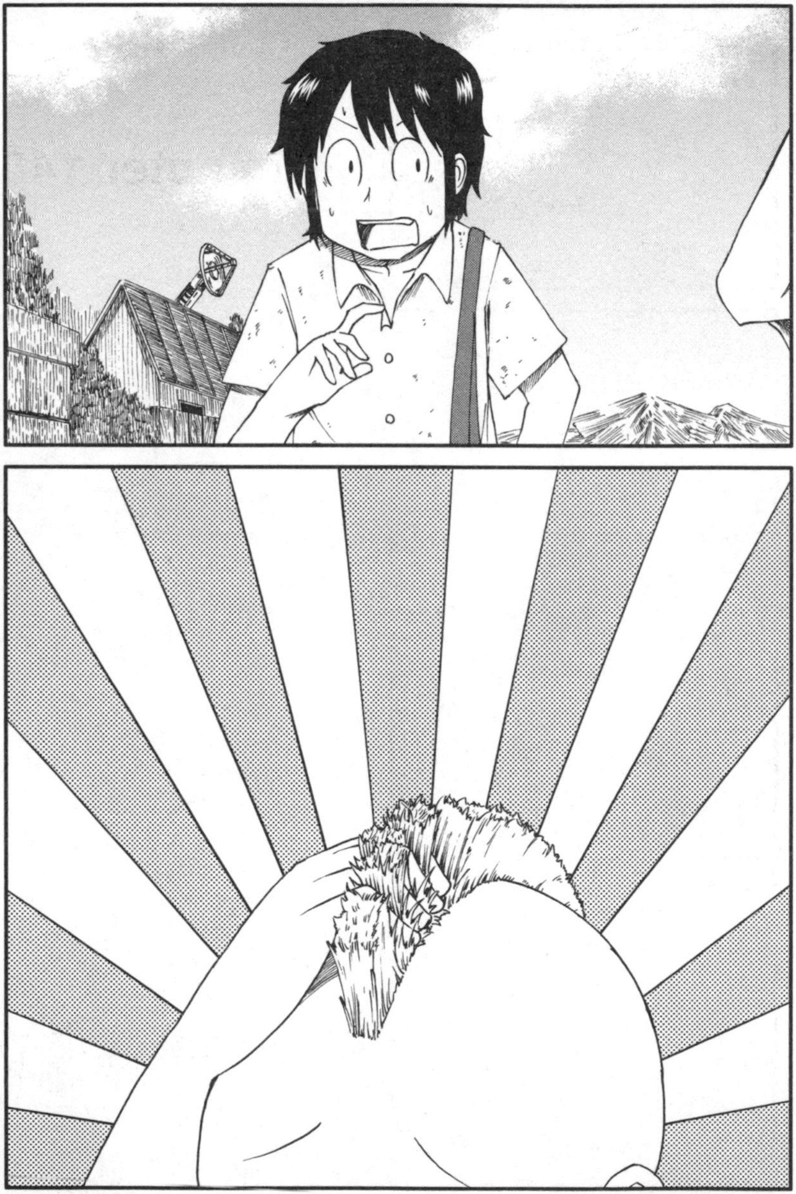

chapter 139: end

chapter 140

Sakamoto, say hi to Yukko!
... ... Hello.
Whoa! He really can talk!!
GLANCE GLANCE
キョロ キョロ
ドキ ドキ
BADUM BADUM
Amazing!! Oh man, what do I say?!
Uhm, uhm, uhmm ...
SHAKE !!
SWIP
スッ
This one ...
isn't very bright, huh?

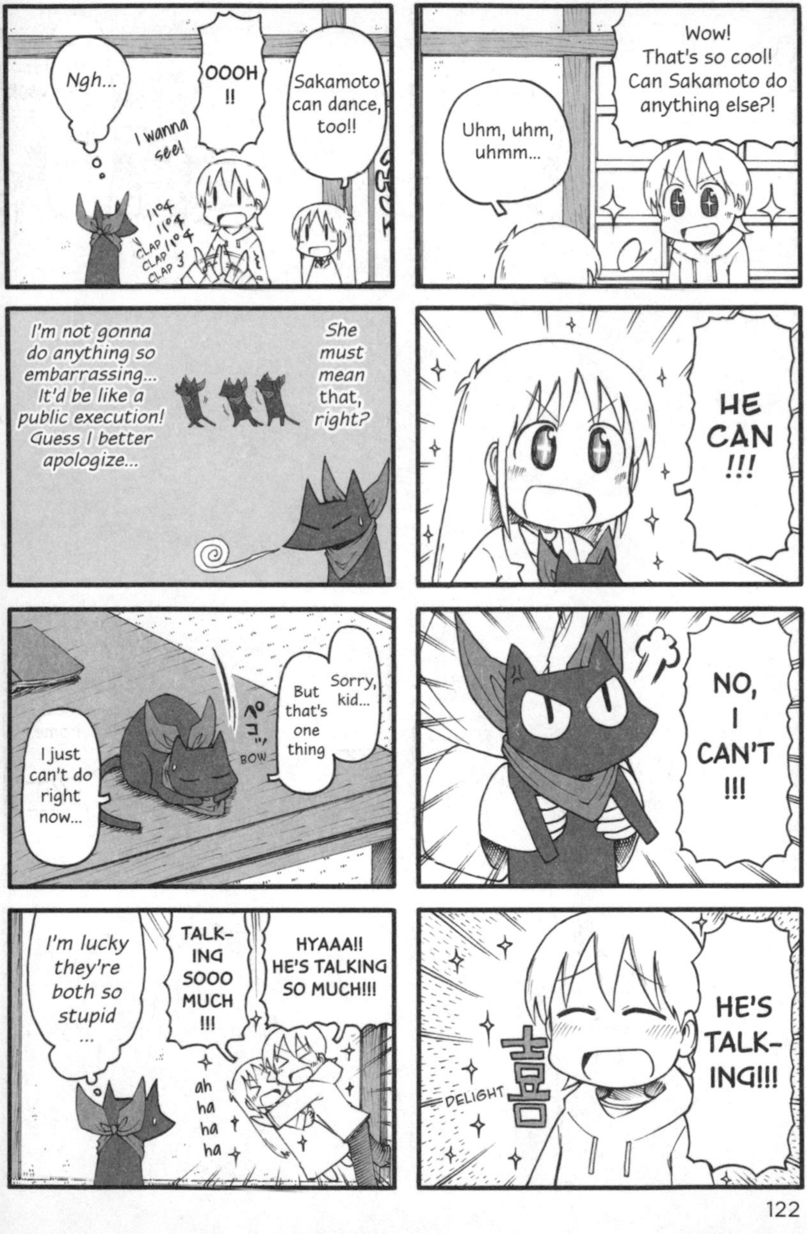
Wow! That's so cool! Can Sakamoto do anything else?!
Uhm, uhm, uhmm...
Sakamoto can dance, too!!
OOOH !!
I wanna see!
CLAP CLAP CLAP
Ngh...
HE CAN !!!
She must mean that, right?
I'm not gonna do anything so embarrassing... It'd be like a public execution! Guess I better apologize...
NO, I CAN'T !!!
Sorry, kid...
But that's one thing
BOW
I just can't do right now...
HE'S TALK-ING!!!
DELIGHT
HYAAA!! HE'S TALKING SO MUCH!!!
TALK-ING SOOO MUCH !!!
ah ha ha ha
I'm lucky they're both so stupid ...

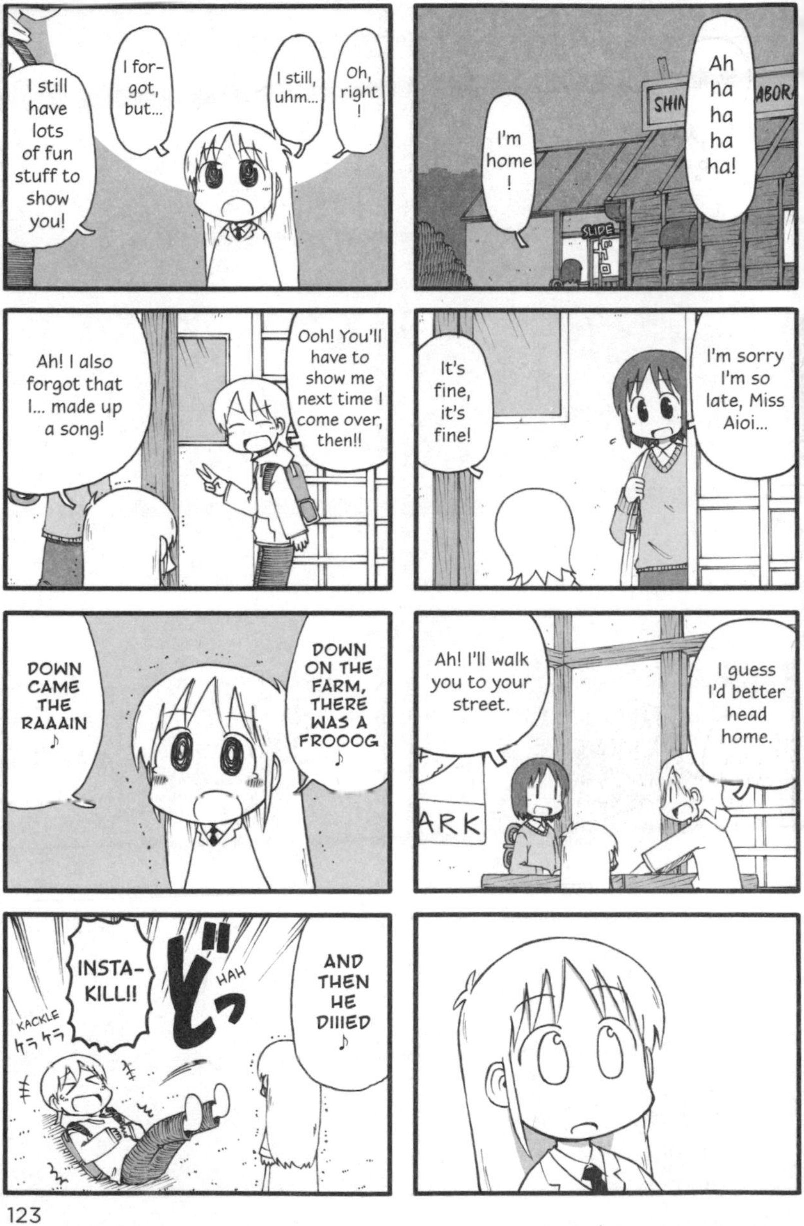

Ah ha ha ha ha!
SHIN ABOR
SLIDE
I'm home!
Oh, right!
I still, uhm...
I for-got, but...
I still have lots of fun stuff to show you!
I'm sorry I'm so late, Miss Aioi...
It's fine, it's fine!
Ooh! You'll have to show me next time I come over, then!!
Ah! I also forgot that I... made up a song!
I guess I'd better head home.
Ah! I'll walk you to your street.
ARK
DOWN ON THE FARM, THERE WAS A FROOOG ♪
DOWN CAME THE RAAAIN ♪
AND THEN HE DIIIED ♪
HAH
どっ
INSTA-KILL!!
KACKLE
ケラケラ

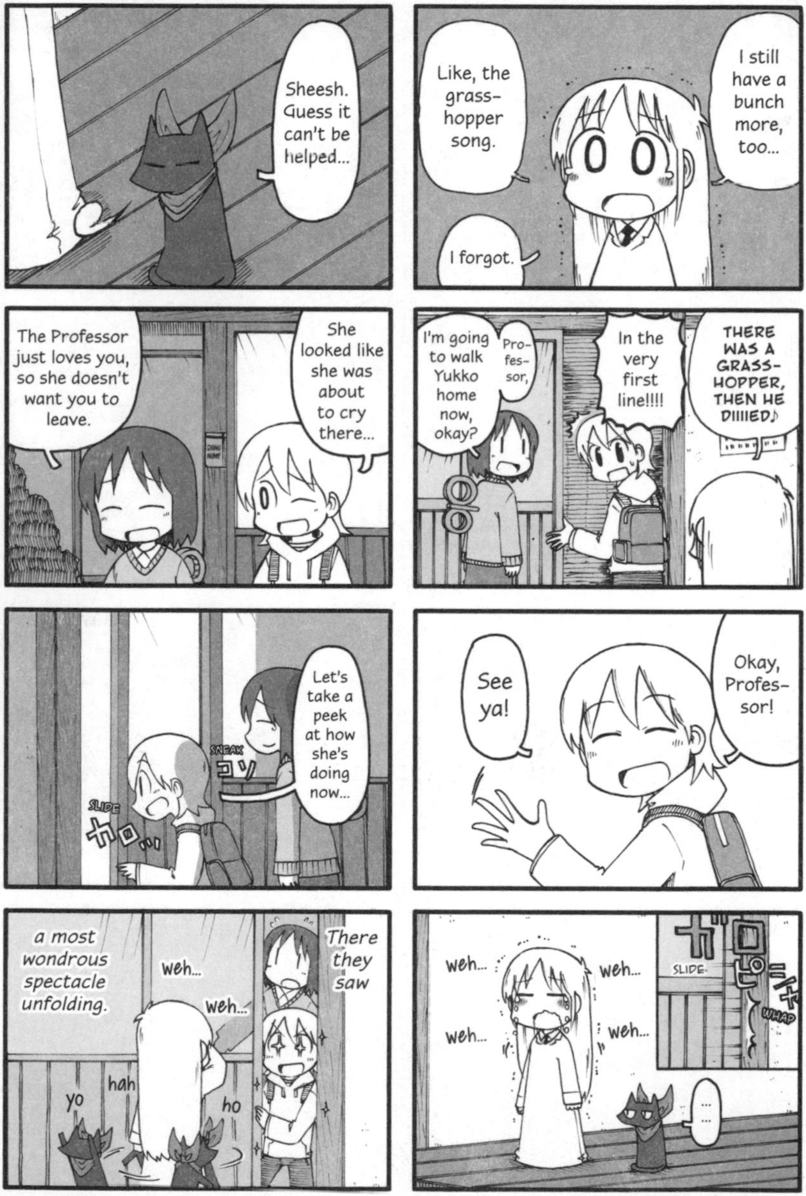
I still have a bunch more, too...
Like, the grass-hopper song.
I forgot.
Sheesh. Guess it can't be helped...
THERE WAS A GRASS-HOPPER, THEN HE DIIIIED♪
In the very first line!!!!
Pro-fes-sor,
I'm going to walk Yukko home now, okay?
She looked like she was about to cry there...
The Professor just loves you, so she doesn't want you to leave.
Okay, Profes-sor!
See ya!
Let's take a peek at how she's doing now...
SNEAK
SLIDE
SLIDE
WHAP
weh...
weh...
weh...
weh...
...
...
There they saw
a most wondrous spectacle unfolding.
weh...
weh...
hah
ho
yo

chapter 140: end

chapter 141

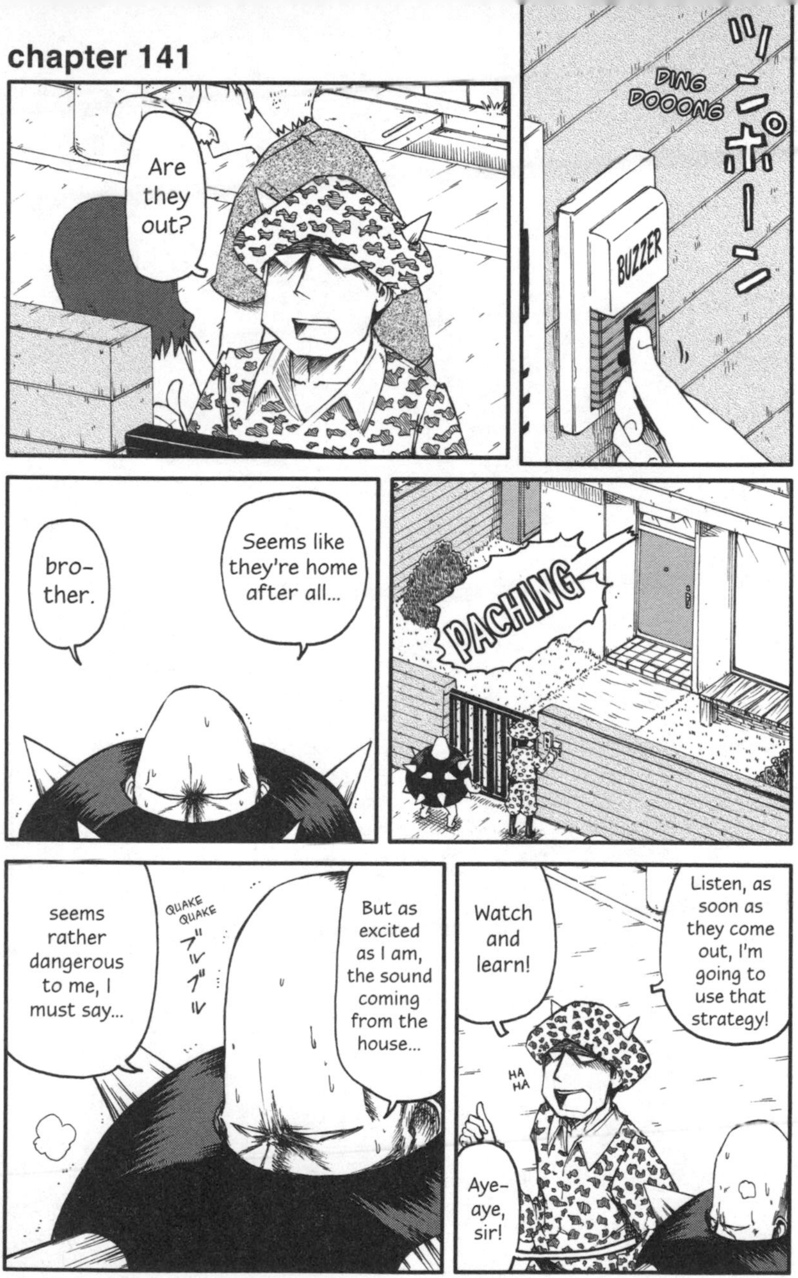

ピンポーン
DING DOOONG
BUZZER
Are they out?
PACHING
Seems like they're home after all...
bro-ther.
Listen, as soon as they come out, I'm going to use that strategy!
Watch and learn!
HA HA
Aye-aye, sir!
But as excited as I am, the sound coming from the house...
QUAKE QUAKE
ブルブル
seems rather dangerous to me, I must say...

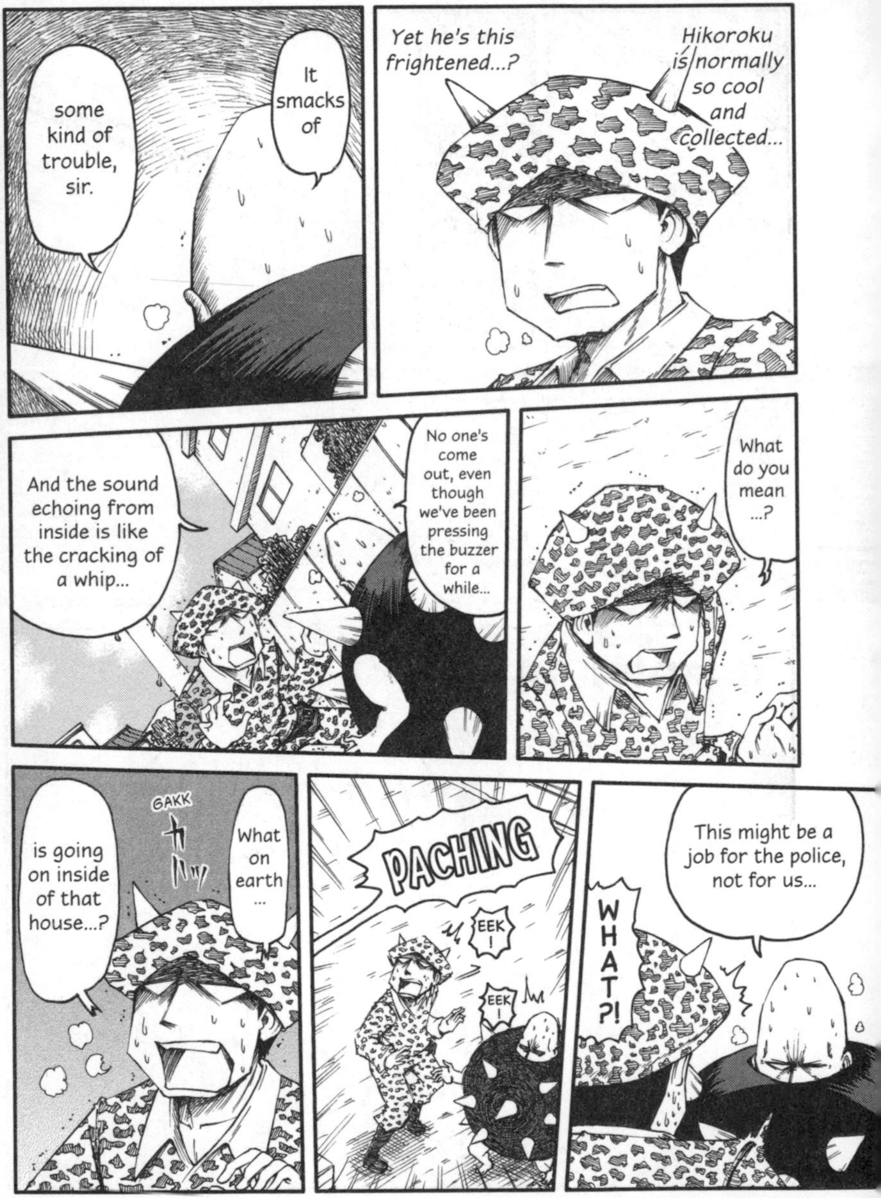
Hikoroku is normally so cool and collected...
Yet he's this frightened...?
It smacks of
some kind of trouble, sir.
What do you mean ...?
No one's come out, even though we've been pressing the buzzer for a while...
And the sound echoing from inside is like the cracking of a whip...
This might be a job for the police, not for us...
WHAT?!
PACHING
EEK!
EEK!
What on earth ...
GAKK
is going on inside of that house...?

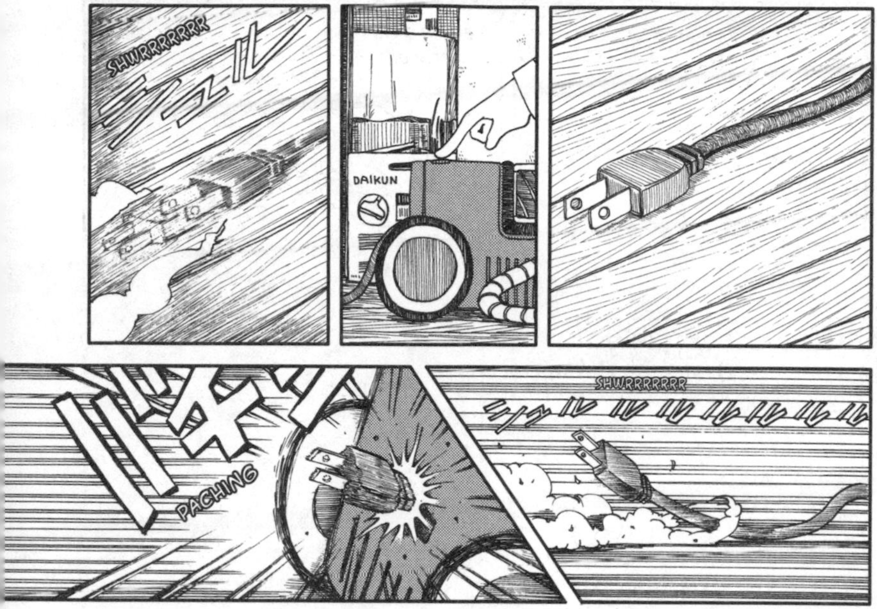
DAIKUN
SHWRRRRRRR
SHWRRRRRRR
PACHING

chapter 141

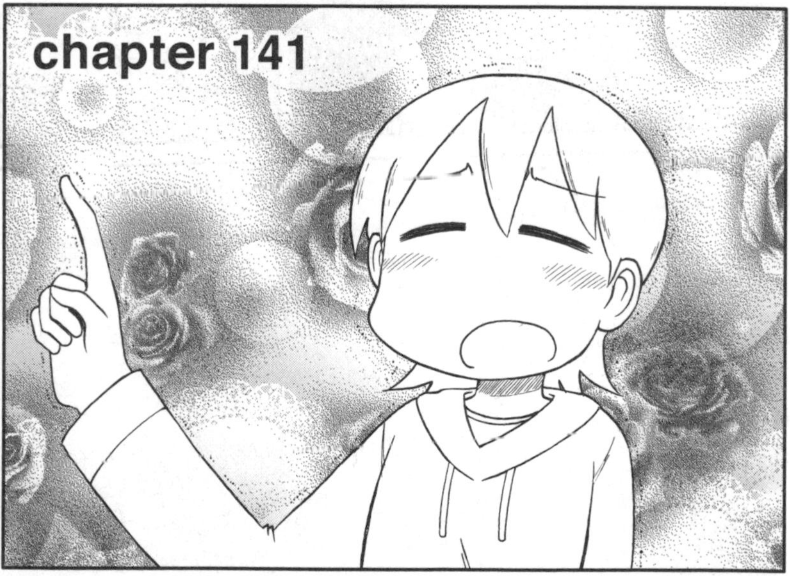

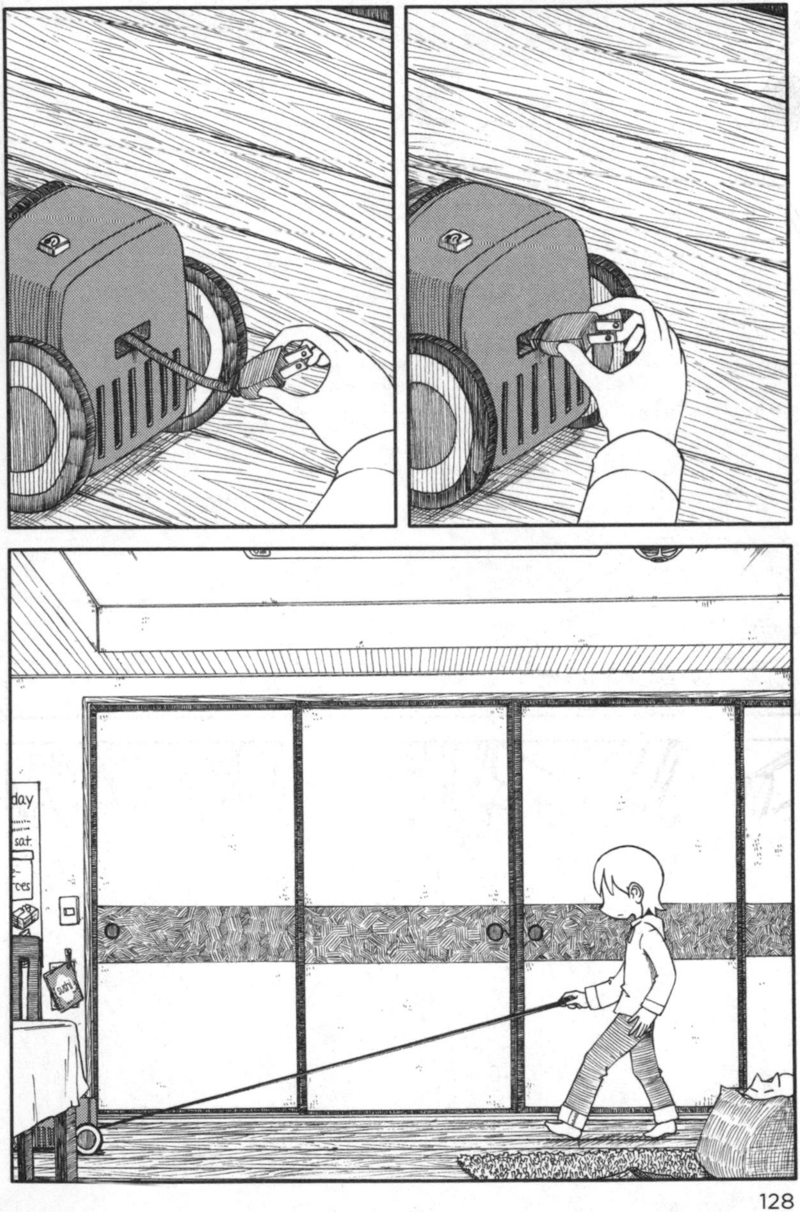
day
sat.
sushi

SWPP

KUN

SHWRRRRRRRRRRRRRRRRRRR

KLAK

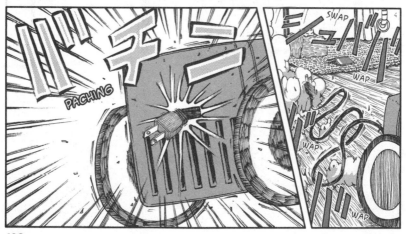

PACHING

SWAP

WAP

WAP

WAP

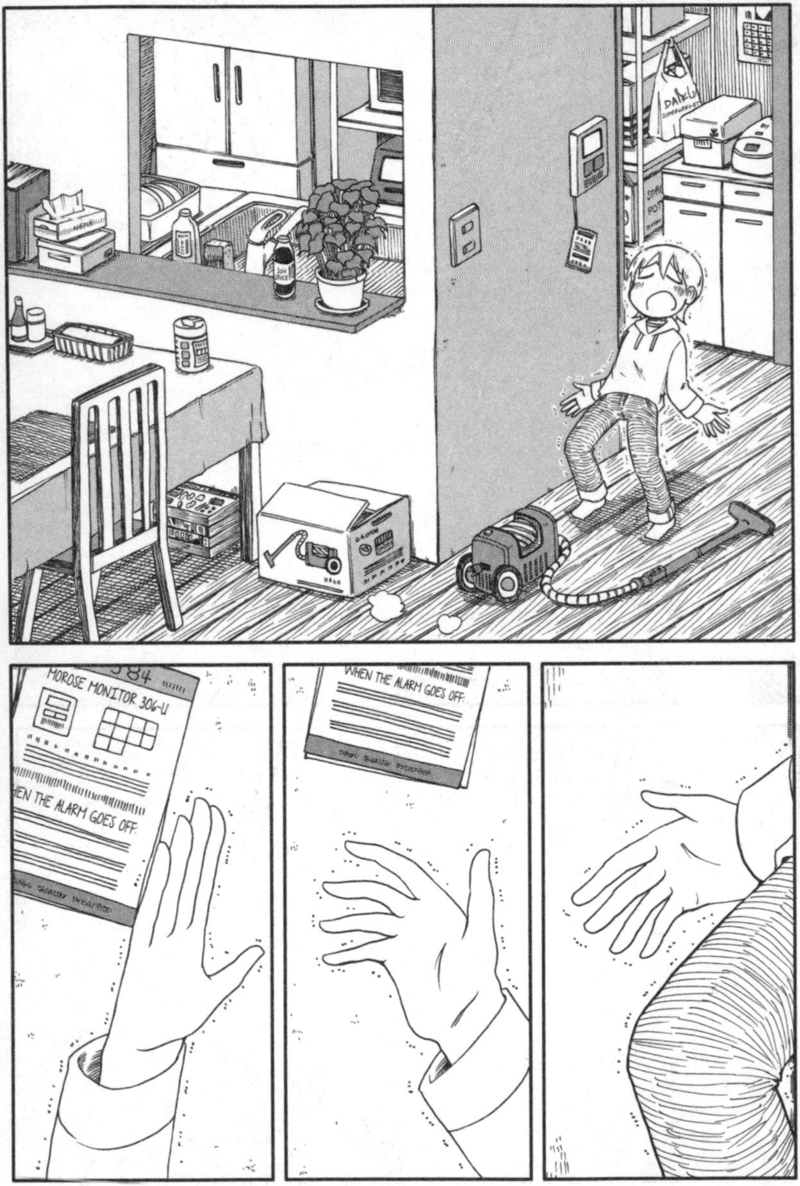
WHEN THE ALARM GOES OFF:
MOROSE MONITOR 306-U
HEN THE ALARM GOES OFF:

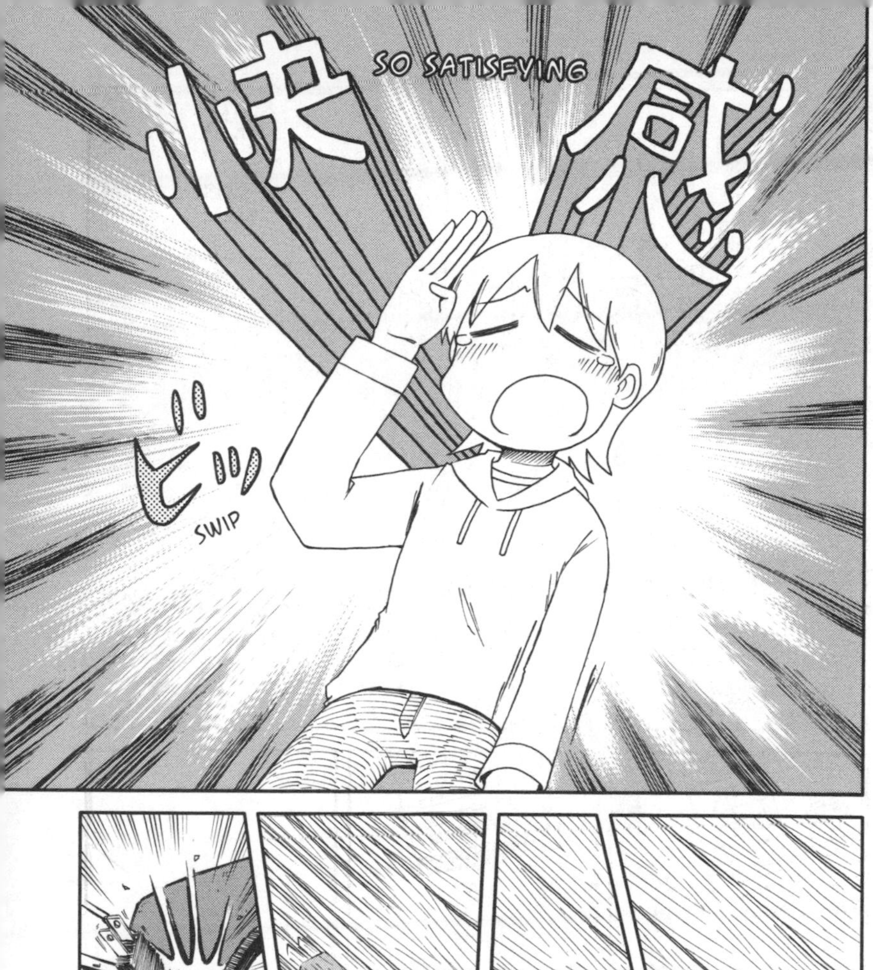
快感
SO SATISFYING
ビッ
SWIP
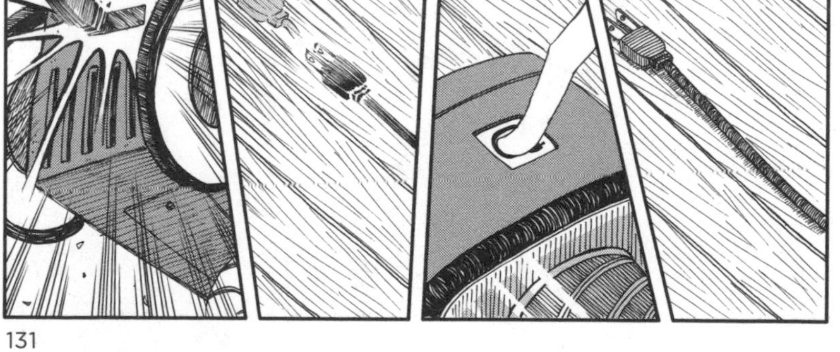

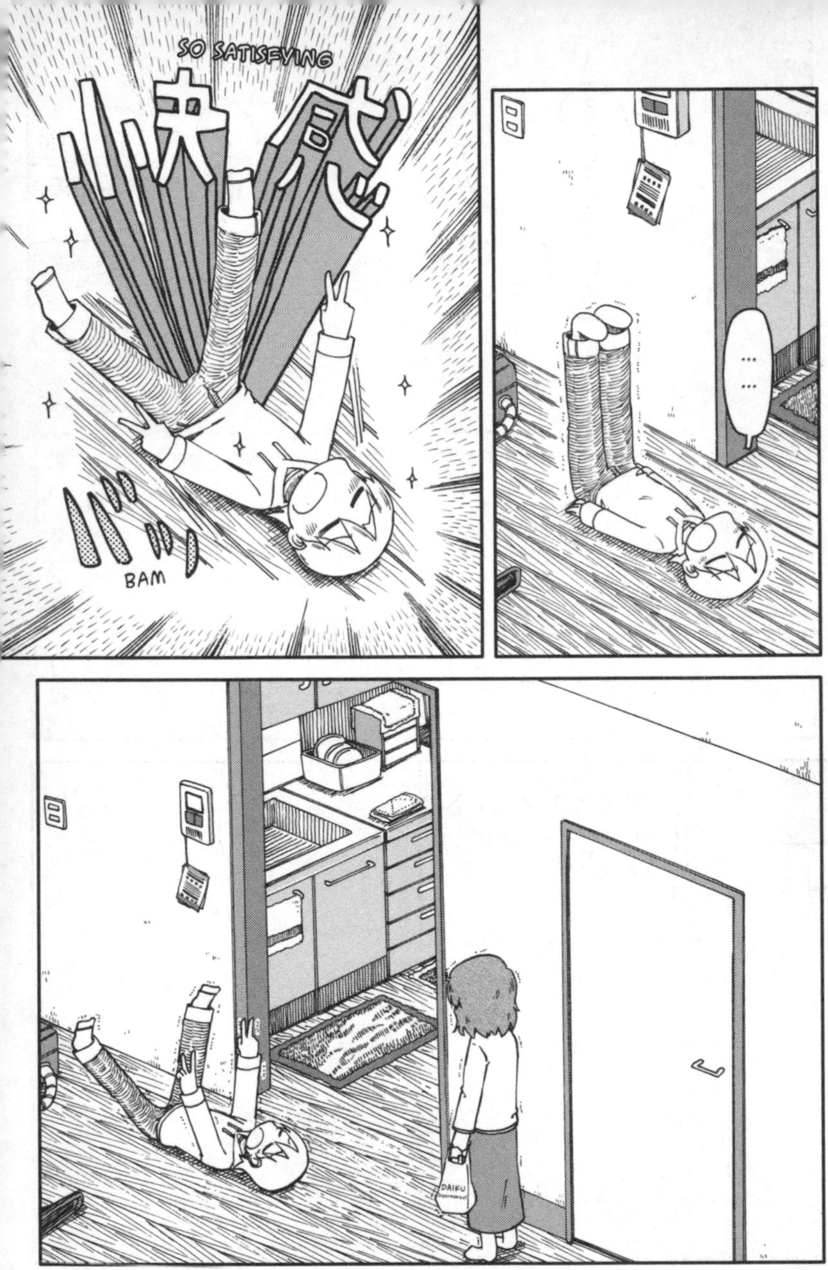
...
...
快感
SO SATISFYING
BAM
DAIKU
Supermarket

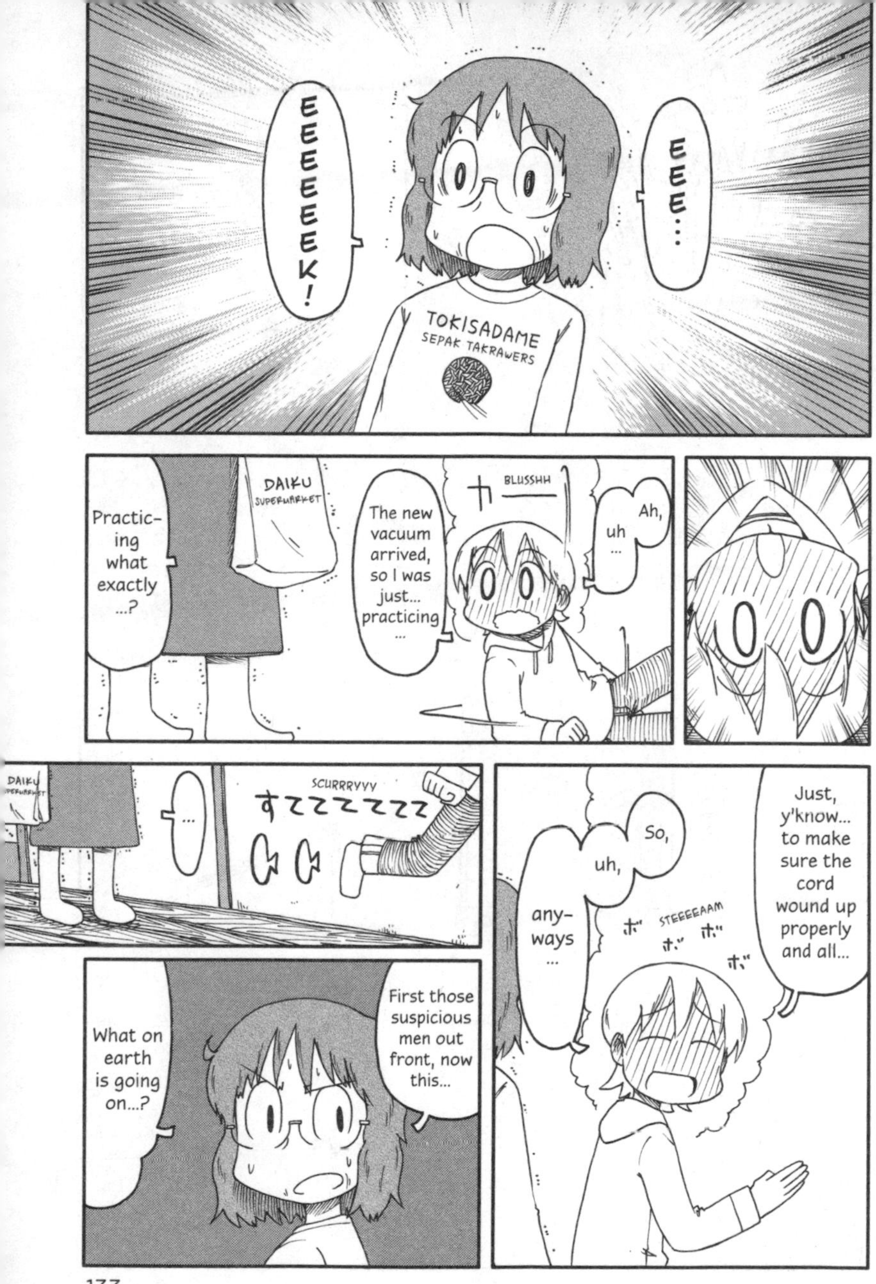
EEE…
EEEEEEEK!
TOKISADAME SEPAK TAKRAWERS
Ah, uh …
カ BLUSSHH
The new vacuum arrived, so I was just… practicing …
DAIKU SUPERMARKET
Practicing what exactly …?
Just, y'know… to make sure the cord wound up properly and all…
So, uh, anyways …
ボ STEEEEAAM
SCURRRYYY
…
DAIKU SUPERMARKET
First those suspicious men out front, now this…
What on earth is going on…?

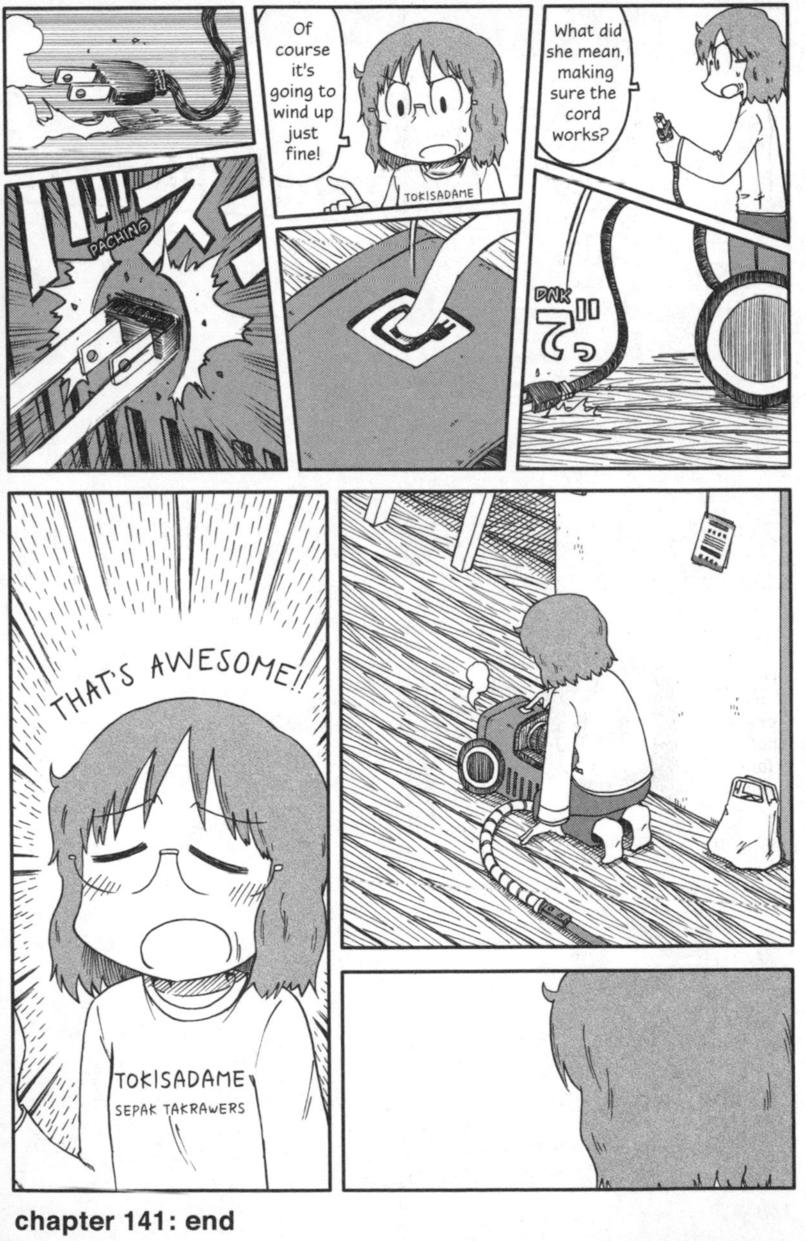
What did she mean, making sure the cord works?
Of course it's going to wind up just fine!
TOKISADAME
DNK
PACHING
THAT'S AWESOME!!
TOKISADAME
SEPAK TAKRAWERS

chapter 141: end

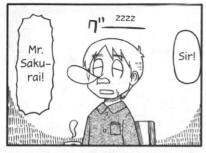

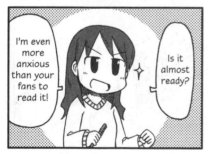

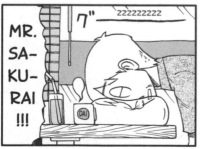

chapter 142

STEAM
MILK SNOW
HAJIME SAKURAI

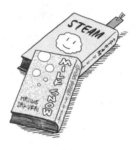

NOTABLE WORKS

■MILK SNOW■
the story of a young man's troubles, actions, and the madness that manifests from within. with just the right note of comedy, this is a refreshing tale of love, friendship, and youth.

■STEAM■
was the sight he saw in the desert a mirage, or nothing more than a wisp of steam...? an ambitious novel that incorporates philosophy in its humor.

zzzz
Sir!
Mr. Saku-rai!
Oh... Ah...
SPOP
Sor-ry, sor-ry.
So, about your next book...
Is it almost ready?
I'm even more anxious than your fans to read it!
zzzzzzzzz
MR. SA-KU-RAI !!!
DAI

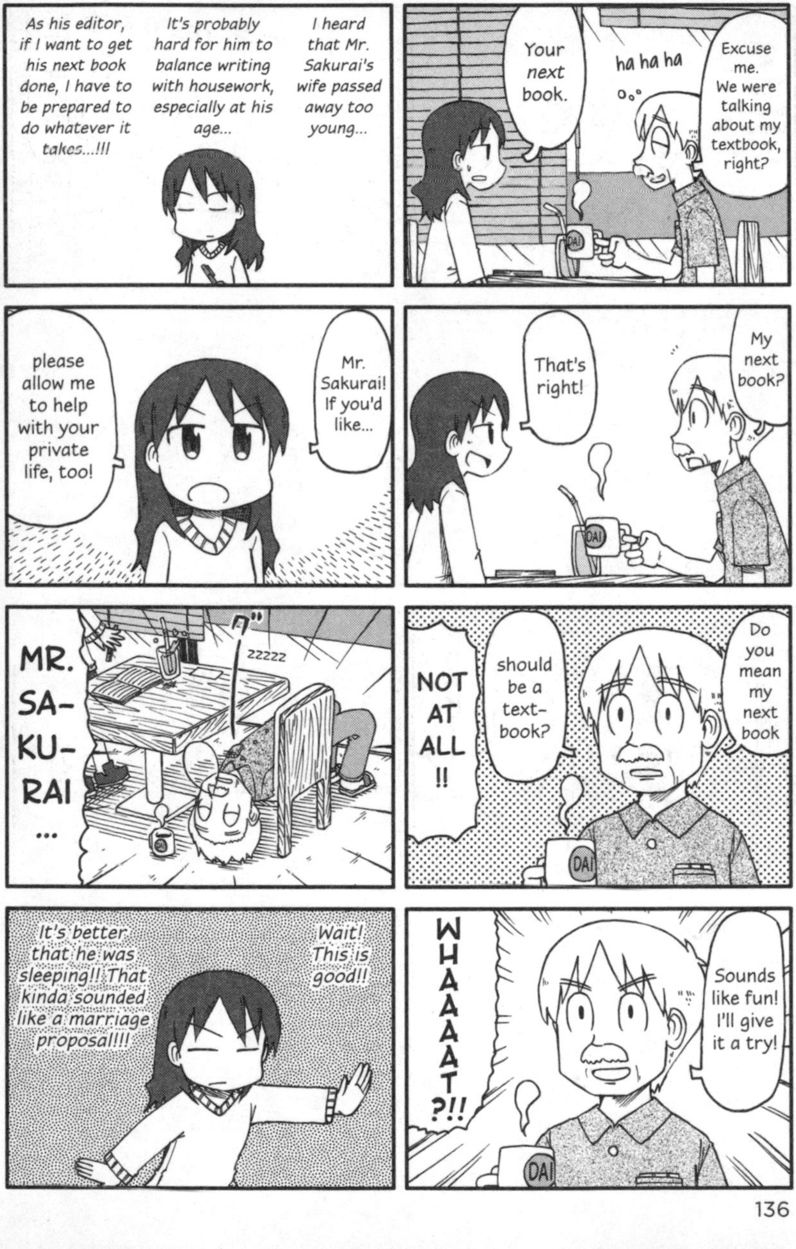
Excuse me. We were talking about my textbook, right?
ha ha ha
Your next book.
I heard that Mr. Sakurai's wife passed away too young...
It's probably hard for him to balance writing with housework, especially at his age...
As his editor, if I want to get his next book done, I have to be prepared to do whatever it takes...!!!
My next book?
That's right!
Mr. Sakurai! If you'd like...
please allow me to help with your private life, too!
Do you mean my next book
should be a text-book?
NOT AT ALL !!
zzzzz
MR. SA-KU-RAI ...
Sounds like fun! I'll give it a try!
WHAAAAT ?!!
Wait! This is good!!
It's better that he was sleeping!! That kinda sounded like a marriage proposal!!!

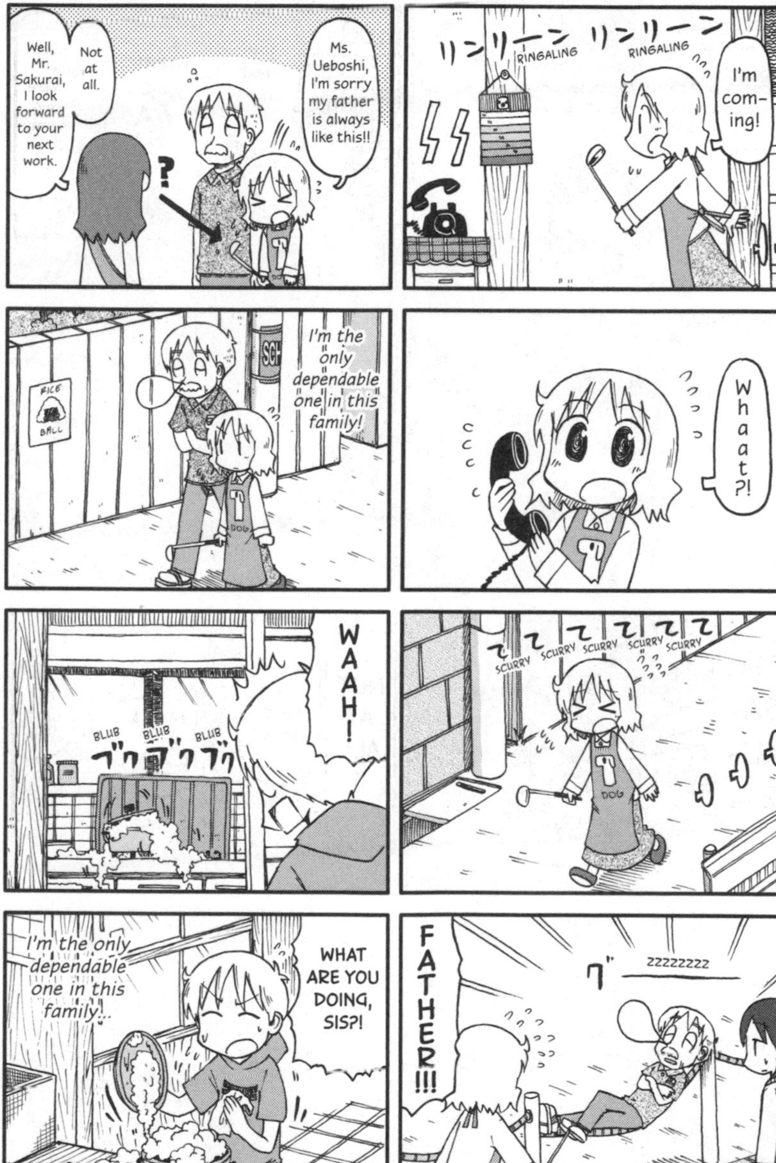
リンリーン
RINGALING
リンリーン
RINGALING
I'm coming!
Ms. Ueboshi, I'm sorry my father is always like this!!
Not at all.
Well, Mr. Sakurai, I look forward to your next work.
?
Whaaat?!
I'm the only dependable one in this family!
SCH
RICE BALL
DOG
SCURRY
SCURRY
SCURRY
SCURRY
SCURRY
DOG
WAAAH!
BLUB
BLUB
BLUB
ブクブクブク
FATHER!!!
グー
zzzzzzzz
WHAT ARE YOU DOING, SIS?!
I'm the only dependable one in this family...

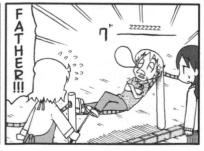

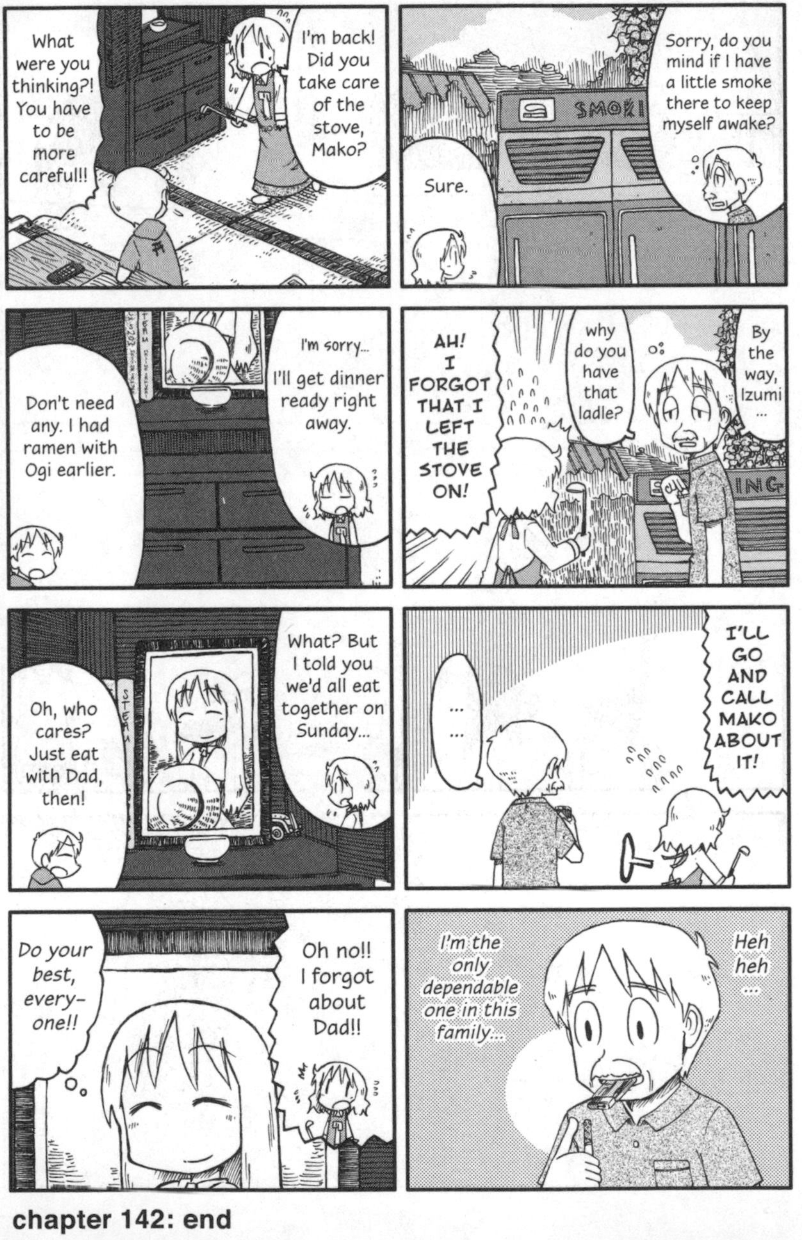

Sorry, do you mind if I have a little smoke there to keep myself awake?
Sure.
SMOKI
By the way, Izumi...
why do you have that ladle?
AH! I FORGOT THAT I LEFT THE STOVE ON!
I'LL GO AND CALL MAKO ABOUT IT!
... ...
Heh heh...
I'm the only dependable one in this family...
I'm back! Did you take care of the stove, Mako?
What were you thinking?! You have to be more careful!!
I'm sorry... I'll get dinner ready right away.
Don't need any. I had ramen with Ogi earlier.
What? But I told you we'd all eat together on Sunday...
Oh, who cares? Just eat with Dad, then!
Oh no!! I forgot about Dad!!
Do your best, everyone!!

chapter 142: end

chapter 143

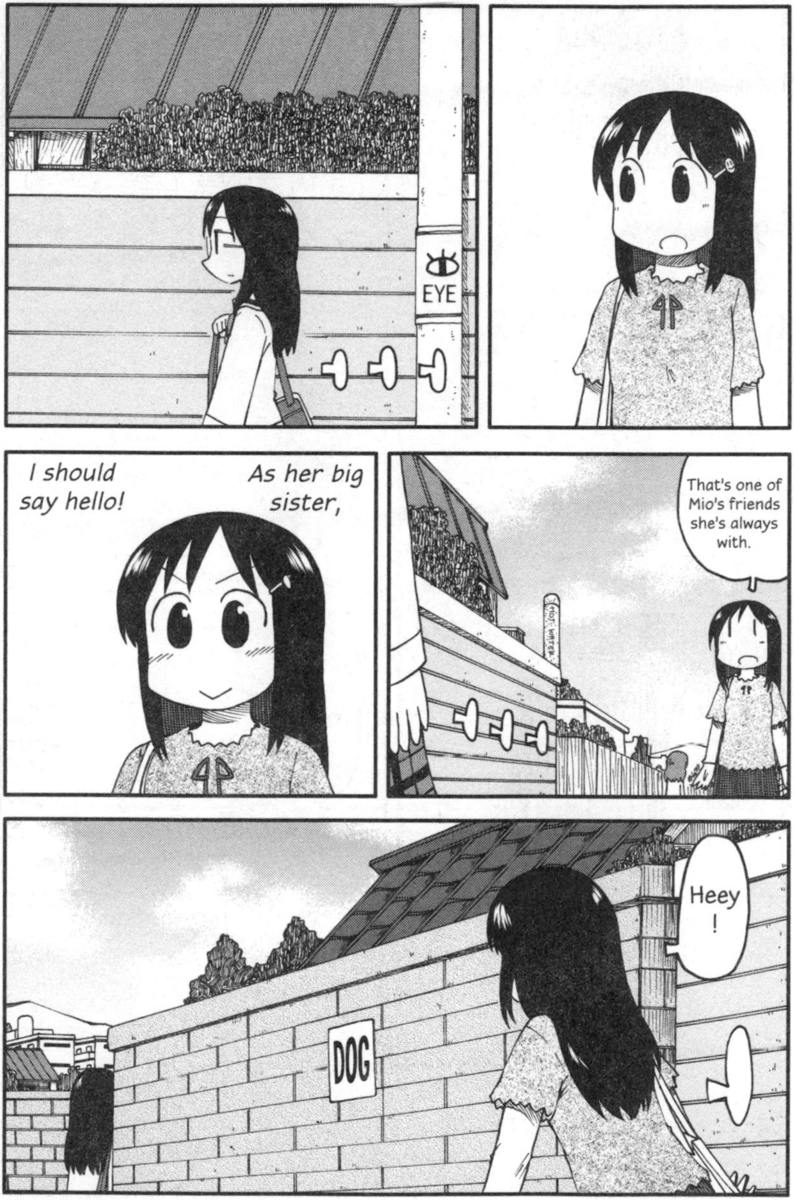
EYE
That's one of Mio's friends she's always with.
HOT WATER
As her big sister,
I should say hello!
Heey !
DOG

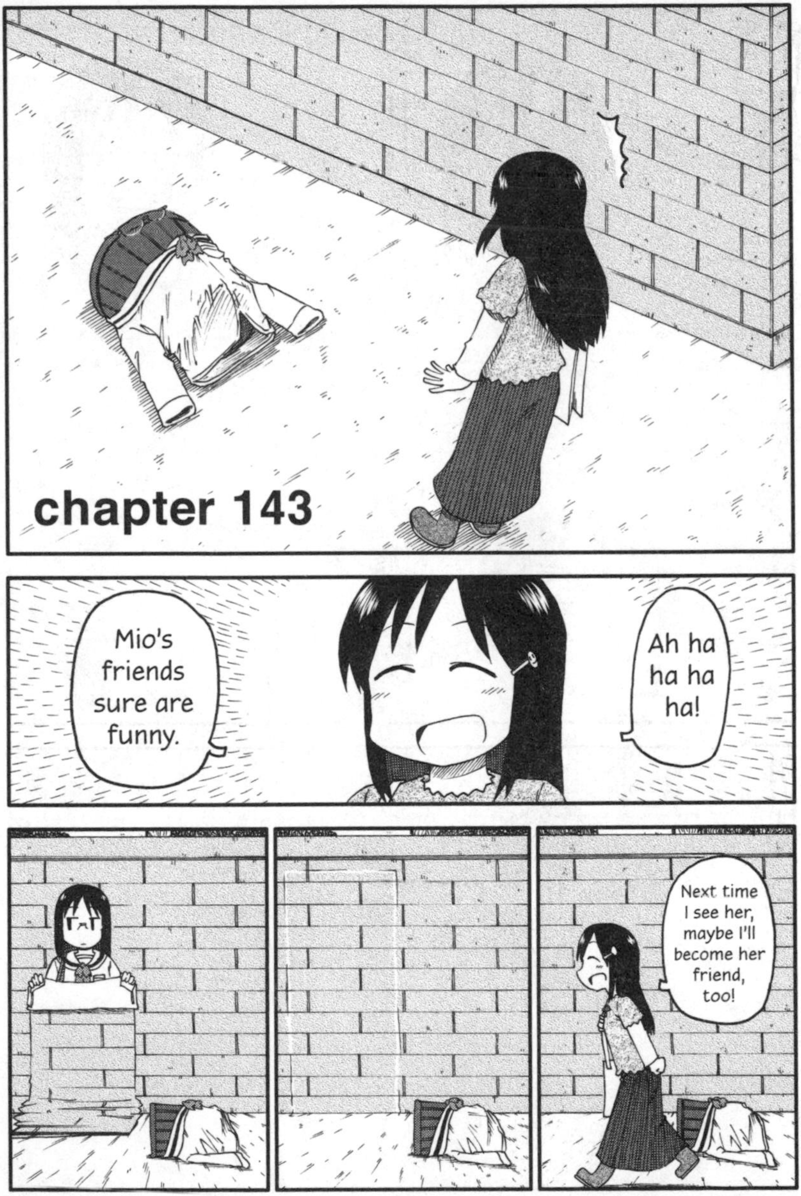
chapter 143
Ah ha ha ha ha!
Mio's friends sure are funny.
Next time I see her, maybe I'll become her friend, too!

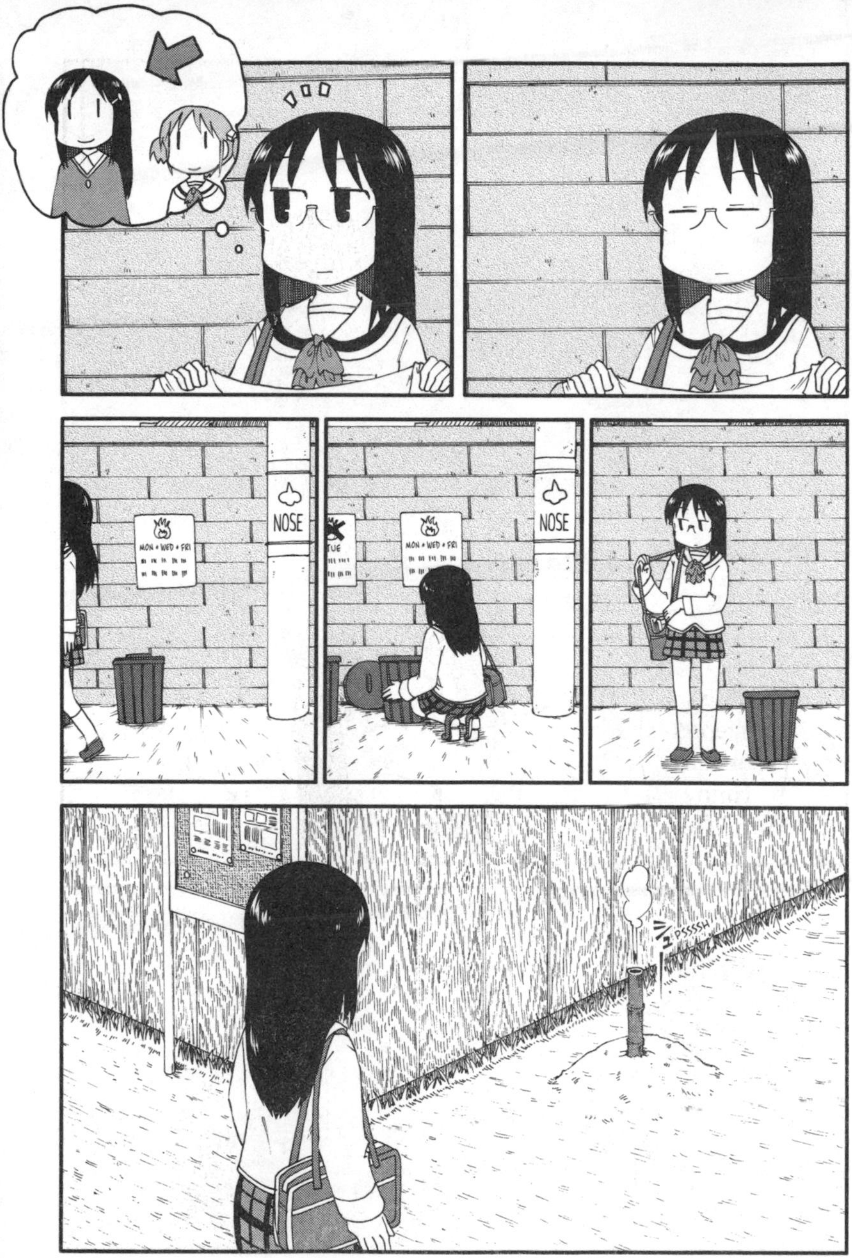
NOSE
MON • WED • FRI
TUE
NOSE
MON • WED • FRI
PSSSSH

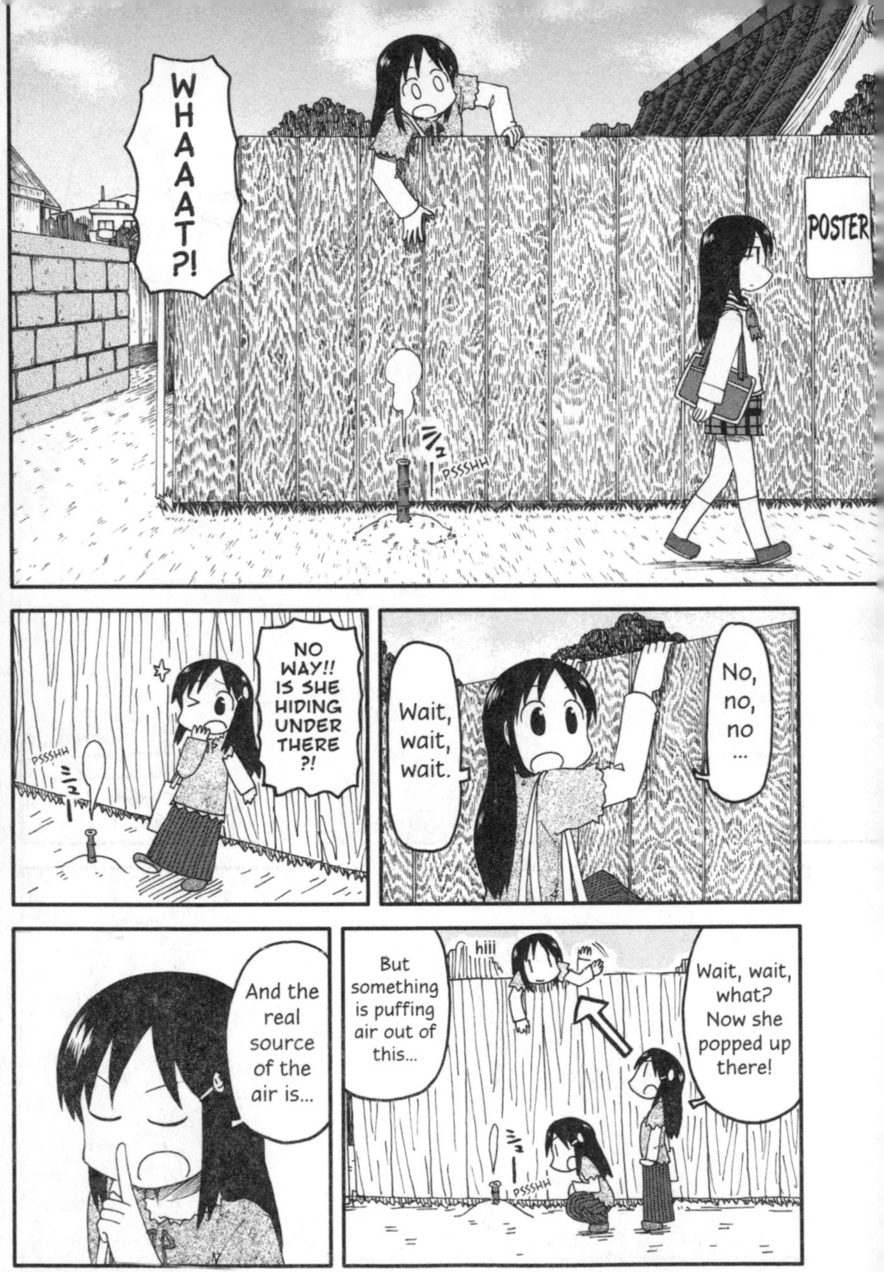
POSTER
WHAAAT?!
PSSSHH
No, no, no ...
Wait, wait, wait.
NO WAY!! IS SHE HIDING UNDER THERE?!
PSSSHH
Wait, wait, what? Now she popped up there!
hiii
But something is puffing air out of this...
PSSSHH
And the real source of the air is...

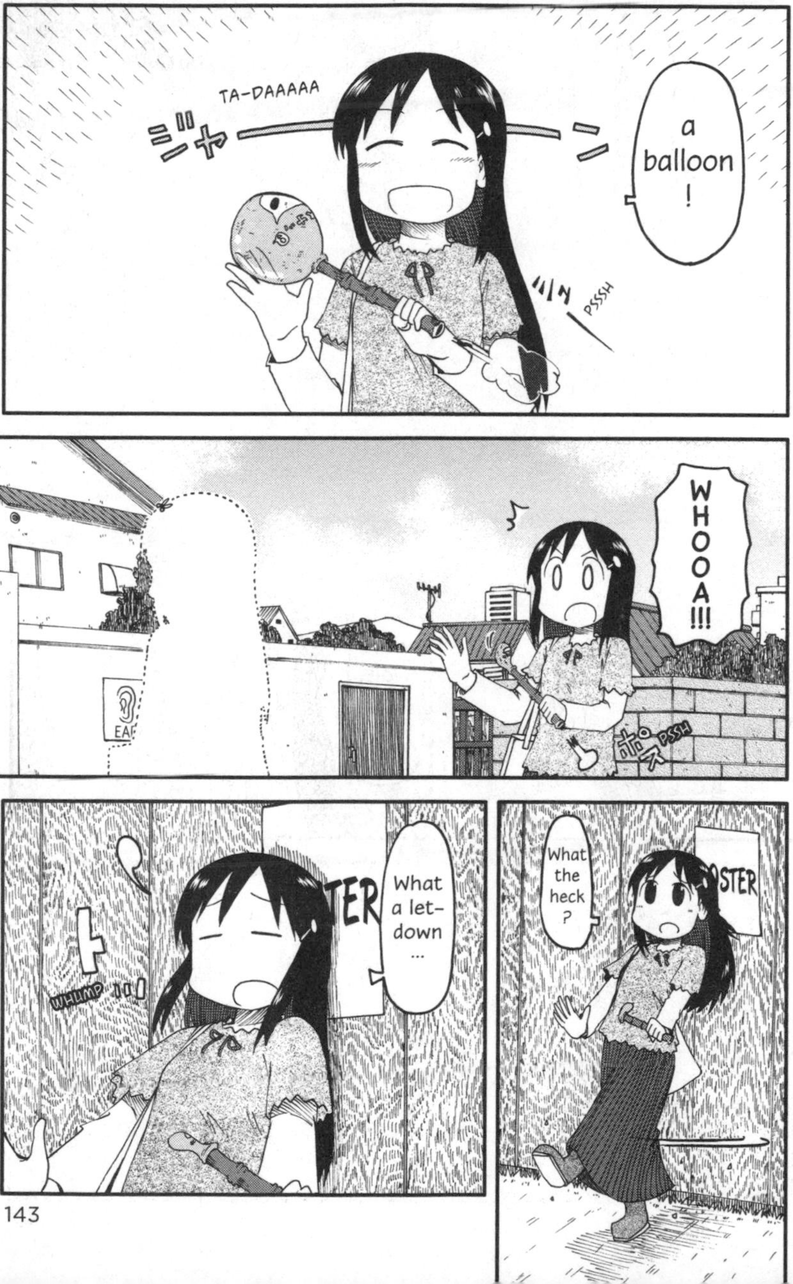
TA-DAAAAA
ジャーン
a balloon!
PSSSH
WHOOA!!!
PSSH
What the heck?
What a let-down...
WHUMP

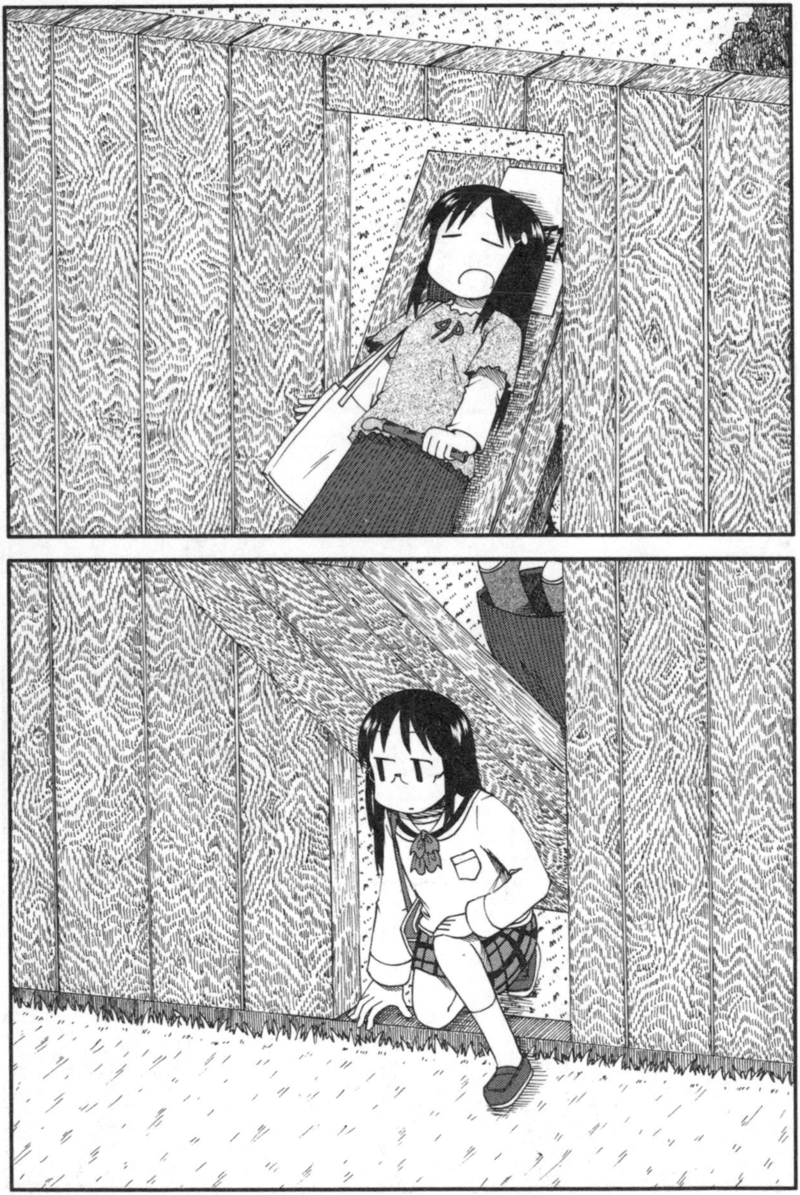

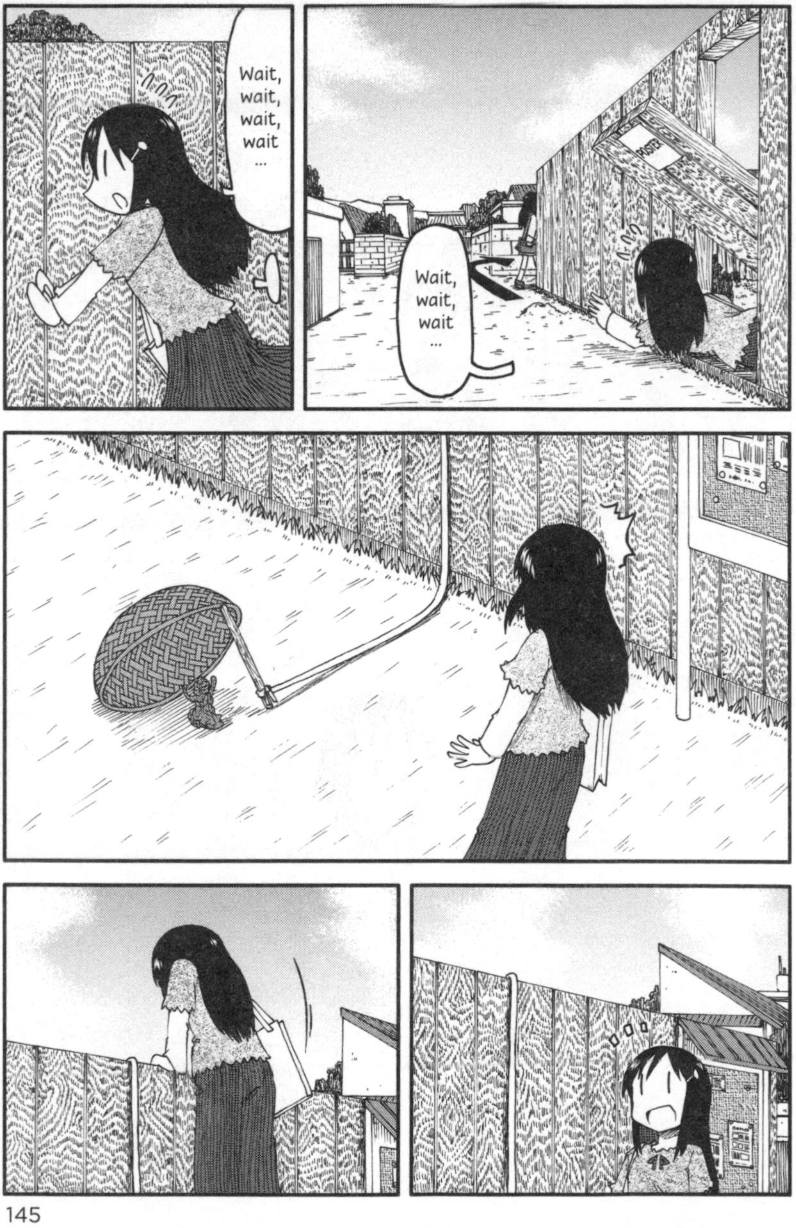
Wait, wait, wait ...
Wait, wait, wait, wait ...

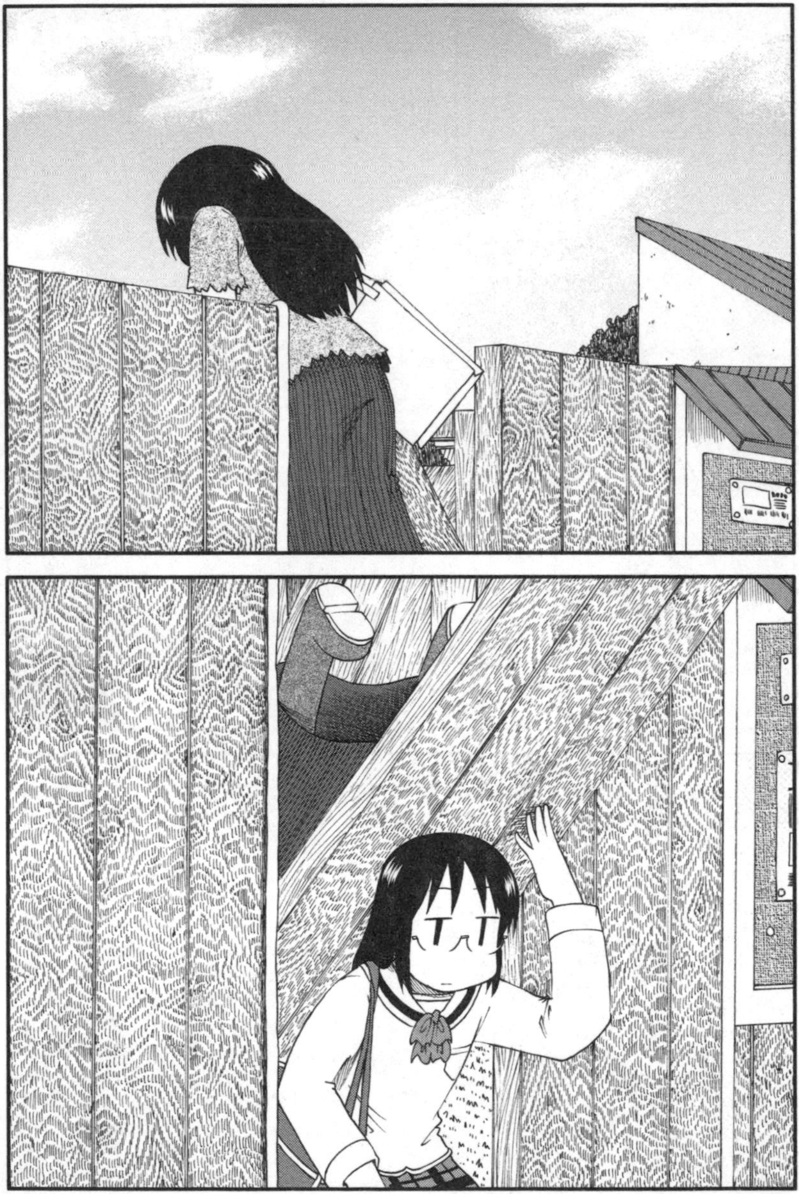

ずぼーっ
ZHA BAAM
...
...
WIND

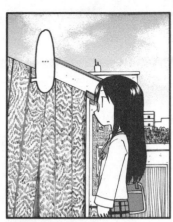

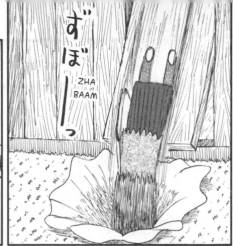

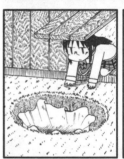

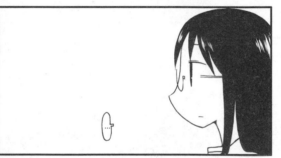

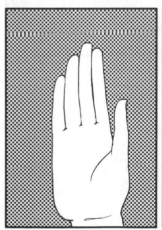

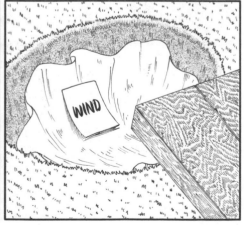

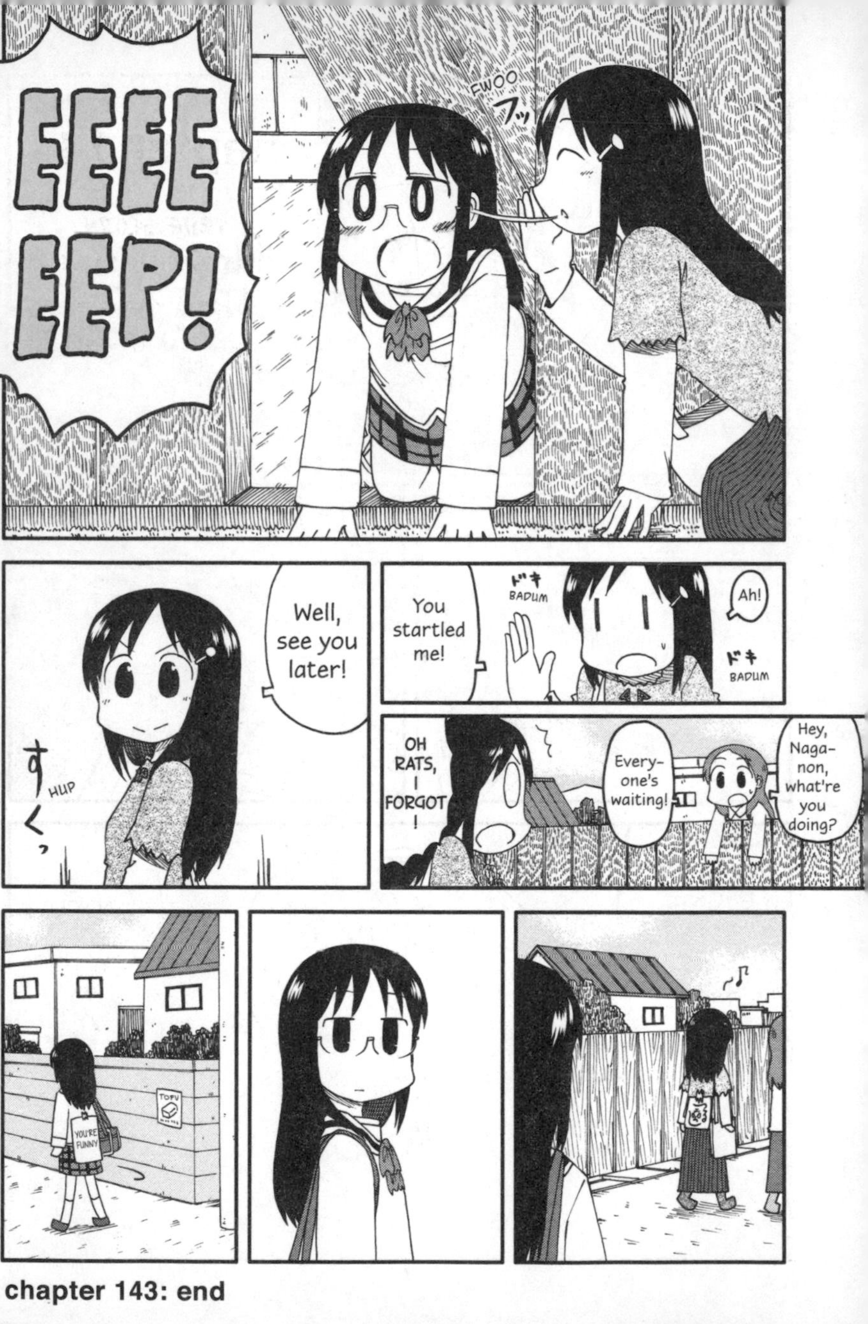
FWOO
フッ
EEEE EEP!
Ah!
ドキ BADUM
ドキ BADUM
You startled me!
Hey, Naga-non, what're you doing?
Every-one's waiting!
OH RATS, I FORGOT!
Well, see you later!
すくっ HUP
TOFU
YOU'RE FUNNY

chapter 143: end

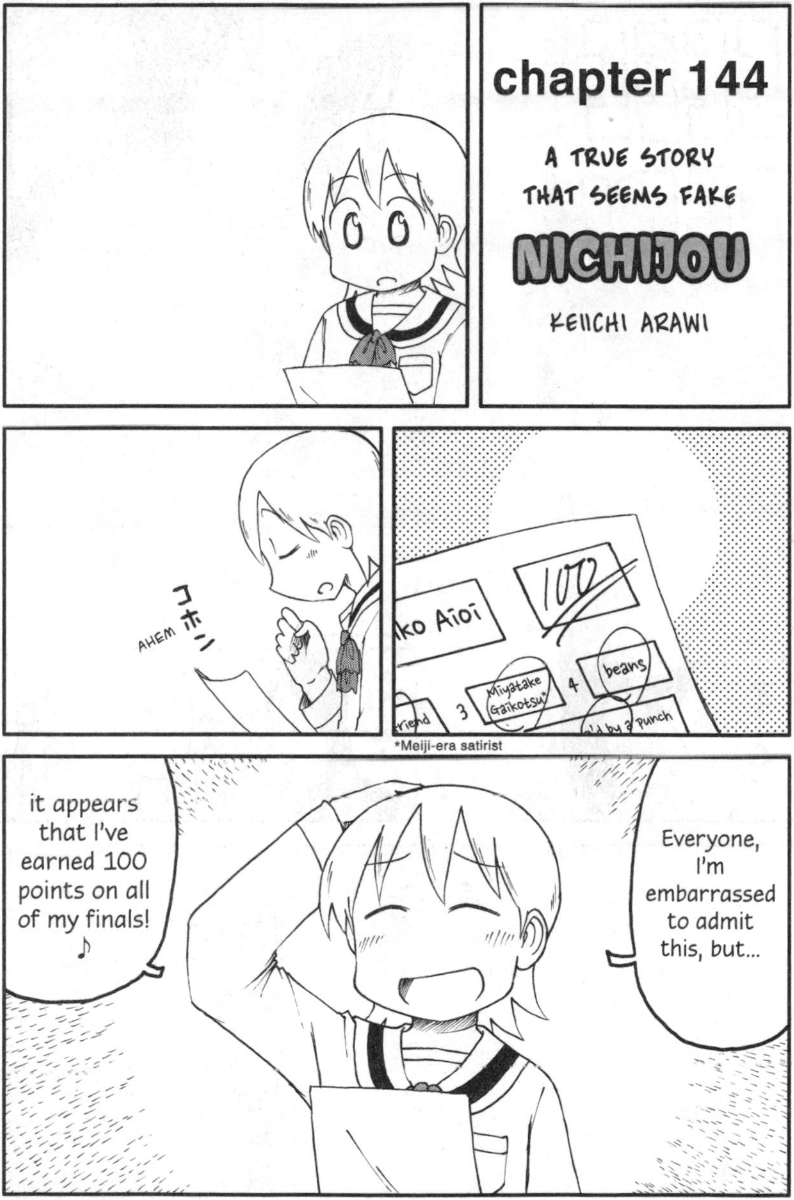
chapter 144
A TRUE STORY THAT SEEMS FAKE
NICHIJOU
KEIICHI ARAWI
100
beans
4
Miyatake Gaikotsu*
3
コホン
AHEM
Everyone, I'm embarrassed to admit this, but...
it appears that I've earned 100 points on all of my finals! ♪
*Meiji-era satirist

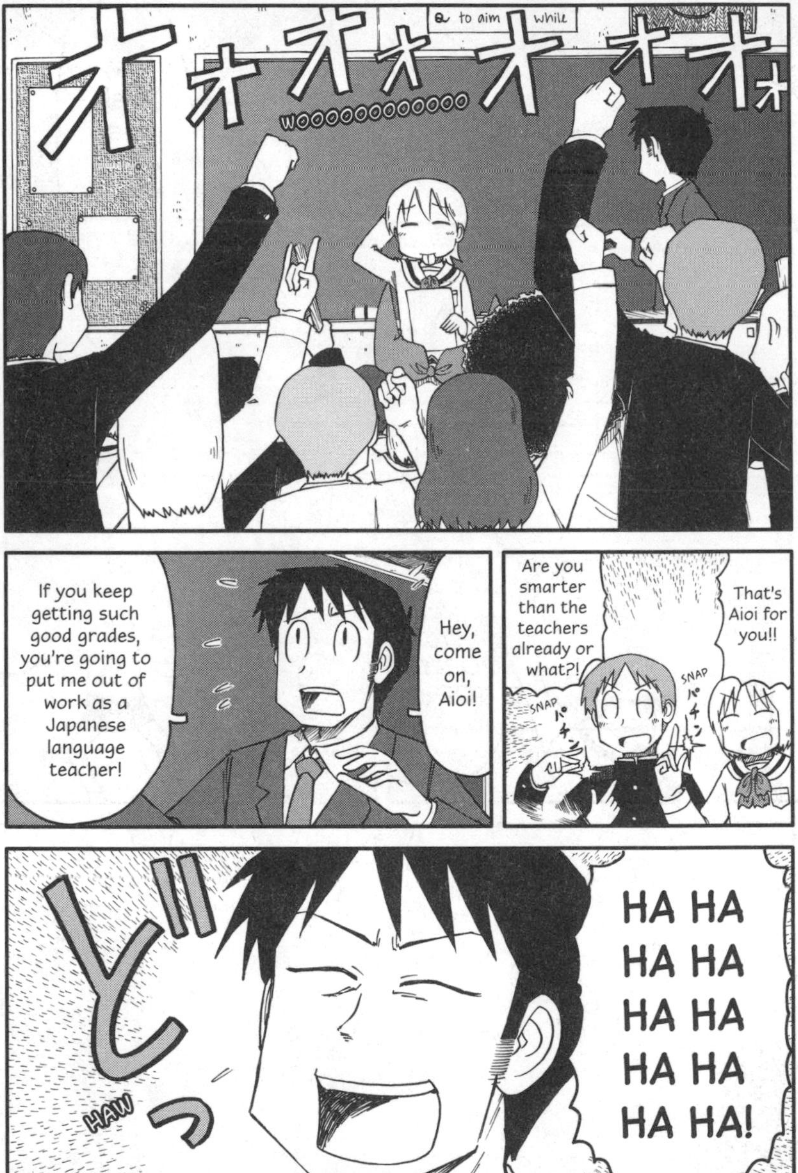
to aim
while
オォォォォォオォ
WOOOOOOOOOOOO
That's Aioi for you!!
Are you smarter than the teachers already or what?!
SNAP
パチン
SNAP
パチン
Hey, come on, Aioi!
If you keep getting such good grades, you're going to put me out of work as a Japanese language teacher!
HA HA HA HA HA HA HA HA HA HA!
どっ
HAW

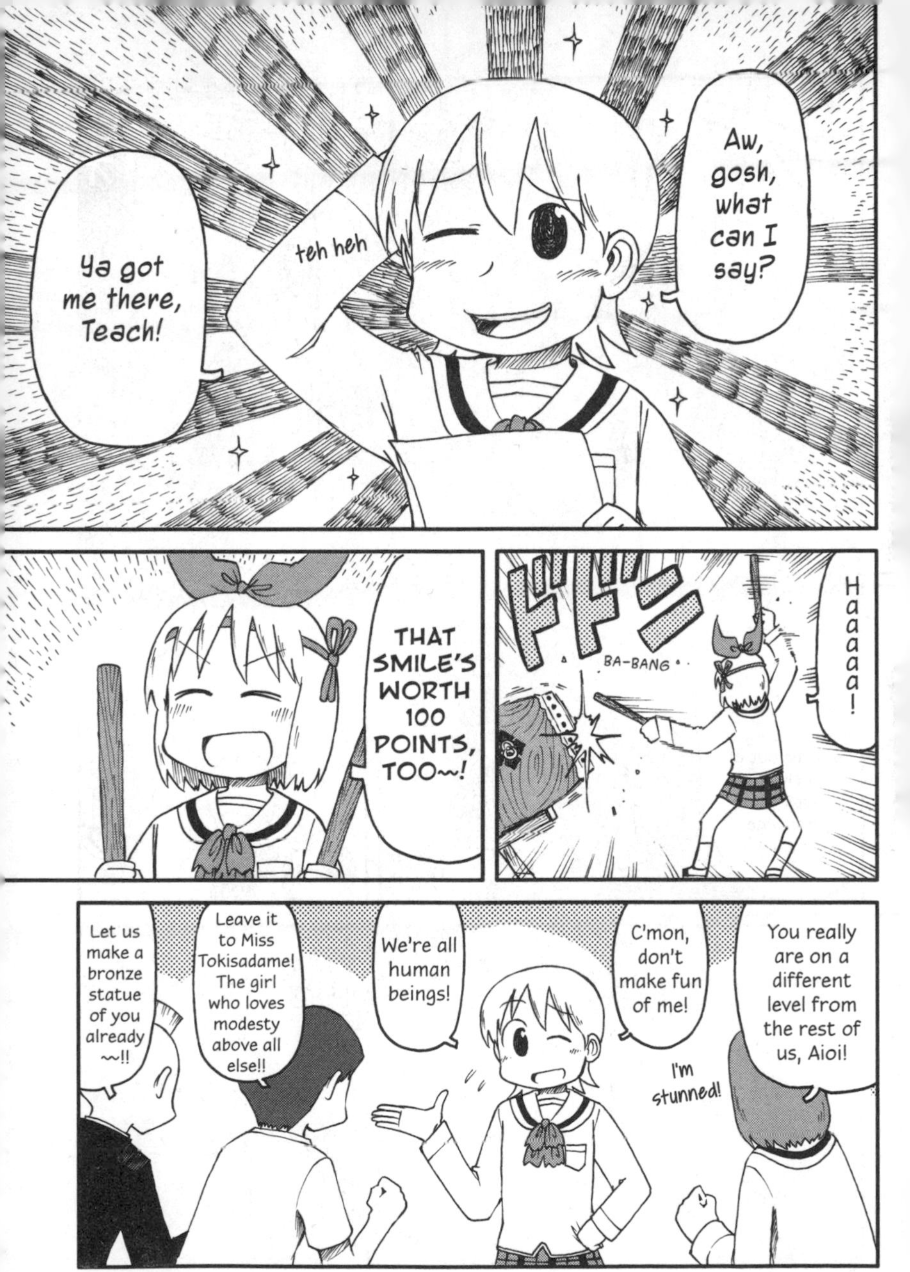
Aw, gosh, what can I say?
teh heh
Ya got me there, Teach!
Haaaaa!
BA-BANG
THAT SMILE'S WORTH 100 POINTS, TOO~!
You really are on a different level from the rest of us, Aioi!
I'm stunned!
C'mon, don't make fun of me!
We're all human beings!
Leave it to Miss Tokisadame! The girl who loves modesty above all else!!
Let us make a bronze statue of you already ~!!

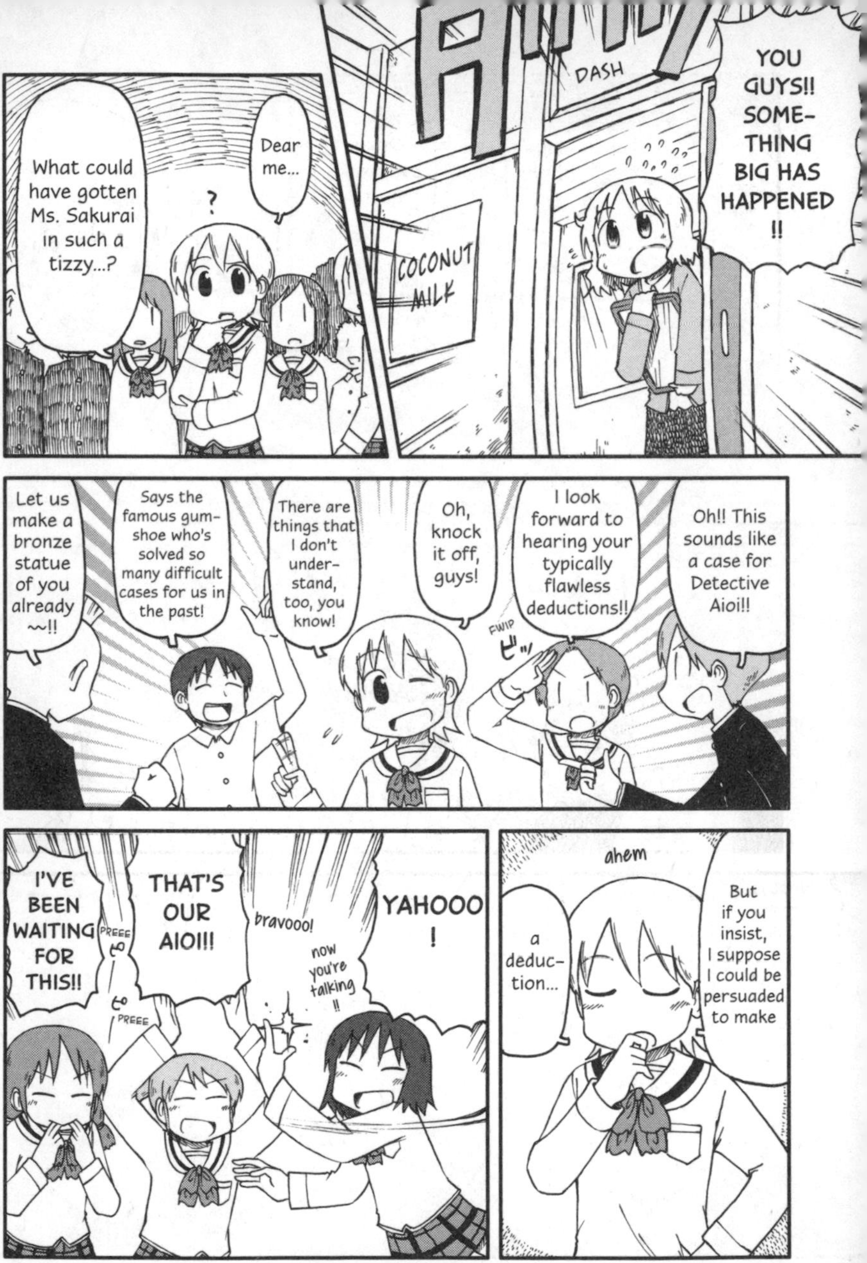
DASH
YOU GUYS!! SOME-THING BIG HAS HAPPENED !!
COCONUT MILK
Dear me...
?
What could have gotten Ms. Sakurai in such a tizzy...?
Oh!! This sounds like a case for Detective Aioi!!
I look forward to hearing your typically flawless deductions!!
FWIP
Oh, knock it off, guys!
There are things that I don't under-stand, too, you know!
Says the famous gum-shoe who's solved so many difficult cases for us in the past!
Let us make a bronze statue of you already ~!!
ahem
But if you insist, I suppose I could be persuaded to make
a deduc-tion...
YAHOOO !
bravooo!
now you're talking !!
THAT'S OUR AIOI!!!
PREEE
I'VE BEEN WAITING FOR THIS!!
PREEE

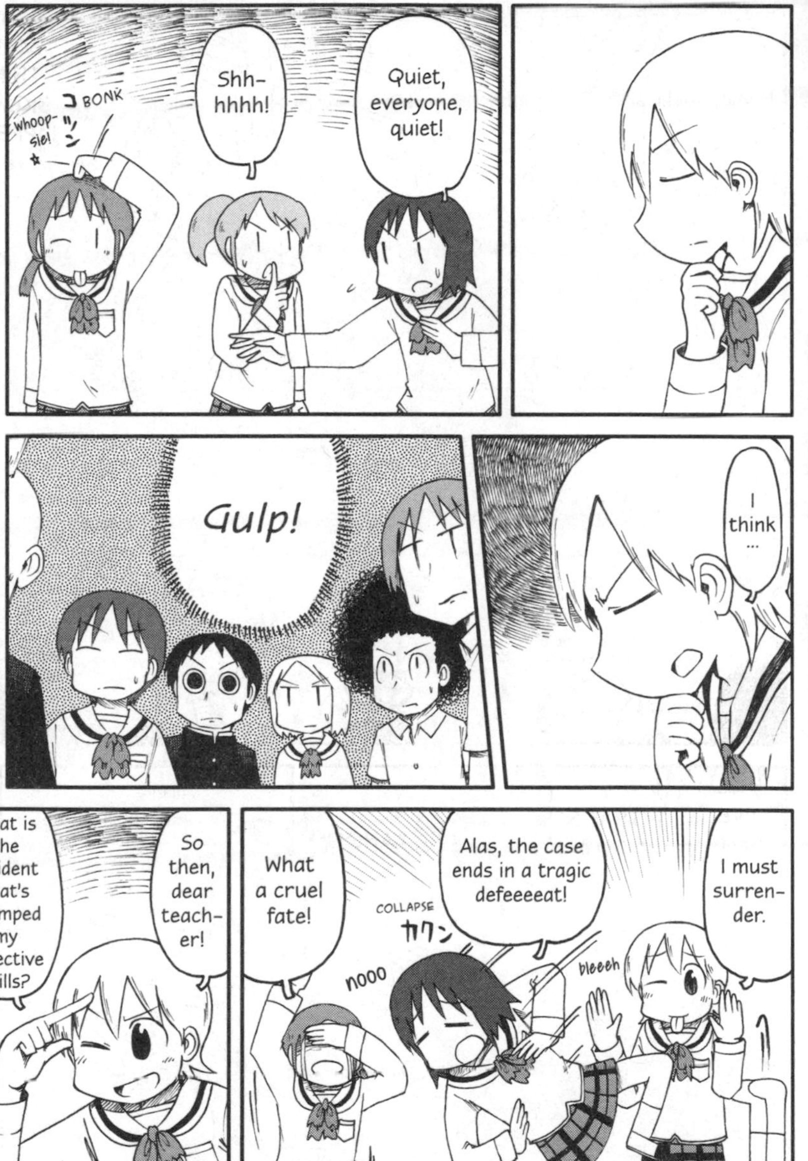

Quiet, everyone, quiet!
Shh-hhhh!
コツン BONK
Whoop-sie! ☆
I think...
Gulp!
I must surren-der.
bleeeh
Alas, the case ends in a tragic defeeeeat!
COLLAPSE カクン
What a cruel fate!
nooo
So then, dear teach-er!
What is the incident that's stumped my detective skills?

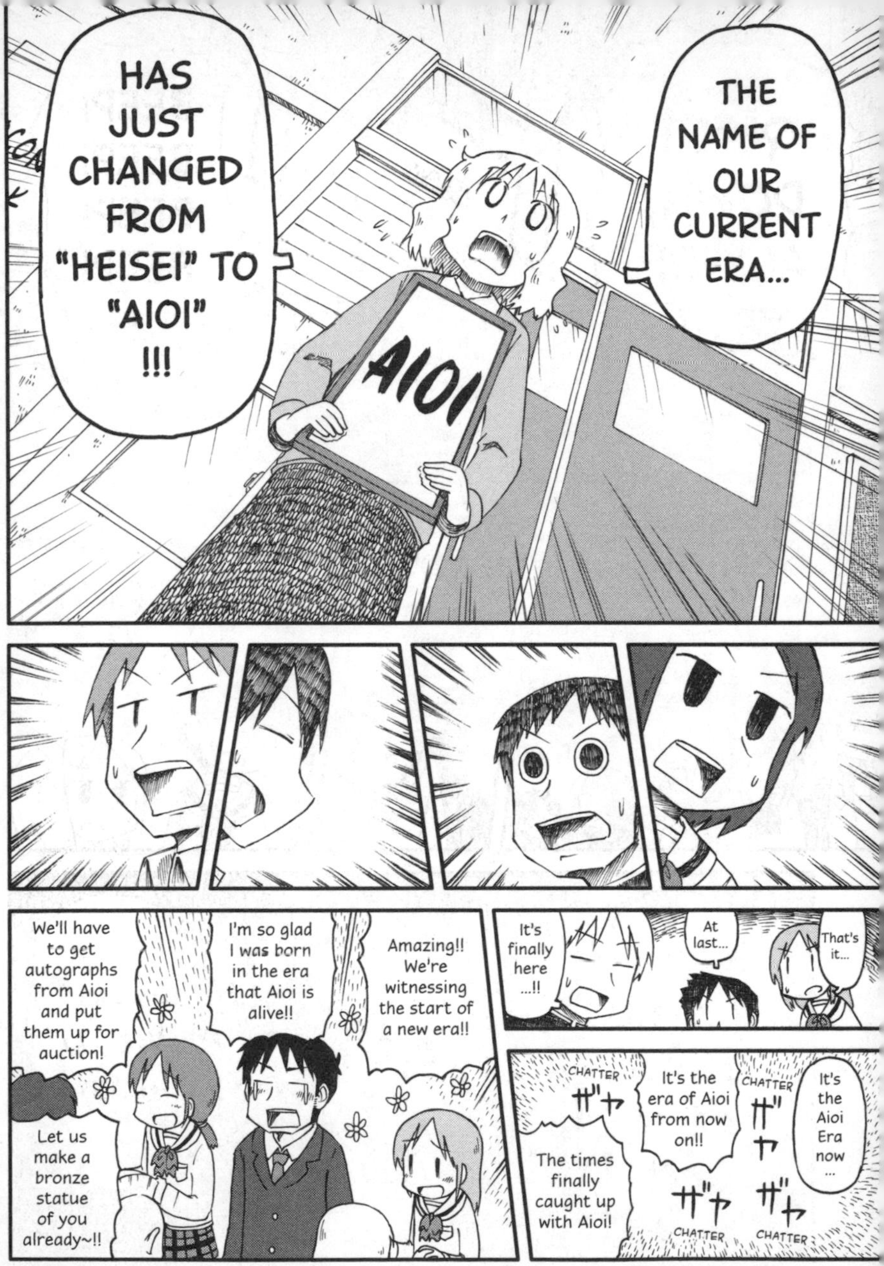
THE NAME OF OUR CURRENT ERA...
HAS JUST CHANGED FROM "HEISEI" TO "AIOI" !!!
AIOI
That's it...
At last...
It's finally here ...!!
It's the Aioi Era now ...
CHATTER ザワ
CHATTER ザワ
It's the era of Aioi from now on!!
CHATTER ザワ
CHATTER ザワ
The times finally caught up with Aioi!
Amazing!! We're witnessing the start of a new era!!
I'm so glad I was born in the era that Aioi is alive!!
We'll have to get autographs from Aioi and put them up for auction!
Let us make a bronze statue of you already~!!

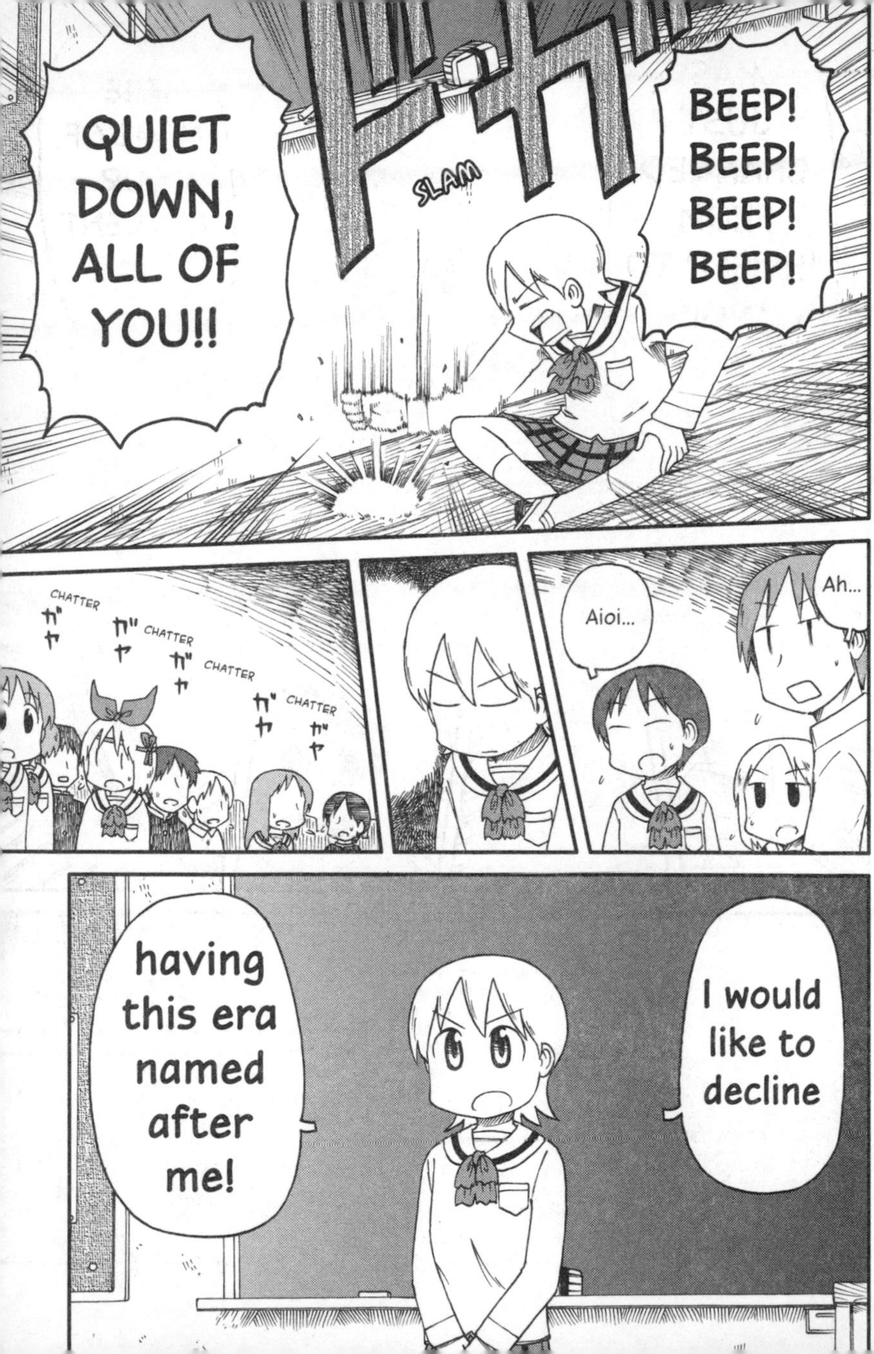
BEEP! BEEP! BEEP! BEEP!
SLAM
QUIET DOWN, ALL OF YOU!!
Ah...
Aioi...
CHATTER
CHATTER
CHATTER
CHATTER
ガヤ
ガヤ
ガヤ
ガヤ
ガヤ
I would like to decline
having this era named after me!

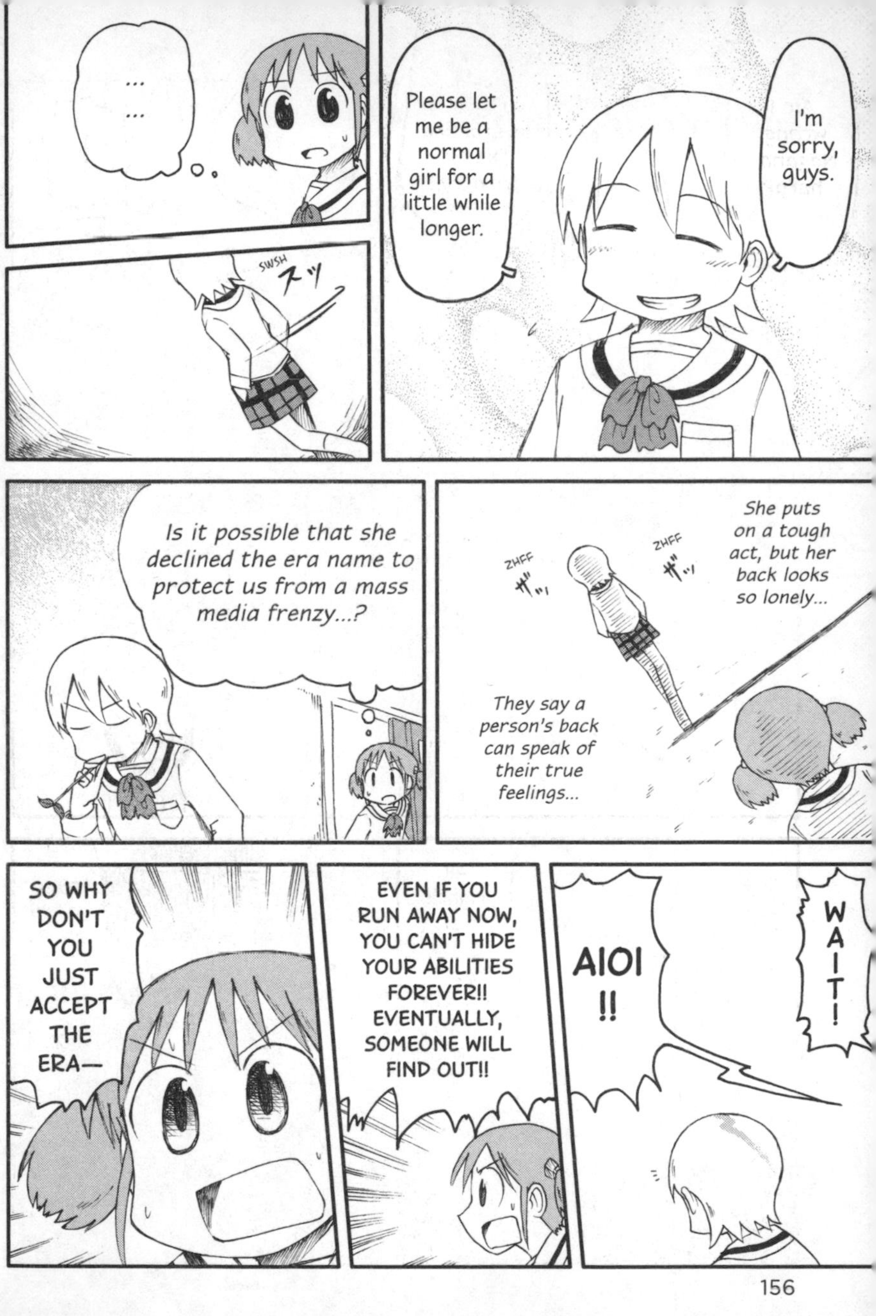
I'm sorry, guys.
Please let me be a normal girl for a little while longer.
... ...
SWSH
She puts on a tough act, but her back looks so lonely...
ZHFF
ZHFF
They say a person's back can speak of their true feelings...
Is it possible that she declined the era name to protect us from a mass media frenzy...?
WAIT!
AIOI !!
EVEN IF YOU RUN AWAY NOW, YOU CAN'T HIDE YOUR ABILITIES FOREVER!! EVENTUALLY, SOMEONE WILL FIND OUT!!
SO WHY DON'T YOU JUST ACCEPT THE ERA—

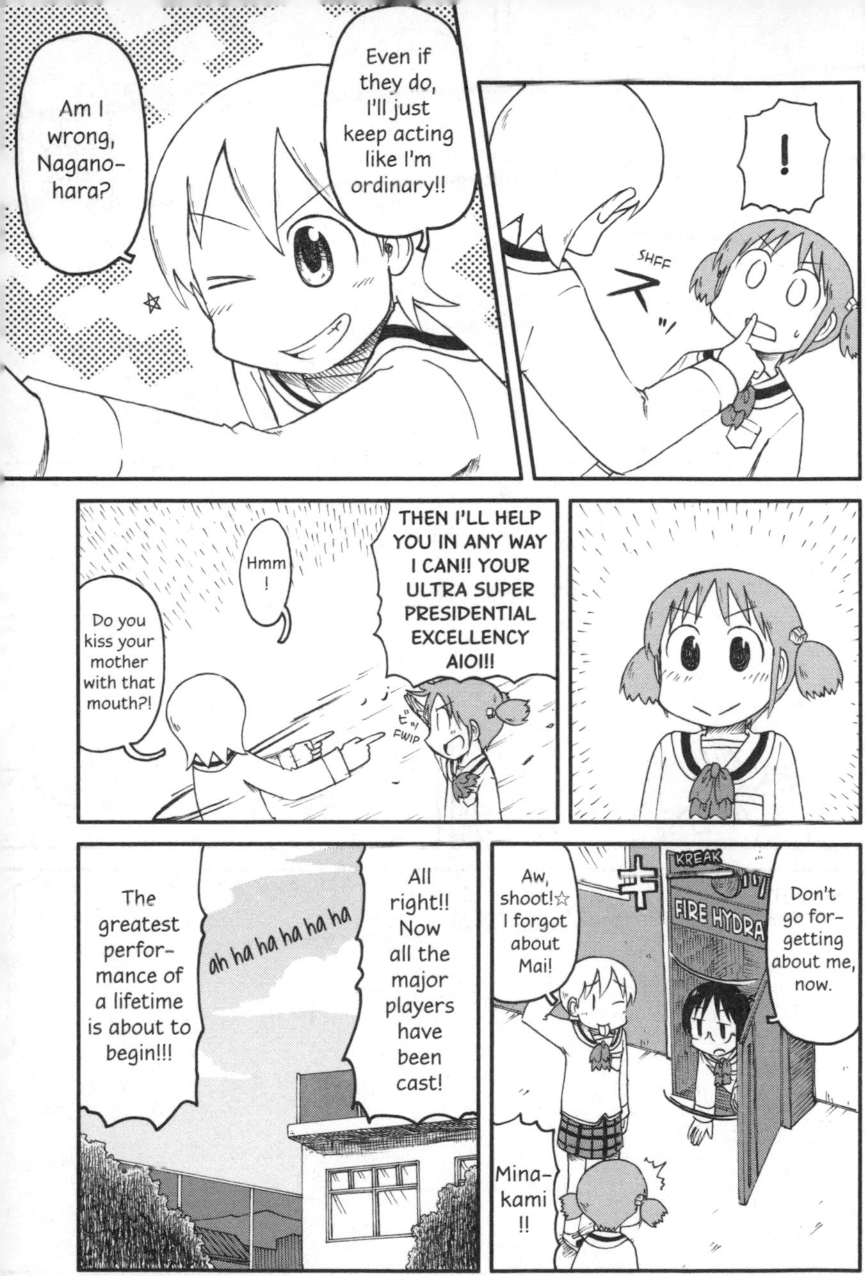
!
SHFF
Even if they do, I'll just keep acting like I'm ordinary!!
Am I wrong, Naganohara?
THEN I'LL HELP YOU IN ANY WAY I CAN!! YOUR ULTRA SUPER PRESIDENTIAL EXCELLENCY AIO!!!
Hmm !
Do you kiss your mother with that mouth?!
FWIP
Don't go forgetting about me, now.
KREAK
FIRE HYDRA
Aw, shoot!☆ I forgot about Mai!
Mina-kami !!
All right!! Now all the major players have been cast!
ah ha ha ha ha ha
The greatest performance of a lifetime is about to begin!!!

...and that's what the school was like before you came here, Nano.
I was trying to respond to Nano's question with a childish fake story, but...
somewhere along the way, my story gained two more audience members...
and so, caught in an atmosphere of choking silence, I quietly closed my mouth.

chapter 144: end

chapter 145

YOUNG AIOI'S TROUBLES

DIE LEIDEN
DES
JUNGEN
AIOI

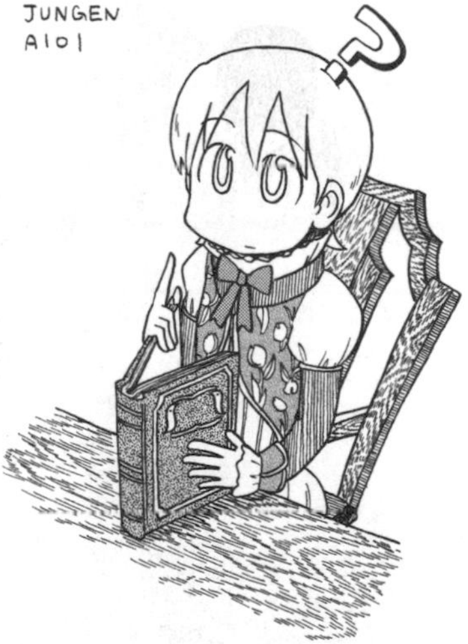

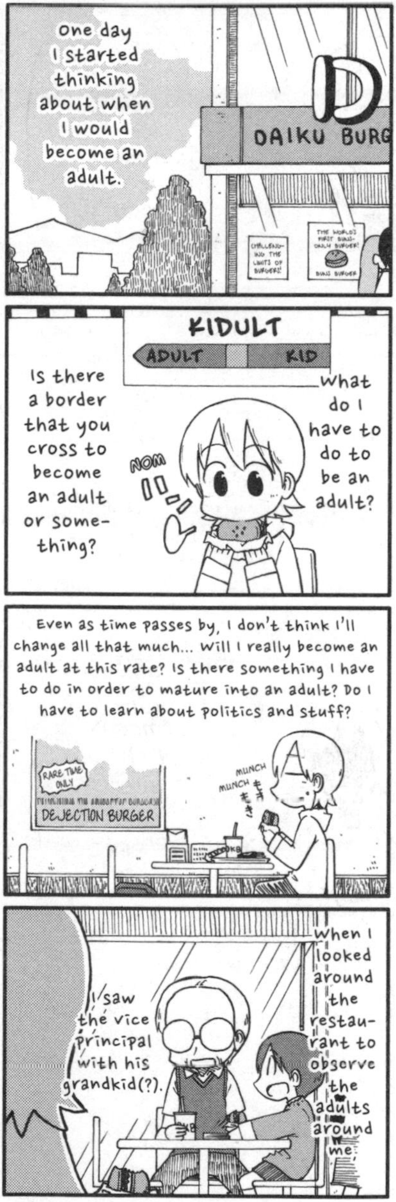
One day I started thinking about when I would become an adult.
DAIKU BURG
THE WORLD'S FIRST BUNS-ONLY BURGER!
BUNS BURGER
CHALLENGING THE LIMITS OF BURGERS!
KIDULT
ADULT
KID
What do I have to do to be an adult?
Is there a border that you cross to become an adult or something?
NOM
Even as time passes by, I don't think I'll change all that much... Will I really become an adult at this rate? Is there something I have to do in order to mature into an adult? Do I have to learn about politics and stuff?
MUNCH MUNCH
RARE TIME ONLY
DEJECTION BURGER
When I looked around the restaurant to observe the adults around me,
I saw the vice principal with his grandkid(?).

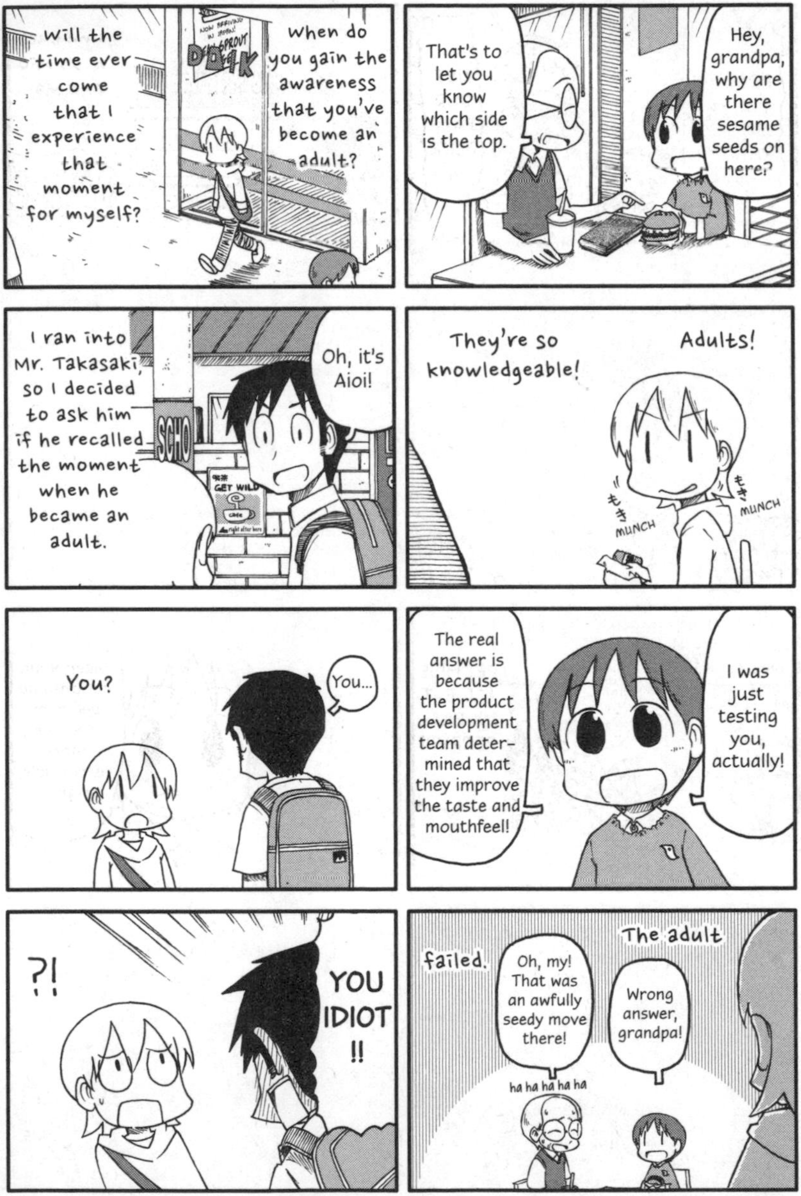
Hey, grandpa, why are there sesame seeds on here?
That's to let you know which side is the top.
When do you gain the awareness that you've become an adult?
Will the time ever come that I experience that moment for myself?
Adults!
They're so knowledgeable!
もき MUNCH
もき MUNCH
Oh, it's Aioi!
I ran into Mr. Takasaki, so I decided to ask him if he recalled the moment when he became an adult.
SCHO
GET WILD
I was just testing you, actually!
The real answer is because the product development team determined that they improve the taste and mouthfeel!
You...
You?
The adult failed.
Wrong answer, grandpa!
Oh, my! That was an awfully seedy move there!
ha ha ha ha ha
YOU IDIOT !!
?!

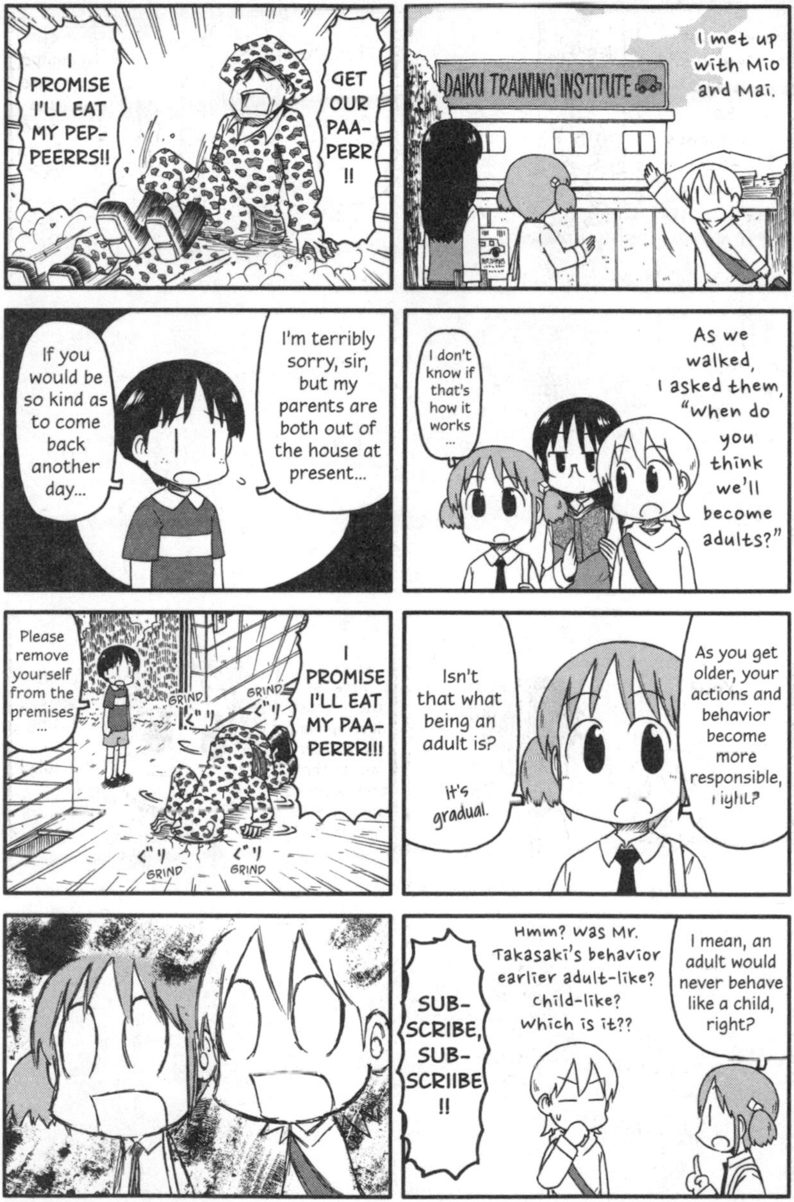

I met up with Mio and Mai.
DAIKU TRAINING INSTITUTE
GET OUR PAA-PERR !!
I PROMISE I'LL EAT MY PEP-PEERRS!!
As we walked, I asked them, "When do you think we'll become adults?"
I don't know if that's how it works ...
I'm terribly sorry, sir, but my parents are both out of the house at present...
If you would be so kind as to come back another day...
As you get older, your actions and behavior become more responsible, right?
Isn't that what being an adult is?
It's gradual.
I PROMISE I'LL EAT MY PAA-PERRR!!!
GRIND
GRIND
Please remove yourself from the premises ...
GRIND
GRIND
I mean, an adult would never behave like a child, right?
Hmm? Was Mr. Takasaki's behavior earlier adult-like? child-like? Which is it??
SUB-SCRIBE, SUB-SCRIIBE !!

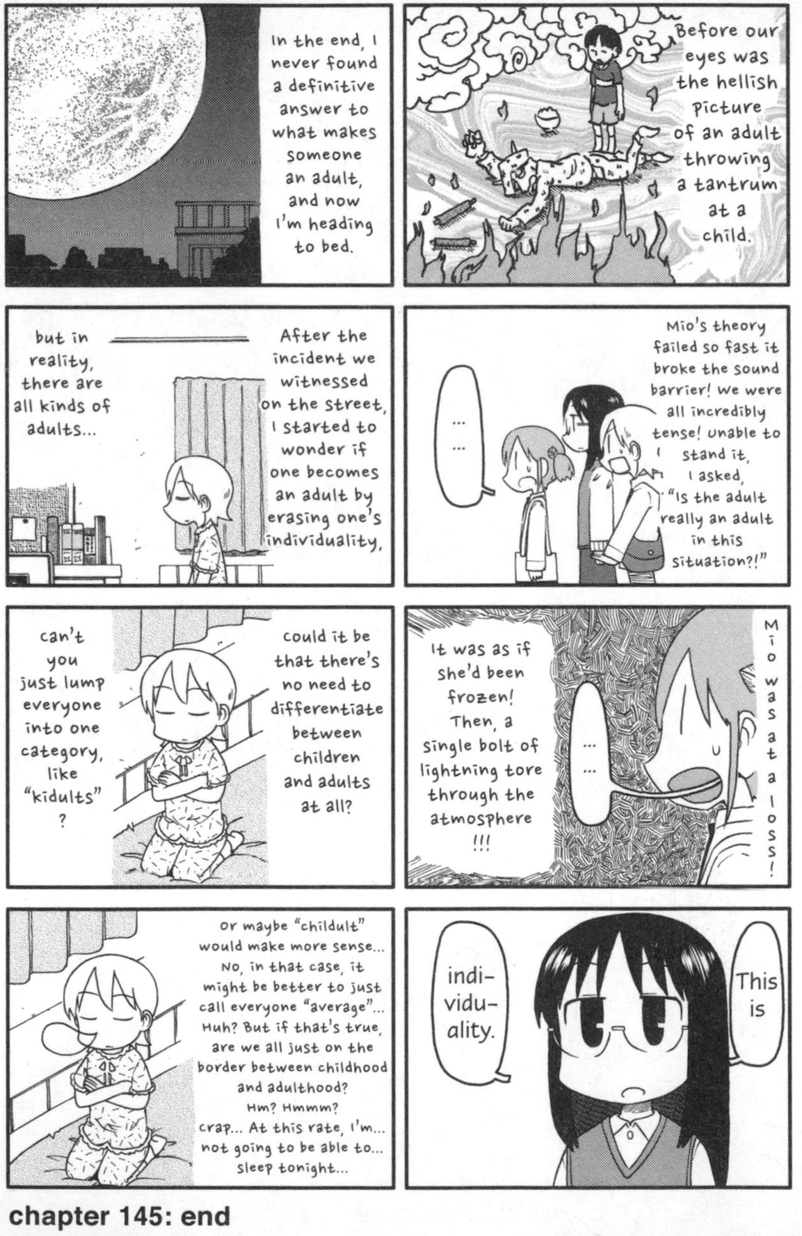
Before our eyes was the hellish picture of an adult throwing a tantrum at a child.
Mio's theory failed so fast it broke the sound barrier! We were all incredibly tense! Unable to stand it, I asked, "Is the adult really an adult in this situation?!"
......
Mio was at a loss!
It was as if she'd been frozen! Then, a single bolt of lightning tore through the atmosphere!!!
......
This is
indi-vidu-ality.
In the end, I never found a definitive answer to what makes someone an adult, and now I'm heading to bed.
After the incident we witnessed on the street, I started to wonder if one becomes an adult by erasing one's individuality,
but in reality, there are all kinds of adults...
could it be that there's no need to differentiate between children and adults at all?
can't you just lump everyone into one category, like "kidults"?
Or maybe "childult" would make more sense... No, in that case, it might be better to just call everyone "average"... Huh? But if that's true, are we all just on the border between childhood and adulthood? Hm? Hmmm? crap... At this rate, I'm... not going to be able to... sleep tonight...

chapter 145: end

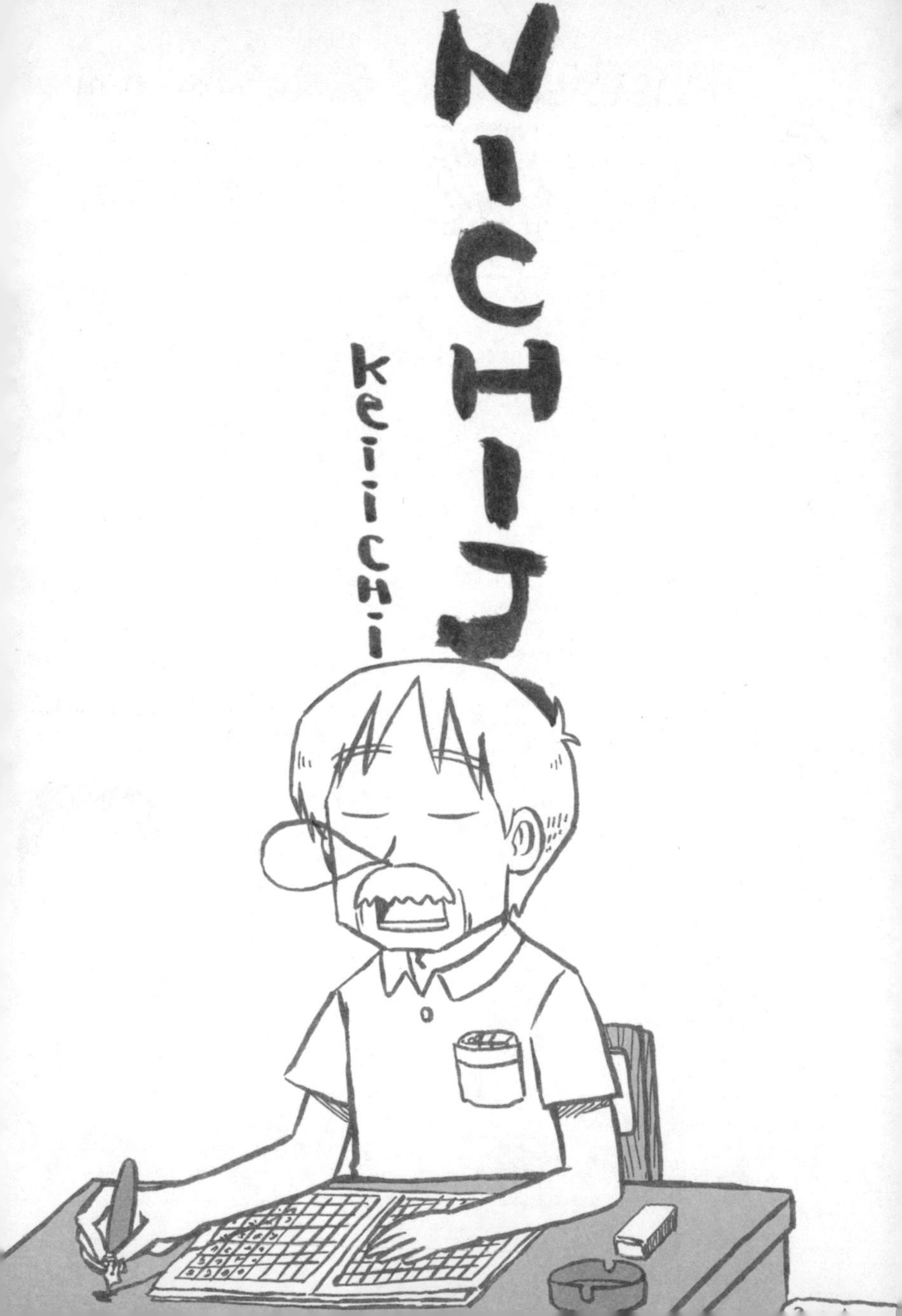
NICHIJ
keiichi

Yukko, Mai, and Mio's

MIDDLE SCHOOL ERA FLASHBACK

classmates and teachers edition!

Mio's friend from middle school

always energetic

Vera

she puts on a brave face in front of her classmates. but at night, she sometimes cries into her pillow. one time, she wanted a beaker from the science lab, so she stole one. but later she regretted it, so at night, she snuck back to the school to return it, but she was caught by security and severely scolded. that night, she cried into her pillow. she sometimes worries about old age and cries into her pillow about it. nobody knows that she cries into her pillow at night, and to this day, Vera continues to put on a brave face.

sat in front of Yukko and Mai

uses a codename

Shirasawa

appears to be a middle school student, but is actually a secret agent sent in by a certain research organization. her objective was to observe the too-flexible person known as "Fujioka."

however, she started to have fun being a student, so she decided to just enjoy her life there.

in the end, she was removed from the position under the pretext of a school transfer, but it's said that the friendships she made in her time in middle school continue to this day.

Yukko and Mai's former classmate

always cheerful

Fujioka

his body is flexible. in fact, it's too flexible. for instance, an expert in the field once came to the school to study just how flexible he is.

the fact that he hasn't hit puberty yet, despite being surrounded by people going through it, is a worry that weighs on him deeply.

as a result, he can often be found resting his chin in his hands and gazing out the window during class.

Yukko and Mai's former teacher

always honest

Mr. Oizumi

he's very serious and passionate by nature, so he tends to worry earnestly about his students' futures, to the point that he once received a complaint from a woman on the PTA.

he always starts his classes with the greeting, "now, let's begin the romance!"

a 35-year-old civics teacher who loves Bavarian cream.

Prepare to be Bewitched!

Makoto Kowata, a novice witch, packs up her belongings (including a black cat familiar) and moves in with her distant cousins in rural Aomori to complete her training and become a full-fledged witch.

"*Flying Witch* emphasizes that while actual magic is nice, there is ultimately magic in everything." —*Anime News Network*

The Basis for the Hit Anime from Sentai Filmworks!

Volume 1 On Sale Now!

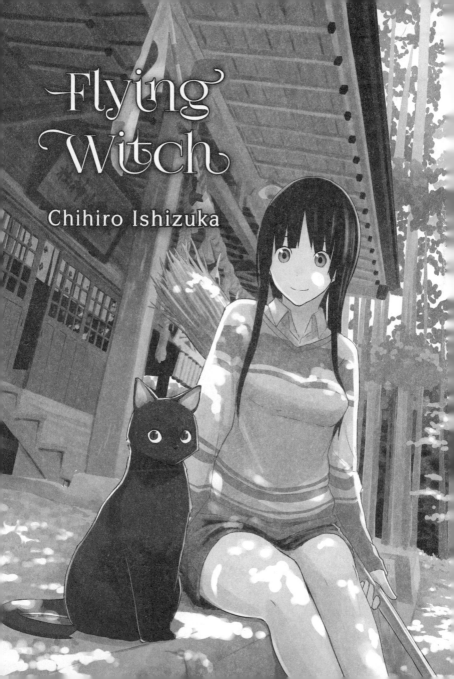

Flying Witch

Chihiro Ishizuka

VANGUARD IS BACK!

A lot has happened to Aichi since we last saw him.
He recently won the Vanguard Asia Circuit and has
enrolled in high school. But as he will soon find out,
high school life may become his biggest challenge yet.
Who knew starting a cardfight club
would be so difficult?

FIRST PRINTINGS INCLUDE A LIMITED EDITION PR CARD!

Volumes 1-8 available now!

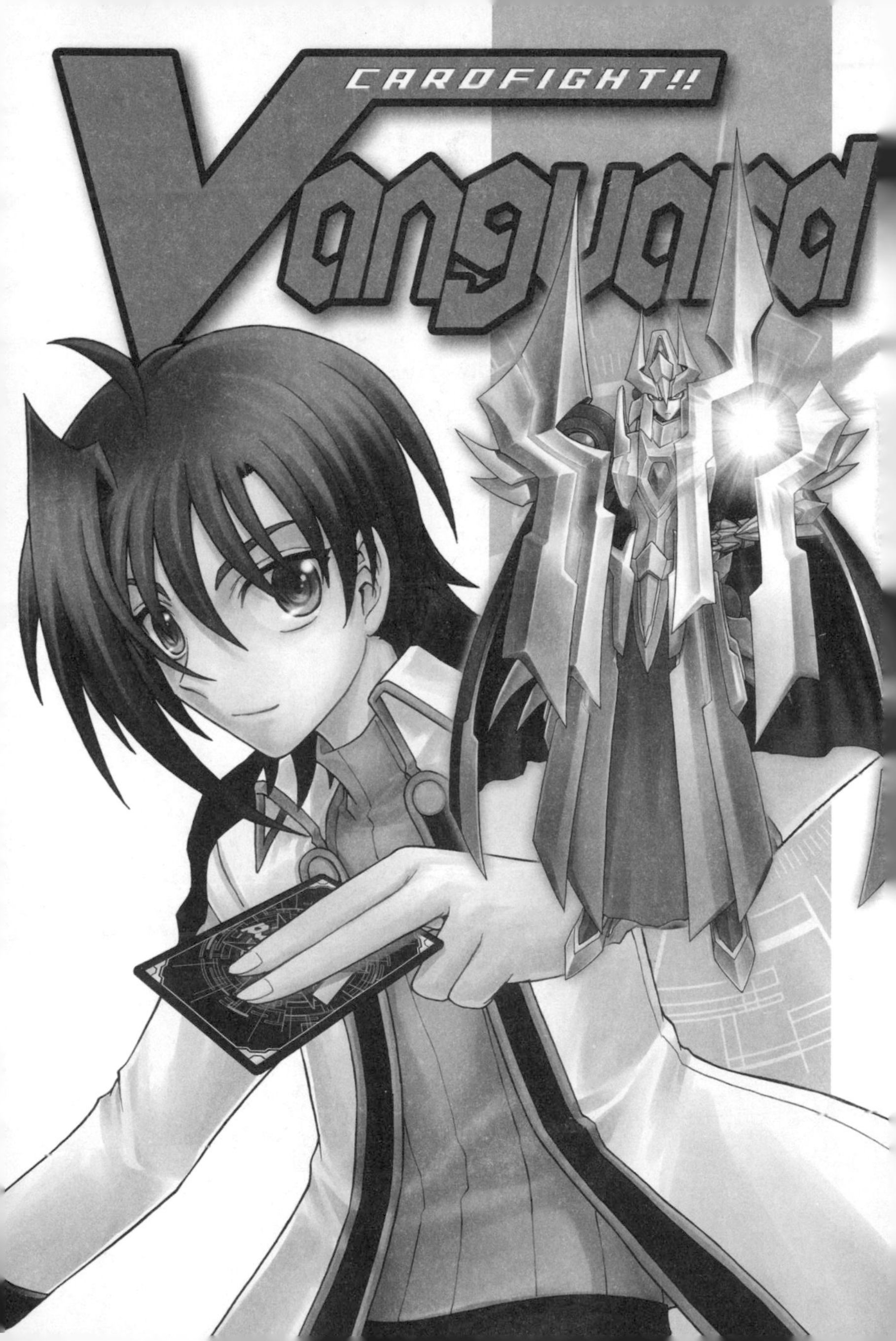
CARDFIGHT!!
Vanguard

The Master of Killing Time

Toshinari Seki takes goofing off to new heights. Every day, on or around his school desk, he masterfully creates his own little worlds of wonder, often hidden to most of his classmates. Unfortunately for Rumi Yokoi, his neighbor at the back of the room, his many games, dioramas, and projects are often way too interesting to ignore; even when they are hurting her grades.

Volumes 1-9 available now!

My Neighbor Seki

Tonari no Seki-kun

Takuma Morishige

nichijou 8

my ordinary life

A Vertical Comics Edition

Translation: Jenny McKeon
Production: Grace Lu
             Hiroko Mizuno

© Keiichi ARAWI 2012
First published in Japan in 2012 by KADOKAWA CORPORATION, Tokyo.
English translation rights arranged with KADOKAWA CORPORATION, Tokyo
through TUTTLE-MORI AGENCY, INC., Tokyo.

Published by Vertical Comics, an imprint of Vertical, Inc., New York

Originally published in Japanese as *nichijou 8* by Kadokawa Corporation, 2012
nichijou first serialized in *Monthly Shonen Ace,* Kadokawa Corporation, 2006-2015

This is a work of fiction.

ISBN: 978-1-942993-67-4

Manufactured in Canada

First Edition

Vertical, Inc.
451 Park Avenue South
7th Floor
New York, NY 10016
www.vertical-comics.com

Vertical books are distributed through Penguin-Random House Publisher Services.